W9-BMC-194

POLAND

THE STRUGGLE FOR POWER

1772–1939

POLAND

THE STRUGGLE FOR POWER

1772 - 1939

By

HENRYK FRANKEL

LINDSAY DRUMMOND LTD.

London 1946

FIRST PUBLISHED 1946
BY LINDSAY DRUMMOND LIMITED
2 GUILFORD PLACE, LONDON, W.C.1

THE TYPOGRAPHY OF THIS BOOK CONFORMS TO THE
AUTHORIZED ECONOMY STANDARD

MADE IN GREAT BRITAIN
PRINTED AT THE ST. ANN'S PRESS, ALTRINCHAM, CHESHIRE

IN MEMORIAM

A. AND D.

PREFACE

THE purpose of this book is to fill certain gaps in the literature on Poland and her people by stressing the analysis of social and economic, rather than that of diplomatic and political factors.

The conclusions arrived at by the present writer differ to a certain extent from those of other works on Poland. Before 1914 autonomous Galicia was the only part of Poland which enjoyed relative freedom of historical research, and the feudal conditions prevailing in that province undoubtedly influenced the work of the Galician historians. Those of them who valued truth above all limited their research largely to delving into the past, without linking up the facts discovered or described by them; on the other hand those whose political outlook influenced their work avoided almost anything which dealt with the serf and peasant problem, that is, with the principle factor in Poland's history.

Objectivity in history is a difficult problem. Prevailing tendencies of time and place cannot fail to affect the historian; often he succumbs to the influences of his social position, education and political opinion. This is well illustrated in many works on Poland; and a leading historian from Warsaw rightly observed some decades ago that " the consequence of seeing the past through the glasses of political interests and of thus drawing practical conclusions from it have had a fatal effect on Polish historical literature."[1]

This statement could also be applied to many works on Poland published in that country and elsewhere in the years before 1939. Apart from internal reasons there were also other considerations which distorted the analysis of events in Poland. The geographical proximity of the Russian Empire and, later, the Union of Socialist Soviet Republics made Poland a question of international importance. In the nineteenth century Poland was the focal point of the international " left wing " campaign against the Russian Absolutist State, and in the twentieth century that of an international " right wing " campaign against the Russian Socialist State, and these political considerations did not fail to exert an influence upon historians.

Apart from these political reasons, which were specific to Polish conditions, works on Poland and her past—as well as works on the history of other countries—suffer from inadequate research. For instance, many works on Poland are little more than biographical studies. The history of any population should, presumably, contain not only an account of the political, or economic, or social elements, but also of other factors relating to its history such as religion, constitution, administration, international relations, art,

[1] W. Smolenski, *Szkoly Historyczne* (Schools of Historical Thought). Warsaw, 1898, p. 160.

science and other expressions of human interests and activity, not to mention climatic and geographical conditions. To isolate one set of facts is undoubtedly necessary for their presentation and analysis; to present them as the history of a people can only be a *malum neccessarium*. The Cambridge Modern History series inaugurated a system of co-operation between men, each of whom was a specialist in a certain epoch, and if this principle be applied "horizontally" and the co-operation of men specialising in the economics, religion or science of a certain epoch be secured, our knowledge and understanding of the past would greatly increase; and also many theoretical questions would probably be better understood.

As many statements and facts described in the present work will be to a certain extent new, it was thought advisable to give frequent quotations and references which, although cumbersome, will enable the reader to follow up the subject. The sources are referred to in footnotes on each page and in the bibliography at the end of each chapter.

The main conclusions of the book are that the economic, social and political oppression of the great majority of the population was largely responsible for Poland's backward development in all spheres and her helplessness in face of foreign aggression both in 1772–95 and 1939.

The writer's acknowledgments and thanks are due for permission to include extracts from the following works: *The Polish Peasant in Europe and America*, by W. I. Thomas and F. Znaniecki, published by Richard G. Badger, The Gorham Press, Boston, U.S.A.; *Theatre of Life*, by Lord Howard of Penrith, published by Hodder & Stoughton; *Poland and Peace*, by A. Skrzynski, published by Allen & Unwin; *New Governments of Eastern Europe*, by Malbone W. Graham, published by Sir Isaac Pitman & Sons, New York; *Peasant Europe*, by H. Hessel Tiltman, published by Jarrolds; *Pilsudski, Hero of Poland*, by Rom Landau, published by Jarrolds; "Memoirs of Unemployed," from *International Labour Review*, published by the I.L.O.; *Unemployment*, Royal Institute of International Affairs, published by Oxford University Press; and from an article on Polish Elections in the *Manchester Guardian*.

The writer wishes to take the opportunity of expressing his deep indebtedness and gratitude to all persons who have given him help and encouragement.

CONTENTS

Part Three

POLAND INDEPENDENT

Part One

THE PERIOD OF SERFDOM

TO KOSCIUSKO:

Good Kosciusko, thy great name alone
Is a full harvest whence to reap high feeling;
It comes upon us like the glorious pealing
Of the wider spheres—an everlasting tone.
And now it tells me, that in worlds unknown
The names of heroes burst from clouds concealing,
And change to harmonies for ever stealing
Through cloudless blue, and round each silver throne.

It tells me too, that on a happy day,
When some good spirit walks upon the earth,
Thy name with Alfred's, and the great of yore
Gently commingling, gives tremendous birth
To a loud hymn, that sounds far, far away,
To where the great God lives for evermore.

John Keats

Chapter I

INDEPENDENT POLAND

OF the early history of Poland little is known. The territories which later formed the Kingdom of Poland were inhabited by various nomadic Slavonic tribes which were often in a state of war with each other. Poland emerges into the fuller light of history in the tenth century, when it seems to have consisted of a loose federation of tribes of peasant landowners under a common king. The first king, according to mythological tradition, was a peasant and wheelwright named Piast. His grandson, Mieszko I, married a Czech princess in 962; it was he who introduced Christianity into Poland.

The first historical figure is Mieszko's son Boleslaw, who is known to have been crowned King of Poland in 1025, to have fought against the Germans and to have gained independence from them. Mieszko and his predecessors seem to have been under the feudal patronage of the German Emperor. Boleslaw extended his rule over non-Polish territories and incorporated in the Polish state so-called Red Ruthenia—the Lwow area—as well as Kiev and the Czech domains. The dynasty of Piast ruled in Poland up to 1370 and was characterised by free peasant proprietorship and the expansion of Polish territory, through the heart of which ran the River Vistula.

During the reign of the early Piasts Poland came into contact with her western neighbours whose influence hastened the development of the Polish feudal system. In contrast, however, to the feudal hierarchy of Western Europe, the Polish barons, who had slowly emerged from the peasantry, considered that they held their land, not from a superior vassal, but direct from the king. This increased the independence of the nobles and, in particular, their influence over those on the lowest rung of the feudal ladder, the peasants, who very soon descended from the level of feudal junior partner to that of servant and slave.

Up to the fifteenth century, however, the economic, social and political development of Poland was progressive in character mainly because the peasantry possessed a large measure of freedom. The knights, occupied with military service and with continuous warfare, sometimes offensive, sometimes defensive, did not concern themselves with agriculture; they depended for their livelihood chiefly on the rents of their peasants, which were paid in kind as well as in money. This form of rental economy facilitated the development of trade and the growth of the towns, which were the markets where the peasants and the knights exchanged their agricultural surplus for the wares made by craftsmen or imported by merchants.

In this period two world trade routes crossed on Polish soil. One was the north-south route from the Baltic to the Mediterranean, the centre of medieval world trade, and the other was the west-east route from Western Europe to the Black Sea, Turkey and reaching as far as India. These routes carried a highly profitable trade, both export and import, and, as the Polish knights rarely descended to robbing merchants, the trade flourished. Cracow, situated at the crossroads, became a very important centre for this trade and, though far from the sea, became a member of the Hanseatic League. There was a steady flow of goods by road and by water to and from Cracow, along the Vistula to Danzig and the Baltic, whence Polish ships sailed to all parts of Europe. The Polish kings established themselves in Cracow, relying on the support of wealthy merchants in the continuous conflicts between the royal power and the increasing ambitions of the knights.

The Jagiellon Dynasty (1386–1572), which followed the Piasts, introduced into Poland the eastern element, which subsequently was to play so important a part in the history of Poland. The first king, Jaggiello, was a Lithuanian;

under his auspices there came into being the union of Poland and Lithuania which survived up to the eighteenth century. During these two hundred years Poland became one of the strongest and most progressive countries in Europe owing to the development of industry and agriculture during the Piast period. On the whole the peasants remained personally free and the towns increased in number and importance.

From the fifteenth century, however, the role of the knights and their relationship to the state was altered. In consequence of the invention and application of gunpowder, methods of warfare were fundamentally changed and the famous Polish Hussars, of whom the Poles were proud, became useless. From then on, there was a general levy of knights only in case of emergency and gradually, having hitherto despised such occupations, the knight retired to his manor and began to organise his estate.

Far-reaching events were taking place at that time in Western Europe which strengthened the position of the Polish gentry. The discovery of America and of the sea route round the Cape to India brought about a complete transformation of world trade by making the Mediterranean basin less important in comparison with Flanders and England, where towns sprang up and the population increased. This led to a large demand for foodstuffs and English and Flemish merchants went to seek grain in the east. Danzig became a flourishing centre for the export of grain, livestock and timber, and the peasants and merchants of Poland began to draw large profits.

All over Europe, Poland included, prices soared. It was the period when, as the result of shipments from newly-discovered America, the amount of silver and gold in Europe was increasing much faster than the quantity of goods for sale. The nobleman did not understand the cause of the rise in prices. He saw his income diminished and regarded as his enemies both the merchants, whom he accused of profiteering, and the peasants, whom he suspected of cheating over rent payments. To compensate for his losses, he began to raise the rents, but even rack-renting could not keep pace with the soaring prices.

At the same time, seeing the possibility of wealth in the export of agricultural products,[1] the gentry began to engage in production and to secure a dominant position in the grain business. But they were immediately faced with an almost insurmountable difficulty, the absence of labour. There was free land, especially in the east, and the peasants preferred to go there rather than to be employed by the barons. The first concern of the nobility was therefore to secure a limitation of the personal freedom of the peasants and

[1] The steadily increasing cost of a last (cargo-loading, about 60 bushels) of wheat in Danzig is shown by the following figures:

Year	Zlotys	Year	Zlotys
1564	21	1660	108
1592	40	1675	216
1616	48	1776	392
1619	56		

The rise in grain prices far exceeded the average rise in prices. Szelagowski, pp. 155–8.

to prevent them from moving from the soil on which they lived and worked; an object which could only be achieved by an aristocracy strong enough to impose its will on the country.

Thus the turning-point in Polish history was reached and the struggle began for complete supremacy in the state. It was a struggle of the gentry against the peasants and burghers as well as against the king. The aims of the gentry were threefold :

1. The concentration of all land in their hands and the creation of large estates for the production of grain for export.
2. The commuting of the rent system into serfdom in order to obtain sufficient labour.
3. The direction and control of the state.

* * *

By a sustained offensive lasting over two centuries, the system of self-government of the village was overthrown and the office of bailiff, who had been the elected representative of the village, became the exclusive privilege of the noble. After 1496 the peasant was made *glebae adscriptus*—tied to the land—without prospect of alleviation; and the towns were deprived of their right to grant protection and freedom to the escaping serf.

By the end of the fifteenth century the process of commuting money rents into labour service—the reverse of what happened in Western Europe—was in full swing. Hitherto rent had been the most important item in the nobleman's budget: now the income derived from grain production was taking its place. In 1520 and 1521, every peasant, notwithstanding his former rights and privileges, had to do " week-work " at the rate of one day a week. The Constitution of 1560 and 1563 forbade the increasing of week-work to more than three days a week; thus the burden of villeinage had trebled in forty years. At the end of the seventeenth century (until the Partitions) week-work consisted of six days per week. The nobles had already, in 1466, acquired the right to expropriate the peasants from their holdings on payment of a compensation according to the value of the land. Later, however, in the process of consolidating their estates, they frequently exercised this right without making any compensation. It was a process similar to the English enclosures, with the difference that the landless peasantry of England later formed the army of industrial workers, while the Polish peasants became absorbed by the manor either as servants or as landless agricultural labourers, in either case losing their personal freedom.

Before the period of serfdom the judicial system in Poland had been liberal. Both native and immigrant (mostly German) peasants were personally free; they had their own courts, and even had the right of appeal to the king. By the fifteenth century, however, the peasant could only appear in a court of law accompanied by the lord of his manor. In these circumstances he could not possibly accuse his oppressor, for even if he had had the courage to do so the noble would hardly have consented to accompany him to court. But the peasant was to lose even this meagre privilege, and after 1532 he became subject exclusively to the jurisdiction of his master.

The peasant revolts of Western Europe hastened the natural process of their emancipation into tenant farmers and freeholders. Their struggles were often successful and the possibility of repetition hampered the landlord, even though as soon as the peasants dispersed he might forget the promises he had made to them. Unfortunately for Poland, her peasant revolts were only local and were easily crushed. Except in the case of the Ukrainian and Polish peasant revolutions in the seventeenth century, these struggles were never successful and were brutally suppressed in order to prevent future disturbances.

The next victims in the struggle for supremacy in the state were the merchants and the craftsmen. The former splendour of the Polish towns which had, like Cracow, entertained kings and emperors, vanished with the transformation of world trade. The Mediterranean lost its importance. The Italian colonies which had long been established on the shores of the Black Sea, ceased, after the Turkish conquest of this area in the fifteenth century, to be the intermediary between Poland, Greece and Asia. The Polish transit trade, which had hitherto been profitable for the towns, came to an end. Nevertheless, the export and import trade and the national market left fairly wide scope for the development of commerce and industry.

It was at this time that the consequences of the subjugation of the peasants became felt by other classes of the population. The creation of landed estates led to the renewal of self-supporting local communities and of local husbandry. The barons had labour at their disposal and began to start small factories. The serfs were obliged to produce for themselves their most essential requirements and, after their master had introduced a monopoly of trade in his estate, were compelled to buy from him any goods which they were unable to produce. Thus the towns not only lost nine-tenths of their customers but also had to face competition from the barons in their own field.

A further blow was dealt by the gentry when they acquired the monopoly of the grain export. The share of the towns in this trade slowly dwindled to nothing. A very small amount of general trade was possible, enough to maintain the population but not enough to bring any prosperity to the towns. It consisted of the import of luxury goods for the gentry and the export of goods manufactured in the towns. But this trade also came to an end. The gentry already possessed the right to fix the prices of goods offered for sale in the towns as well as the margin of permissible profit (7 per cent for native merchants, 5 per cent for Germans and others, 3 per cent for Jews). In 1493 the barons acquired the right to import goods, duty free, for their own consumption. The English and Dutch shippers, who came to Danzig for grain, brought with them everything the gentry needed from abroad. No customs duties were paid if the imported goods were destined for a noble. This privilege of exemption from import and export duties (the grain export of the gentry was also duty free) is almost unique in the history of Europe.

The barons in addition wanted to get the goods manufactured in the towns at the cheapest prices. The right to fix prices was not sufficient since the towns preferred to export their goods when the fixed price was too low. So the Diet passed a law prohibiting the export of all goods manufactured in towns.

Manufactured goods were either produced on the baron's estate or imported from abroad. No independent activity was left to the towns, which gradually declined and the centres of Polish culture and civilisation, of architecture and science, slowly fell into decay.

The importance of the Polish towns up to the fifteenth and sixteenth centuries was recognised even in England. When Queen Elizabeth expelled the members of the Hanseatic League from England in 1596, she made exceptions only in favour of those who were " subjects of the Polish King." Cracow, the old capital of Poland, had 80,000 inhabitants in the sixteenth century; in 1787 it had little over 9,000. " With every year the towns became poorer; their pavements sank under a new layer of dirt; the means of communication, bridges and roads, already ill-famed, deteriorated. The stone churches and monasteries, showing signs of the growing fanaticism, became more and more numerous, and the land within their walls grew more and more extensive."[1]

With the peasantry and towns thus weakened, the only force which might have rallied them and prevented the complete supremacy of the barons was the king, but the system of electoral kingship fatally impaired his position. This electoral system, though inaugurated in the fourteenth century, came into full force in the sixteenth century, after the death of the last Jagiellon king. The electors, an assembly of nobles and of the higher dignitaries of the Church, sought to impose their terms upon the candidates for election and, since it was easier to impose them on foreigners, the great majority of the Polish kings after the sixteenth century were of foreign blood. During the last two centuries of her independence (1572–1772) Poland was ruled mainly by non-Polish kings, such as Henri Valois of France, Stephen Batory of Transylvania, the Swedish Vasas and the Saxon kings. Every attempt to limit the influence of the barons was thus doomed to failure, especially since any power exercised by the king was discontinued during the interregnum following his death, during which time the gentry, the wealthier members in particular, controlled the country.

Even in the period of the hereditary monarchy, the kings were sometimes compelled to grant privileges to the barons in return for their services. For instance, in 1422, at Czerwiensk, on the eve of a battle with the Teuton Knights, the assembled nobility laid down conditions for their participation. The king, Wladislaw Jagiello, had no option but to confirm all their former privileges and also to declare the hereditary estates inviolable. After 1466 the nobles gained the exclusive privilege of possessing land; and the word " *nobilis* " became synonymous with " *haeres*."

[1] Bruckner, p. 196.

The aim of the barons, in their successful efforts to limit the power of the king, was twofold: to keep complete control of the state machinery, and to divide among themselves the Crown Lands which covered large stretches of country. In the first half of the sixteenth century, when the estates were being organised, the barons succeeded in securing vast parts of the king's demesne, partly in return for their support and partly by fraud.

After the death of the last Jagiellon the monarchy was no longer hereditary and the kings were naturally not interested in the preservation of the Crown Lands. According to feudal theory these were part of the king's property, and even the most public-spirited kings, such as Jan Sobieski, who defeated the Turks at Vienna, disposed of them without any thought that he was diminishing the country's public resources.

Not only political but also purely personal considerations, played a considerable part, therefore, in the choice of the future king. The magnates looked out for a suitable person who would confer on them political and personal privileges and who would not be in danger of becoming too strong; for political and personal reasons the neighbouring kings and princes each tried to get hold of the Polish throne. No king so elected could count on having any considerable moral authority in the country. "The election to the throne often resulted in the choice of foreign princelings, who were placed at the head of affairs in Poland, without previous knowledge of the country, and without any sense of permanency of the throne in their families. This led to violent competitions and contests. Neighbouring states were greatly concerned in them. It was of great importance to obtain the influence and support of Poland in their rivalries with one another. Factions were therefore formed and subsidised in Poland by the most powerful of its neighbours, and when a vacancy to the throne occurred the country was thrown into a turmoil by these rival interests. Bribery was largely resorted to, and force, or threats of force, were used to secure the election of a candidate favoured by some neighbouring power. Not infrequently a foreign army marched into the country in support of some candidate."[1]

The gentry itself was not a homogeneous class. Wealth became concentrated among the nobles themselves. Where there is no law and no justice, the object of oppression depends on the immediate interests of the despot. The right of might was used against the poorer noble as well as against the peasant, and the magnates had no qualms about depriving a lesser noble of his land. The custom of dividing up property among the heirs gradually created smallholdings, hardly superior to those of the peasants, which could not provide a reasonable livelihood according to the standards of the gentry. No more peasant land was available for appropriation and the owners of these small estates were compelled to enter the household of one of the magnates or even to become serfs.

A Polish writer of this period thus described the process: ". . . by a continual dividing up of the estates one inevitably arrives at poverty; it even

[1] Eversley, p. 20.

happens that the noble becomes a peasant. I know many who already consider as peasants their relatives, brothers and uncles, whose land they have bought and whom they force to do week-work. Thus it comes about, as was said by the old philosophers, that after a long time the kings are become slaves and the slaves kings."[1]

So strong, however, was the distinction between nobles and peasants, between free men and serfs, that even if a nobleman was driven to the same economic level as a peasant, he still considered himself as belonging to a higher class and blindly followed his wealthier " brother."

* * *

At the height of this fateful struggle (in the sixteenth century) when the peasants, the town middle classes and the kings began to feel the grip of the enemy within their gates, a vital spark of patriotism[2] flared up from the lower ranks, especially among the free burghers and the poorer nobles. Their resistance against despotism introduced into the life of the Polish state a breath of fresh air.

As elsewhere in the Middle Ages, the struggle against the aristocracy took religious forms, and Renaissance and Reformation found fertile soil on the shores of the Vistula. At that time there were such violent religious disputes in Poland, and so many denominations, that in Western Europe it was said that " if anyone had lost his religion he should go to Poland, for if he could not find it there he would not find it anywhere." The Anabaptists and the Socinians, known as the Polish Brethren, had definite " Socialistic " leanings and created a centre of religious thought in Rakow. " Its teachers were able scholars with a reputation throughout Europe. It grew rapidly and became famous. Young men were sent there from both Catholic and Protestant sources until it had about a thousand students, nearly a third of them from the nobility. Rakow became known as the ' Sarmatian Athens.' So many came here even from Germany that special services in the German language were held for them. In this school young men were trained for the Socinian ministry under teachers whose fame survives among scholars to this day."[3]

Some of the Polish Brethren came to England through Holland after their expulsion from Poland in 1660; Voltaire mentioned that Sir Isaac Newton was sympathetic to them.[4] Faustus Socinius, the founder of the Western Unitarian Church, lived in Poland and was buried there.

[1] Gornicki, pp. 790–1.

[2] The meaning of the word " patriot " has been different at different periods of history. In ancient Rome it described a person " *amans patriae et salutis publicae*." In eighteenth-century England, according to Macaulay, it was a " by-word of derision," and according to Dr. Johnson it was the term for a " factious disturber of the Government " (*Murray's English Dictionary*). During the French Revolution it applied to those who fought for a new France against the established government. In the nineteenth century the word came to mean anyone who loved his country, regardless of whether he oppressed his own or other peoples. In the present book the word " patriot " reverts to its original sense, as modified by the French Revolution, and it describes a person who loves his country and people and works for their social and cultural progress.

[3] Wilbur, pp. 151–2. [4] Voltaire, p. 37.

The greatest achievement of the Reformation in Poland was to create a body of literature in the Polish language. The use of Polish was a reaction against the Latin of the Catholic Church. Hitherto it had been regarded as barbaric; but now the situation required a literature to stimulate the resistance of the people against the magnates. Italian Humanists, expelled from their own country, found a new home at Cracow, where the intellectual life of Eastern Europe was concentrated at that time, and thousands of students came from abroad to study at the university where Copernicus worked upon his theory.

Polish literature and thought of that period rebelled against the aristocracy and concerned itself with the future of the Polish state. " Among the Germans," wrote Andreas Fricius Morevius, " and among almost all Christians you will not find slaves. The Mohammedans also forbid anyone to be considered as a slave except the Christians whose religion they despise. And we, who claim to possess God's true faith, are not ashamed to have slaves of the same confession as ourselves . . . and among other evils, the nobles want the right to take the land from the peasants whenever they wish and yet do not allow the peasant to depart from the land whenever he will; more than that, they want to tie down the peasant and his children as well. God, the creator of the world, is so good that He gave food enough for all, whether rich or poor. But the rich, in their selfishness, dare to consume all. They proclaim that the world belongs to them, and that what the peasant owns he possesses only on their behalf."[1]

The magnates were not moved even by the prophetic homilies of the preacher Peter Skarga (" Skarga " in Polish means a " complaint ") who thundered against their atrocities from his pulpit and in the Diet.

" Oh God! How much has our earth absorbed, and is still absorbing, of the blood of the innocent Abels, which continually cries out of the soil for the vengeance of God. And this blood and sweat of living subjects and peasants, which flows unchecked, what retribution does it have in store for the kingdom? You say yourselves that there is no country where subjects and peasants are more oppressed under such absolute dominion, which the gentry exploit without any legal hindrance . . . the angry noble or the king's prefect takes what the poor man possesses and kills him when he likes and how he likes, and will not hear reproach."[2]

The Opposition, however, was too weak and the sixteenth century outburst of literary and political activity came to an end. The Reformation was suppressed and the oligarchy of the barons continued almost unchallenged throughout the next two centuries. In the course of time the conditions of the peasants became almost undistinguishable from that of animals.

" In a short period of the seventeenth century several million people perished. About one million escaped to the Cossacks and others to Silesia. The country was gradually depopulated. Many villages disappeared and

[1] Modrzewski, p. 117. [2] Skarga, p. 368.

almost all the others suffered a serious diminution in numbers. In the villages where there were previously hundreds of houses, often less than a third remained. The fields, once cultivated so carefully, became covered with woodland. One no longer saw meat on the peasants' tables. Sometimes there was even a lack of bread. The unhappy poor, to forget their misery, sought a narcotic in vodka. They were liable at any moment to lose all their property and their meagre earnings. The peasant was considered to be of a species inferior to the noble, to whom he belonged unconditionally and who had therefore the right to seize all the peasant owned. In their blindness the barons spurned the poor peasants, who worked exclusively for the profit of the gentry. They forgot that these people were once equal to them, were their brothers, who spoke the same language. They forgot that only blind fate and unrestricted violence put them in a subordinate position. The greater their poverty, their indigence, the greater the reason to respect their earnings, their property. Humanity, as well as the interest of the Republic, required this. But the nobles were so blind that they impaired their own advantage and, indeed, transformed the old Republic, famous for its liberty into an inferno of slavery. . . . For many years Poland offered the sorry sight of a nation in which the privileged minority, not satisfied with the seizure of land which formerly belonged to the majority of the population, usurped for itself the right to appropriate everything which this majority might acquire by diligence or economy, and in the end actually acquired unconditional power over the life and personal freedom of the working population. This monstrous state lasted up to the fall of the Republic."[1]

The death-rate increased considerably in the seventeenth century and whole villages were depopulated. In 1660 Poland had 15 million inhabitants; in 1700, 12 million. In 1660 in Crown Poland (i.e. without Lithuania and East Prussia, which was then a Polish vassal) there were about 60,000 villages and hamlets, in 1676 only 23,657. Attempts to bring colonists into the country failed on many accounts. In 1633 a law was passed which transformed into a serf every colonist who lived at least one year on the nobleman's land. "There were cases where men and women were given away as presents, as a dowry for the daughters, and on the occasion of sales of land the barons often unceremoniously took away the peasants' holdings. Socage, taxes, statute labour, oppressed the peasant on all sides. From his fifteenth year, often from his eighth, as long as his strength lasted, the peasant had to work for the noble, and in his old age, expelled from his holding, he was forced to beg for his living. The peasants' work was the best revenue in Poland."[2]

The situation was similarly described by English writers.

"The Polish nation is divided into two sorts of People: The Gentry or Freeborn Subjects, who are hardly a tenth part of the Kingdom, and the Vassals, who are no better than Slaves to the Gentry, for they receive no Benefit from the Laws, can Buy no estates, nor enjoy Property any more than our Negroes in the West-Indies can.

[1] Lelewel, pp. 184–6, 491. [2] Grabiec, pp. 155 and 195.

" . . . By a Gentleman or Nobleman of Poland, is understood a Person who either himself, or his Family, has a possession in land; for they never intermarry with the Common People. All the Gentry from the King's Son to those that are but only Masters of an Acre of land, are equally Noble.

" . . . Every Gentleman is a Sovereign, Lord and Master in his own lands, for he has the Power of Life and Death over his Tenants, or (as the Poles term them) his Subjects, tho' I may better call them his Slaves, for they have neither Privilege nor Law to protect them, but are to be governed absolutely by the Will and Pleasure of their Lord. They dare not leave his Lands to go to another's, under Pain of Death, unless he sells them to his Neighbour, as he has the power to do, or has violated or ravish'd their Wives or Daughters; in so much that I have heard that some have wish'd to have had a fine Wife or Daughter, that their Lord might thereby have given them occasion to get rid of him.

" If a Gentleman kills another Gentleman's Slave, he is neither to be try'd nor punished for it, and is only oblig'd to give that Gentleman another Slave in the Room of him, or as much Money as will buy one."[1]

" The Country People are poor and miserable, and are Masters of nothing they have, but are subject to their Lords, who treat them as tyrannically as Galley-Slaves. A Gentleman there has Power of Life and Death over those of his Family, and Tenants: And if a Neighbour kills one, and pays the Value set upon him, all is well again: And when they speak of a Gentleman's Riches they reckon them by his Number of Tenants. The Houses of these miserable slaves who work hard, and live upon little, are only of Mud and some Trees to hold up the Roof."[2]

The inclination towards crime and drunkenness amongst the peasants (habits which survive to some extent in modern Poland) was the natural reaction to their tragic life. The peasant was whipped for nightly dawdling in the inns, for being in a neighbouring village at night, for playing cards, for not observing socage; he was whipped when he was late at his work and put in irons for leaving his hamlet without permission, even for a short time. The peasant sought revenge in crime and the manor replied by devising yet more severe penalties, thus creating a vicious circle. The peasants found some relief in alcohol and, since many of the nobles enjoyed the monopoly of the sale of spirits, drinking was encouraged. " The condition of the Polish peasants during the eighteenth century was undoubtedly the worst in Europe. They lived in the most abject discomfort; and their filth and misery exposed them to the horrors of epidemics, against which they could make no resistance. Of personal liberty they had none; they were forbidden to leave their villages, and the forced labour on their lords' estates left them scanty leisure to cultivate their own diminutive plots; so that in seasons of bad harvest the mortality amongst them, from starvation alone, was frightful."[3]

With the political and economic life of the country in ruins, seventeenth-

[1] Connor, Vol. II, pp. 5 and 168.
[2] Whitlock, p. 2.
[3] Whitton, pp. 205–6.

and eighteenth-century Poland was at the mercy of the oligarchy of the magnates and of the frequent outbursts of enmity amongst them. That this state of affairs was known abroad is shown by a verse of Daniel Defoe's:

> " Pride, Plenty's Handmaid, deeply taints their Blood,
> And Seeds of Faction mix the crimson Flood.
> Eternal Discords brood upon the Soil,
> And universal Strifes State embroil.
> In every Family the Temper reigns,
> In every Action Seed of Gall remains.
> The very Laws of Peace create Dispute,
> And makes them quarrel who shall execute.
> Their valu'd Constitutions are so lame,
> That governing the Governments inflame.
> Wild Aristocracy torments the State,
> And People their own Miseries create."[1]

According to Nisbet Bain the degradation of the yeomanry to the condition of serfs was one of the blackest blots on Polish history.

> " It was monstrous that this vast Republic, considerably larger than the whole of the modern German Empire, abounding in corn of all sorts, with vast forests full of precious pelts, with immense pastures covered by fine cattle, with a network of countless rivers which a proper system of canalisation could so easily, at a relatively trifling expense, have connected with the Baltic and the Euxine—it was monstrous that such a country, intended by nature to be the granary of Europe, should be rotting away in obscurity without ships, without trade, without commerce, without money, obliged to import many of the necessaries of life at most exorbitant prices. The monopolising of the land by a greedy and ignorant gentry was the chief cause of this deplorable collapse. After destroying the whole country politically, the magnates and the *szlachta* had proceeded to ruin the individual provinces, one by one, financially and economically. Their fixed determination that no other class but themselves should have any privileges had led, gradually but inevitably, to the disappearance of the native merchants and the trade guilds, and the enslavement of the peasantry."[2]

* * *

Demoralised by their success, the gentry began to neglect national defence. The towns were in ruins and presented no danger to the aristocracy. The peasants, their resistance broken, had already been turned into serfs, and the private armies of the magnates were sufficient, when necessary, to remind them of their duties. The king presented a potential source of danger to the aristocracy, but this danger was successfully averted by depriving him of any means of forming a national army or of having control of the state machinery. From the sixteenth to the eighteenth centuries the Polish Commonwealth was

[1] Defoe, p. 4.

[2] Bain, pp. 41, 46.

so vast that the aristocracy, which alone decided national policy, did not consider any foreign Power as its rival. Poland covered 280,000 square miles and was the third largest country in Europe; it dominated the Ukraine, Lithuania, Prussia, White Russia and the Baltic States, and the king bore the title, " King of Poland, Grand Duke of Lithuania, Russia and Prussia."

The advantages of such conditions of anarchy (" in disorder Poland stands " was the watchword of the magnates), which enabled the barons to do exactly as they pleased, outweighed any possible external risk. As early as the sixteenth century, Skarga warned the nobles of the possible consequences.

> " This mother (Poland) has united in the Commonwealth such great and honourable nations (Lithuania and Ukraine) as extend her domain from sea to sea . . . She gave you riches and wealth and leisure. She gave it to you so that you have money enough, food enough, free clothes, hordes of servants, numbers of horses and carriages. Everywhere profits and incomes are increased.
>
> " In such a state of prosperity nobody troubles about castles and walls. The whole country is poor; it is only some families which are rich. There is nothing to cover what our forefathers spent on defence. There is nothing for the army, for building ramparts, for cannons and ammunition, for supplying the fortresses.
>
> " Oh! Horrible Sodom! With your luxury, your sloth, with your cruelty to the subject and the poor, soon may you be consumed and destroyed by fire! Nobody has the country at heart! Such a *peculatus* (appropriation of public goods) has multiplied in this kingdom that people have ceased to be remorseful over it. The choicest morsel is to take away public income, and there is no fear that the culprit will be punished."[1]

The army was small and consisted mainly of mercenaries at the time when Frederick the Great was laying the foundations of the Prussian Army, and Maria Theresa in Austria and Peter the Great and Catherine II in Russia were introducing the mercantilist policy and creating bases for the development of industrial production.

The gentry were obliged to do military service in case of war. When the levy had been called, however, they directed themselves often against the king rather than against the enemy. So the king preferred not to have recourse to such a double-edged weapon. " The Polish army with its large number of officers and handful of undisciplined, badly armed privates, became a mere parade of troops, useless in time of need."[2]

The backward economic system made recruitment for the national army an impossible task. " To go with the drum " (enlist volunteers for the army), was forbidden on the private estates of the magnates, who feared a reduction in the number of their serfs and thus of their property. When the patriotic " Four Year " Diet (1788–92) decided in January 1789 to increase the army to 100,000 men, the magnates succeeded in introducing an amendment for-

[1] Skarga, pp. 263–5, 369–70.

[2] Bruckner, p. 34.

bidding recruiting on their estates. Recruiting was only allowed in the towns and on the royal and ecclesiastical estates.

Nevertheless, for the first time in Polish history, the Diet passed resolutions against the interests of the magnates, and, to encourage the serfs to escape, promised them liberty when they had served twelve years with the colours. But this half-hearted effort could not create a powerful national army, nor uphold national independence. Only the complete liberation of the peasant and his exclusive possession of the land could have created a barrier against foreign invaders.

There were sufficient signs that aggression was being planned by Poland's neighbours. Yet reaction was still triumphant. In 1776 the Diet was trying to solve the peasant problem by peaceful methods and worked out a project of peasant rule. The magnates, however, managed to have the plan rejected in 1780, proclaiming, " we destroy these laws and they shall not be resurrected nor receive our consent." No wonder Rousseau exclaimed that " on reading the history of the government of Poland it is difficult to understand how a state so curiously constituted has been able to exist for so long. A large body composed of a number of dead members and a small number of disunited members, of which all the movements, almost independent one from another, far from having a common aim, mutually destroy each other . . . The vast disparity of fortune which separates the great lords from the lesser nobility is a large obstacle to the reforms necessary to make love of the homeland the dominating passion.

". . . The Polish Republic, as has often been said and repeated, is composed of three orders : the knights, the senate and the king. I should prefer to say that the Polish nation is composed of three orders : the nobles who are everything, the bourgeois who are nothing, and the peasants who are less than nothing."[1]

William Coxe, Archdeacon of Wiltshire, visited Poland on the eve of her loss of independence.

> " Notwithstanding their boasted liberty, the Poles are by no means free . . . the shadow rather than the reality of freedom which is in fact merely a turbulent system of aristocratic licentiousness, where a few members of the community are above the control of law, and the majority excluded from its protection. . . . The name of Poland still remains but the nation no longer exists; universal corruption and venality pervade all ranks of people. Many of the first nobility do not blush to receive pensions from foreign courts; one professes himself publicly an Austrian, a second a Prussian, a third a Frenchman, and a fourth a Russian.
>
> " The present situation of the Polish nation impressed my mind with pathetic ideas of fallen greatness; and I could not behold without a mixture of regret and sympathy, a people, who formerly gave law to the north, reduced to so low a state of weakness and misery. The nation has few

[1] Rousseau, Vol. II, p. 404.

manufactures, scarcely any commerce, a king almost without authority; the nobles in a state of uncontrolled anarchy; the peasant groaning under a yoke of feudal despotism worse than the tyranny of the absolute monarch. I never before observed such an inequality of fortune, such a sudden transition from extreme riches to extreme poverty; wherever I turned my eyes, luxury and wretchedness were constant neighbours. . . . As they lose their nobility if they follow trade or commerce, the most needy devote themselves to the service of the richer nobles who, like the old feudal barons, are constantly attended by numerous retainers. The generality, indeed, of the Polish nobles are not inclined either to establish or give any regulations in favour of the peasants whom they scarcely consider as entitled to the common rights of humanity. A few nobles, however, of benevolent heart and enlightened understanding, have acted upon different principles, and given liberty to their vassals. The event has showed this project to be no less judicious than humane, no less friendly to their own interests than to the happiness of their peasants; for it appears that in the districts in which the new arrangements have been introduced the population of the villages is considerably increased, and the income of the estate augmented in a triple proportion."[1]

Stanislas I, Leszczynski, Duke of Lorraine and father-in-law of Louis XV, King of France, was one of the few kings of Poland who were Polish by origin. The magnates, however, drove him into exile, being horrified by his views.

" What creates our fortune and our substance," Leszczynski wrote, " if not the true plebei, who give us bread, who continuously dig for us in the earth and bring forth treasure? From their work comes our comfort, from their laborious occupations, the abundance of the country . . . they bear the burden of the taxes, the army is recruited from them; in sum, they work instead of all of us so that if there were no peasants we would become peasants ourselves, and when we elevate somebody saying he is a noble among nobles, we should rather say he is a noble thanks to the peasants."[2]

Leszczynski belonged to the group of Polish patriots of the eighteenth century who realised that something would have to be done to change the régime, and the condition of the peasant. These patriots who brought new life into the oppressed country were professional men, landless and poor nobles, state officials, sometimes merchants and craftsmen, and even aristocrats. But their weakness was that they were not representative of one solid class. They could not represent the peasants' interests because they were not peasants and instinctively despised them; they could not represent the middle class because this did not exist. If they were nobles or aristocrats they realised that the selfish interests of their class were contrary to the national cause and as patriots they were ready to make sacrifices to save the country and its people from foreign domination.

Out of a population of 8.7 millions Poland had approximately 6,350,000 serfs and semi-serfs (peasants on Royal estates who were less oppressed).

[1] Coxe, p. 13.

[2] Leszczynski, p. 101.

However, the age-long prejudice againt the peasants, whose active participation in the defence of the country was obviously of vital importance, prevented the patriots from formulating any clear-cut programme. The following two extracts from King Stanislas Leszczynski's writings show this well:

> ". . . God forbid *hunc casum* (this case) that somebody should abolish *Absolutum dominium* (the absolute right over the serfs). Could he find a better means than to promise privileges of liberty to our peasants? I say, would this attraction not incite them to a general mutiny and would they not sacrifice our liberty for theirs?"

The fear of the consequences of a sudden liberation of the peasants, so long oppressed and humiliated, strove against his clear vision of the impending catastrophe:

> ". . . fruitless will be all our labours and care *ad firmandum regimem* (to strengthen the state) of the Commonwealth so long as it shall be like the statue of Nebuchadnezzar, made of the most precious stones, but frail because of its feet of clay. The common people, what are they if not the feet, or rather the base, upon which stands the Commonwealth? If this base be of clay, then the whole *moles* (burden) which rests upon it will collapse."[1]

The same hesitation can be observed in all actions of the Opposition. Even the armed Confederation of Bar (one of its leaders, Casimir Pulaski was killed when fighting as a colonel under Washington in America) which represented its views and was formed on the eve of the Partitions (February 1768) could not draw up plans of its own and therefore sent a delegate to the French encyclopaedists, Jean-Jacques Rousseau and Bonnot de Mably, asking for a programme for Poland's reorganisation. Their views, however, were not less hesitant than those of the enquirers. All that Rousseau could propose was a reform of the educational system and the limitation, not the abolition, of the *liberum veto* (all actions of the Polish Diet had to be unanimous), rejecting even an hereditary kingship.

> " I am aware that the project of enfranchisement is beset with difficulties. What I fear is not only the mistaken self-interests, the vanity and prejudice of the masters. Even were this obstacle overcome, I should still fear the vices and meanness of the serfs. Liberty is a strong food, but it needs a stout digestion; it demands a healthy stomach to bear it. I laugh at those degraded peoples who rise in revolt at a word from an intriguer; who dare to speak of liberty in total ignorance of what it means; and their hearts full of every slavish vice, imagine that, to be free, it is enough to be a rebel. High-souled and holy liberty! If these poor men could only know thee, if they could only learn what is the price at which thou art won and guarded; if they could only be taught how far sterner are thy laws than the hard yoke of the tyrant—they would shrink from thee a hundred times more than from slavery; they would fly from thee in terror as from a burden made to crush them."[2]

[1] Leszczynski, pp. 12, 151. [2] Rouseau, Vol. II. pp. 382–3.

Bonnot de Mably saw only one remedy, though he considered it premature for Poland: " Begin by setting up a legislative force and give it a power which nothing can resist. If the prejudices of the Poles are such that it is impossible to begin reform by this operation, or if the politics of their neighbours are opposed to it because they fear that the republic may be cured of its errors, then it is useless to think of the salvation of your country. One could perhaps apply a few palliatives; but do not count on any efficacious remedy. For there comes an end to the abuse of a nation. The Poles, continually a prey to the same disorders, will in the end get tired of defending the shadow of a republic which is fatal to all the citizens and which produces only despots and slaves."[1]

With but a small group of patriots having a vague programme, and with a group of aristocratic families determined to fight against all " French " innovations, the old republican kingdom of Poland was doomed; and when the neighbouring Powers " affected the first Partition of Poland in 1772 they did not require to conquer a kingdom, but only to take each a share of a state which had fallen to pieces."[2] The first Treaty was signed at St. Petersburg between Prussia and Russia in February 1772, and the second Treaty, which admitted Austria also to a share of the spoil, in August of the same year; the formal consent of the Polish Seym was extorted in 1773. Russia obtained some of the eastern territories of the Polish-Lithuanian Kingdom, including Vitebsk; Prussia some of the western territories, without Torun and Danzig; and Austria the greater part of Galicia, less the town of Cracow. In all, Poland lost about one fifth of her population and one quarter of her territory.

References

Alison, Sir Archibald, *History of Europe*. London, 1860.

Bain, R. Nisbet, *The Last King of Poland*. London, 1909.

Bonnot de Mably, *Du Gouvernement et des lois de la Pologne*. London, 1781.

Bruckner, A., *Geschichte der polnischen Literatur*. Leipzig, 1901.

Connor, Bernard, *The History of Poland*. London, 1698.

Coxe, William, *Travels in Poland, Russia, Sweden and Denmark*. Fifth edition. London, 1802.

Defoe, Daniel, *The Dyet of Poland*. London, 1705.

Eversley, Lord, *The Partitions of Poland*. London, 1915.

Gornicki, L., *Dziela* (Works). Warsaw, 1828.

Grabiec, J., *Historja, etc.* (The History of the Polish Nation). Cracow, 1909.

Lelewel, J., *Geschichte Polens*, Leipzig, 1846.

Leszczynski, S., *Glos Wolny* (A Free Voice Safeguarding Liberty). Cracow, 1858.

Modrzewski, A. Frycz, *De Republica Emendanda*. Przemysl, 1857.

Rousseau, J-J., *Considérations sur le Gouvernement de la Pologne et sur sa Réformation projetée*. Paris, 1793. (English translation by C. E. Vaughan, Cambridge, 1915.)

Skarga, P., *Kazania* (Homilies to the Diet), edited by Professor Chrzanowski. Warsaw, 1912.

Szelagowski, A., *Pieniadz i Ceny* (Money and the Revolution in Prices in Poland in the sixteenth and seventeenth centuries). Lwow, 1902.

Voltaire, *Letters concerning the English Nation*. London, 1926.

Whitlock, E., *The Ancient and Present State of Poland*. London, 1697.

Whitton, F. E., *A History of Poland*. London, 1917.

Wilbur, E. M., *Our Unitarian Heritage*. Boston, 1926.

[1] Mably, pp. 14–15.
[2] Alison, Vol. III, p. 514.

Chapter II

THE STRUGGLE FOR FREEDOM

THE first Partition had a profound effect on Polish public opinion and stirred the remainder of Poland into action. The danger of complete destruction was now not merely hypothetical but threatening and imminent. Conferences between the Emperors and their diplomats were numerous and were all directed to one end—the wiping out of Poland, which was becoming a centre of " dangerous " revolutionary propaganda.

From the point of view of intellectual life in Poland the twenty years between the First and the Second Partitions were more fruitful than had been the previous two hundred years. The Polish Opposition directed their first efforts to cultural reform, which was facilitated by the dissolution by the Pope of the Jesuit Order and the consequent expulsion of its members from Poland. Albeit unjustly, the Jesuits were accused by the patriots of having been the sole cause, by their virtual monopoly of education, of the sterility of Polish intellectual life in the seventeenth and eighteenth centuries, at a time when the English, French and Dutch were making brilliant contributions to science, art and literature.

Through the efforts of Kollontai, who was a fervent propagandist of freemasonry and an apostle of Jacobinism in Poland, a governmental body was set up to concentrate the patriots' work in the field of culture. One of the principal achievements of this Ministry of Education (1773), which was in fact the first in Europe, was the replacement of the " Catholic " language of Latin by Polish as the language of instruction. The up-to-date methods of teaching introduced by the Ministry produced groups of well-educated nobles, relatively free from medieval superstition, who became an asset to the country's struggle for freedom. There was a revival of political thought; hundreds of pamphlets began to circulate, thousands of young nobles and bourgeois, seeing the need for the progressive reform of the State, began to spread democratic propaganda in the country and to urge peasant reforms and the creation of favourable conditions for industry.

All discussion centred round the question of the constitution. On one point the patriots were unanimous: the whole régime was rotten and had to be changed at all costs. Against the advice of Rousseau, the Poles accepted the hereditary monarchy as a vital necessity, for it was obvious that the electoral system was disastrous in its consequences. They decided, also against the advice of Rousseau, that the ill-starred *liberum veto* would have to be completely abolished if the Diet were to have any real life. They accepted the principle of the division of executive, legislative and juridical powers; but they did nothing for the liberation of the peasants.

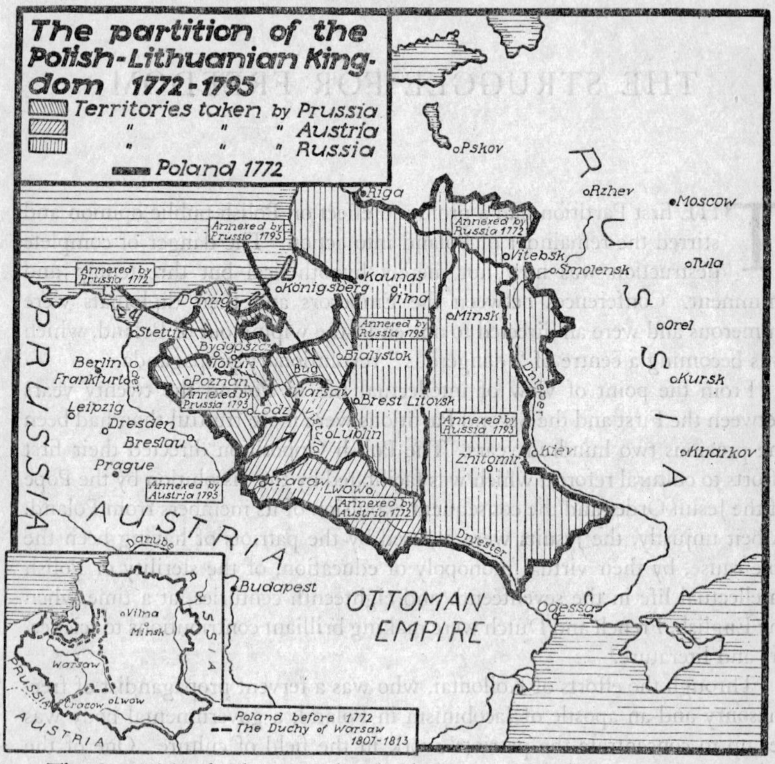

The Opposition leaders were headed by Ignacy Potocki, one of the leading figures of the Ministry of Education and an organiser of Polish freemasonry, who, according to the chronicler Czacki, "in spite of his ideas of social equality, which appeared sometimes to be his chief creed, always yielded to his hereditary traditions." They all possessed one thing in common, they could not rise to the situation at a time when higher and wider interests than those of a single group were at stake, when the fate, even the existence of the country was entrusted to them because they were bound by the ties of their private life, by their family relationships.[1] Like Rousseau, the patriots feared a peasant rising, and produced a draft constitution for a reconstructed Polish State, a project full of half-measures, satisfying no large class of the population, and actively opposed by the aristocracy. The Constitution of 3rd May 1791 provided:

[1] Morawski, p. 387.

"Art 1. The State Religion: The National Religion of the State is and will be the Holy Roman Catholic Faith. Conversion from the State religion to another one is prohibited.

"Art. 2. The Landed Gentry: Honouring the memory of our Ancestors as Founders of the Independent Government, we most solemnly promise to the Nobles' Rank all liberties, privileges, priorities in private and public life; we recognise the Nobility as the foremost Defenders of liberty and of this Constitution.

"... Art. 4. The peasants: We take, in justice, humanity and Christian obligation as well as for our own Interest, under the protection of Law and the National Government the agricultural people, from whose hand flows the most abundant source of the country's riches, who represent the most numerous population in the Nation, and thus the bravest force in the country.

"Having in this way guaranteed the nobility all advantages due to them from the peasants, and wanting most effectively to encourage the multiplication of the country's population, we proclaim complete freedom for all people who may settle in the country or who, having previously left, would now like to return."

Such a Constitution could obviously not save Poland nor liberate the sleeping forces of the peasantry, although conditions were more favourable than they had been before. The serfs began to recover their faith in their own power and to forget their defeat during the uprisings in 1648–50. The aristocrats began to complain that the peasants "threatened continually to imitate the French action, that they talked about 'better times' and believed that the king ordered them not to do week-work."

Some revolutionary nobles were already going round the country, as the Russians did a hundred years later, to mobilise the peasants, and King Stanislas August, a pawn in the hands of Catherine II, Empress of Russia, issued an edict on 11th August 1791 drawing the attention of the authorities to the "agitators who incite the people to disobey their masters, to refuse services in kind and in labour." The King was in 1756 attached to the suite of the British Ambassador at St. Petersburg, who, "blending diplomacy with intrigue, deliberately threw the charming young Pole in the way of the impressionable Grand Duchess with the result which might reasonably be expected ... Later he was for political reasons sent back to Poland; but Catherine had not forgotten her former lover."[1]

The answer of the magnates, even to the innocent Constitution of 3rd May 1791, was rebellion. The Constitution was adopted against their will—and they began to fear lest a precedent had been created. All the available evidence points to the fact that any patriotic feeling was alien to them. According to Prof. Bruckner, "The arrogance of the magnates sometimes took the form of pronounced megalomania."[2] In order to fight against the "innovations" and against the King, who rallied for a short time to the camp of the patriots, the magnates organised the Confederation of Targowica

[1] Whitton, p. 132. [2] Bruckner, p. 195.

and turned for help to Russia, because a clause had been inserted in the treaty signed by Russia and Poland after the First Partition, prohibiting any change of the Polish Constitution without Russia's consent.

The members of the Targowica Confederation, mainly big landowners, rushed with their private armies against " revolutionary " Warsaw to finish off " the anarchy created by the wretched conspirators, crazy with the spirit of the French Revolution." Catherine II sent Russian armies to their assistance (under the command of a Pole, General Branicki) and the spectre of the Revolution which they saw in the timid and abortive Constitution of 3rd May 1791 was banished. The King of Poland, at the command of the Empress of Russia, went over to the barons and " order was restored " in Warsaw. The patriots who had tried to introduce reforms were defeated, and with the active help of the leading aristocratic families of Poland, the Second Partition took place in 1793. Russia annexed all eastern provinces from Livonia (Latvia) in the north to Moldavia in the south; Prussia, the greater part of Western Poland, including Torun and Danzig. As a result, the Polish-Lithuanian Union was reduced to one third of its original dimensions. In a manifesto addressed to the world, Frederick the Great justified the Partition saying that " the spirit of French democracy and the ideas of this terrible sect are spreading more and more in Poland, so that the intrigues of the Jacobin envoys receive strong support there."[1]

How great was the egoism of the gentry is shown by the fact that when the Swedish Ambassador praised the monarchic revolution carried through in Sweden (Sweden with the help of France chose her own king against Russia's advice), Tadeusz Czacki answered : " I would prefer to be the slave of a foreign power than of my own king." The writer Suchorzewski had said in 1790, " If the chains which the succession to the throne put on the Poles cannot be thrown away by another means than by becoming Prussian, Muscovite or Austrian then such will I be." During the vote in the Diet on the Constitution of 3rd May 1791 the same noble declared: " I want to defend my country because I am free, but if she will be the bed of despotism, I proclaim myself the enemy of Poland."[2]

Characteristic of the barons' outlook was their behaviour in Galicia, which had been occupied by Austria since 1772. Dr. Morawski related how a large landowner, Madame Potocka-Kossakowska, declared to her Austrian friends : " If you leave me my wealth and my religion, what shall I have to regret? "[3] On the whole, the loss of independence had no influence on the mood of the nobility who, on the contrary, gave itself up to an orgy of feasting. The first few years of the Austrian régime were marked by fêtes, in the towns as well as in the country. The magnates even, " seeing suspicious movements among the peasants, denounced the conspirators to the Austrians."[4] According to Prof. Tokarz, " The Galician gentry after the Partition asked only for religion, property, the punishment of the apostate with death and confisca-

[1] Kalinka, p. 18.
[2] Korzon, Vol. IV, p. 631. [3] Morawski, p. 377. [4] Grabiec, pp. 244, 248.

tion of his estates, and the prevention of nobles living outside Galicia from acquiring estates there."[1]

When the Austrian monarch in 1782 relieved the peasants of some feudal burdens, abolished the nobles' profitable trade monopoly, and even divided up some land among the peasants, the majority of the Galician peasants were lost to the national cause. For centuries they had been treated like animals, beaten, oppressed and humiliated by their Polish masters. Now there came a stronger, foreign master who brought them some relief. It is not surprising, therefore, that during the whole of the nineteenth century Polish peasants in Galicia used to say "Our Emperor."

* * *

After the Second Partition (1793) Poland ceased in fact to exist. The king was still nominally in Warsaw as head of an independent state, but the Russian garrison and Catherine's Ambassador took care to prevent any further *faux pas* on his part. Even before 1791 the Ambassador, Count Repnin, was daring enough to arrest four leading Polish senators and bishops of the Opposition and to send them to prison in Russia.

The patriotic opposition came to the conclusion that in these circumstances the only possibility was an armed struggle, the success of which depended, as they gradually realised, on the co-operation of the serfs as well as of democratic elements outside Poland. Soon after 1791 armed groups of peasants were formed. They chose the Kosciuszko Cap, a Polish counterpart of the French Tricolor, which later became famous as their democratic revolutionary badge.

Thaddeus Kosciuszko, a small nobleman by origin, had left Poland in 1776, as had several other Poles who were disgusted with the misrule of the aristocrats, and had gone to fight for American independence. He reached the rank of colonel and gained valuable military experience during the war, especially at the siege of New York. Later he returned to Poland and took part in the struggle against the Targowica Confederation.

Kosciuszko's views were reflected in his will, which he drew up before leaving America: "I, Thaddeus Kosciuszko, on the eve of my departure from America, do declare and direct that should I make no other testamentary disposition of my property in the United States, I hereby authorise my friend Thomas Jefferson to employ the whole thereof in purchasing negroes from among his own or any others, and giving them liberty in my name; in giving them an education in trade or otherwise, in having them instructed for their new condition in the duties of morality, which may make them good neighbours, good fathers and mothers, husbands and wives, in their duty as citizens; teaching them to be defenders of their liberty and country, of the good order of society and in whatsoever may make them happy and useful." According to Thomas Jefferson, Kosciuszko was "as pure a son of liberty

[1] Tokarz, p. 30.

as he had ever known, and of that liberty which is to go to all and not to the few and rich alone."[1]

In January 1793 Kosciuszko went to Paris " to induce the revolutionary government to espouse the cause of Poland. In return for assistance he promised to make the future government of Poland as close a copy of the French Government as possible."[2] The Revolution made him a " *citoyen français*," an honour which was also bestowed on Bentham, Klopstock, Paine, Schiller, Washington and Wilberforce. The patriots chose him as leader of the insurrection in March 1794 in Cracow. He issued a proclamation to the whole nation (not only to the nobles; for the first time in Polish history the peasants became acknowledged citizens and not merely subjects and slaves), summoning it to the armies of independence. A few days later his peasant battalions, armed only with scythes, defeated Russian infantry and artillery forces at Raclawice. As soon as the news of the outbreak of the insurrection reached Warsaw the common people of the capital (again for the first time in the history of Poland) began a spontaneous mass struggle against the Russian occupants. " The whole night, the whole day," says a former officer of King Stanislaw August's bodyguard in his Memoirs, " the army fought against overwhelming odds. The guilds struck like lions, one with swords, a second with knives, a third with spears, others with scythes and axes. One could see workers, apprentices, blindly throwing themselves, axe or hatchet in hand, on armed Russian columns and crushing them with bravery and doggedness."[3]

The Russians were driven out of Warsaw. The *Warschauer Zeitung*, published for the German-speaking merchants and craftsmen of Warsaw, wrote on 14th May 1794: " The ambitions of patriotic citizens are thus fulfilled. Already some of the traitors have paid the penalty; henceforth treacherous sons of the country will know that the crimes of arrogant magnates will not remain unpunished in Poland." (In 1939–40 the *Warschauer Zeitung* reappeared again after a lapse of about 150 years, this time under Nazi editorship, in order to " continue the German tradition of Warsaw.")

While even Germans took part in Kosciuszko's insurrection, not one " famous " Polish name appears in the list of the officers and men of Kosciuszko's army. " The insurrection had from the first a purely popular character. We find none of the great historic names of Poland in the list of original confederates. For the most part the confederates of Kosciuszko were small squires, traders, peasants and men of low degree generally. Yet the comparatively few gentlemen sacrificed everything to it."[4]

Kosciuszko prepared his insurrection in close touch with the French Revolution. He concluded his alliance with the French Revolutionary Government in January 1793, the month when Louis XVI was sentenced to death and executed, but he could not foresee that when he called the Polish

[1] Haiman, pp. 24–25.

[2] R. N. Bain in *Encyclopaedia Britannica*, XIth Edition, Vol. XV, p. 914.

[3] Kosmowski, p. 17.

[4] *Encyclopaedia Britannica*, ibidem.

people to arms a year later, hoping for help from revolutionary France, Robespierre, with whom he had made the alliance, would be annihilated and the reaction of Thermidor triumphant.

The success of the insurrection thus depended mainly on the mass support of the Polish serfs. However, the lieutenants of Kosciuszko were mainly noblemen and, unfortunately, their aristocratic prejudices compelled him to resort to half-measures.[1] He went back on his plans and proclaimed (in the so-called Polaniecki Manifesto, May 1794) the diminution of the serfs' week-work from five or six days a week to a maximum of three days. This did not satisfy the peasants and, moreover, it made the gentry angry. To his humiliation Kosciuszko saw Polish nobles seeking out the victorious " Scythes " (who escaped from the estates to enlist in Kosciuszko's army) and beating and dragging back into slavery these rebellious subjects who, only shortly before, had conquered Russian guns. The gentry were furious at Kosciuszko's Manifesto and they considered it beneath the dignity of a Polish noble to be saved by " slaves," even if they were of Polish stock. Small wonder that after six months of fighting the insurrection was crushed. The third Partition followed as a direct result of the failure and the 800-year-old Kingdom of Poland ceased to be.

The fates which befell Kosciuszko, the Polish democrat, and King Stanislas August, the Polish aristocrat, were symbolic. Both were taken to live in St. Petersburg, Kosciuszko as a prisoner in the St. Peter Fortress, the King as the guest of honour at the Tsar's Court. " The King was received at St. Petersburg," said Prince Adam Czartoryski, " with all the honours due to a sovereign. On approaching the capital he was met by chamberlains and other high dignitaries, who complimented him on behalf of the Emperor and the members of the Imperial family. Paul offered him one of his palaces, furnished it magnificently, and did all he could to make the king's stay at St. Petersburg agreeable. There were mutual receptions and banquets." While he was rendered harmless in prison, " Kosciuszko, oppressed by a feeling of sadness, covered with wounds which were not yet healed, and bearing on his face an expression of despair, of touching resignation, almost of remorse at being still alive and having failed to save his country, greatly interested the Emperor and did not inspire him with the least fear or suspicion. He often used to visit Kosciuszko, accompanied by the whole of the Imperial family, which showed real interest and almost affection for the unfortunate patriot."[2]

* * *

Kosciuszko's insurrection was the first attempt to re-establish Poland's independence on a broader social basis. The history of all subsequent struggles for the liberation of the Polish people shows the gradual absorption of democratic principles into the minds of those who organised and fought

[1] *Encyclopaedia Britannica*, ibidem. [2] Czartoryski, Vol. 1, pp. 148–152.

against the occupying powers and their Polish allies; after each defeat the Polish democratic leaders were able to enlist the support of larger sections of the population, and also came more and more to distrust the sincerity of most of the nobility.

Three years after Kosciuszko's insurrection his friends and former officers and soldiers formed in Italy the so-called Polish legions whose aim was "an alliance with the revolution which preached the war of the peoples against the kings." These legions (1797–1804) were organised by General Dombrowski and the soldiers wore on their epaulettes the words, "Free men are brothers." The cavalry was commanded by Joselevitch, a Jew. This fact alone was a symbol of the democratic spirit of the legions, since the cavalry was the branch of the army in which nobles served by preference and tradition. The same spirit was to be seen in the following proclamation of the Administration of the province of Lombardy, signed by President Porcelli and the people's representative Visconti:

> "Virtuous Poles! Your nobleness of heart awoke the wonder and admiration of the whole world; and while the unworthiness of your oppressors is well known, the courage and firmness with which you fought single-handed against the allied tyrants is remembered with awe. There is much blood being shed in Europe for the sacred principle of Liberty. It is the aim of kings to bring all nations under their yoke; thus it is the common task of all peoples, who know their own rights, to answer force by force. The people of Lombardy hold out their brotherly hands to you and ask you for your co-operation in the struggle for freedom. Victorious France challenging all peoples to liberate and to trample down chains, fit only for slaves, shows by her unceasing triumphs how to stabilise, arms in hand, on an invincible base the only right government: the government of the people."[1]

The mistake the legionaries made was that, like many others at that time, they believed in the democratic intentions of Napoleon, and they followed him blindly all over Europe. Thousands lost their lives in Spain, some even overseas, in San Domingo.

In 1807, by the Treaty of Tilsit, Napoleon formally created in return for services rendered a substitute for Poland in the form of the Grand Duchy of Warsaw. Its constitution accorded personal freedom to the peasants, but not the soil upon which their families had toiled for centuries. Thus the peasant lost not only his chains, but also his boots, according to a witticism of the time. He could move away without his master's permission, but he had to leave everything behind him. This "liberation" of the peasants, however, by providing a supply of labour which had hitherto been lacking, provided an incentive for the introduction of industrial methods of production into Poland.

After Napoleon's defeat, the Congress of Vienna divided Poland once again. The Russian part was established as a separate kingdom (the Tsar bore the

[1] Limanowski, *Polish Democracy*, p. 52.

title King of Poland), and in May 1815 Tsar Alexander I announced the creation of a provisional government headed by a Pole, Prince Adam Czartoryski, his friend and former Russian Foreign Minister. The kingdom received its own constitution, and the civil service and the army were recruited exclusively from Poles. On the other hand, all Napoleonic reforms were abolished, the peasant's burden increased, and thousands of small nobles became serfs.[1]

Nevertheless, the struggles of Poland's democrats went on unceasingly. In August 1821 Czartoryski had to report to the Tsar that " everything seems unsettled; every institution is in danger, and the most lamentable changes of system are expected."[2]

Yet the period between 1820 and 1830 is one of the most brilliant chapters in the history of Polish culture. It was a period when Polish literature reached a very high degree of development; when Adam Mickiewicz and Juliusz Slowacki wrote their immortal works; when the great historian Lelewel taught the young people in the Universities the mistakes and lessons of the past; when Polish journalism was born; when hundreds of patriotic secret societies met all over Poland; and the whole country devoted itself to reading and learning in order to be better prepared to fight in the future. As in the sixteenth century the moving spirit was the struggle against despotism and on behalf of the people.

Organisations similar to the Italian " Carbonari " and German " Tugendbunde " were created by the Polish democrats; they also introduced Freemasonry, of which the Grand Master, W. Lukasinski, was one of the most staunch of the Polish revolutionaries. He perished in the fortress of Schluesselburg after spending more than forty years in prison (1824–68).

The programme of those secret societies which prepared the Revolution of 1830 was democratic. They did not regard the co-operation of the peasants merely as a useful contribution to the struggle for Poland's freedom. Their conception was of a Poland free from the aristocratic rule which had oppressed her own people and served the foreign invader. The free peasant, owning his land, in a free Poland, was their slogan, and the people regarded these societies as their own: " The student, at any time, was heartily welcomed to the home of the poorest peasant; to talk with the student was comforting to the peasant; and his visit was considered as an augury of happiness to come."

The Polish revolutionaries were conscious of the difficulties of a local uprising in the face of the " Holy Alliance." Although, like Kosciuszko,

[1] There is a story of how, during a Russian census, the small peasant-nobles, in fact just freeholders, were turned into serfs and expropriated with the help of the nearest Polish landlord. In the Russian language the words " peasant " and " Christian " have almost the same pronunciation. Thus the small nobles, who did not understand Russian, when asked whether they were peasants or not, answered, " Yes, we are Christians." The Russians themselves did not understand Polish and put them down as peasants. It was afterwards very easy for the neighbouring landlord not only to enclose the property of the small nobles but also to convert them into serfs.

[2] Czartoryski, Vol. II, p. 311.

they were inspired by the ideals of the French Revolution, they lacked a clear, positive plan of what to do " afterwards " and this omission proved to be fatal.

In July 1830, revolution broke out in Paris; in August Belgium rose in revolt. The time had come to act in Poland. The Paris revolution inspired the people of Warsaw to become more courageous and firmer of purpose, and even to proclaim openly that there would be a revolution in Poland. The conspirators fixed the time, and on the evening of 29th November 1830 the cadets from the officers' school in Warsaw went to the Belvedere Palace to arrest the Grand Duke Constantine who, however, managed to escape. At the same time Warsaw rose. The following proclamation was posted in the streets of Warsaw the next morning:

> " Poles,
>
> " The sad events which took place yesterday evening and during last night have determined the government to co-opt into its service some persons of outstanding merit, and to address to you the following proclamation: His Imperial Highness the Grand Duke and Tsarewicz has just prohibited the Russian soldiers from undertaking any action because Poles alone should be charged with the reconciliation of their countrymen. The Pole cannot cover his hand with the blood of his brother; and it cannot be your intention to give the world the spectacle of a civil war. Only moderation can turn away the calamities which threaten to come upon you. Thus return to order and to calm. Let the veil of night cover the passions which broke loose. Reflect upon the future and upon your country, threatened from all sides: remove all that could imperil its existence. We on our side shall fulfil our duty to maintain public order, the laws and the liberties, assured to the country by its constitution. (Signed) Czartoryski, Radziwill, Chlopicki."[1]

The situation was clear to the revolutionaries who had been preparing the revolt for many years and who, only two months before, had seen Belgium become free. They would have no negotiations with the Tsar and his Polish government, but appealed to the Polish serfs for a general peasant revolution in Poland which would develop and spread over into Tsarist Russia.

General Chlopicki had distinguished himself in his youth at Raclawice and in Italy, Spain and Russia with the " Grande Armée " of Napoleon. As a former officer of Kosciuszko he had naturally much authority amongst the young revolutionaries who consented to follow his leadership when he declared his allegiance to the insurrection. Sir Archibald Alison has described Chlopicki's rôle: " As his patriotism was undoubted, and his character elevated and disinterested, his rule was for some time unresisted even by the burning democrats of the capital. He despised and detested them as much as Napoleon did the ' avocats et idéologues ' of Paris; and it was his great object without their aid, and while retaining the direction of their movements, to work out the independence of Poland by negotiation with the Tsar, and without coming to open rupture with his authority."[2]

[1] Alison, p. 19. [2] Alison, p. 21.

The Russian Government delayed the negotiations for a few months and, when they were ready for military action, asked the insurgents to surrender unconditionally. War broke out in February 1831, and again private interests were stronger than the public welfare; the peasants were asked to help, but there was no mention of their liberation. In consequence it was difficult to expect them to join in any large numbers; the insurrection was doomed in the face of the overwhelming power of the Russians. After six months, in the autumn of 1831, the vanquished remnants were forced to leave the country.

* * *

Of the insurgents, only a few escaped to Austria; the great majority retreated in an orderly fashion towards Prussia and crossed the frontier. They were imprisoned, and only after several months were they allowed to proceed into exile in France, Belgium and England. They travelled on foot and in groups through Germany, and were everywhere warmly welcomed; people eagerly helped them on their march and poets wrote songs in their honour.[1]

" Then for the first time we felt who we were; for what great common cause we fought; why we had to go into foreign lands. And we understood that our mission would be to lead the peoples in their struggle against despotism. And we were ready to shed our blood in each fight for liberty. We said to ourselves : ' Through humanity to Poland.' " This march through Germany had some influence upon the Germans. Many years later one of the first German Socialists, J. Philipp Becker, answering an invitation from the Poles, wrote that the " enthusiasm with which the Polish exiles were received in Germany kindled in his heart the sentiment of liberty which would not cease to burn until his death."[2]

The insurrection of 1830–31 had links also with America. When the revolution broke out the American people sent a representative, S. G. Howe, to present two flags and an address from the U.S.A. to Polish regiments in Warsaw, but he arrived too late. On 29th November 1831, the first anniversary of the revolution, he expressed the opinion that had it lasted longer a large number of volunteers from America would have arrived in Poland.

The Polish democrats received from within Russia itself great support in the struggle developing against Tsarist tyranny. Adam Mickiewicz was one of the first Poles to welcome the Russian revolutionaries as allies in the common struggle against the oppressor. Monica Gardner, in her book on Mickiewicz, described his attitude to these Russians, who were later to become participants in the Decembrist plot (December 1825) : " The Russian liberals and poets became his friends, or rather, loved him as brother. He was on terms of affectionate intimacy with Pushkin, Bestushev, Ryleyev . . . At the meetings of the Russian poets and writers, he dreamed with them of a Utopian future for the human race . . . ' he lived among us ' sang Pushkin, ' among an alien race. There was no hatred for us in his soul. We loved him.

[1] The famous *Polenlieder*, one of which is printed on page 182.

[2] Limanowski, p. 207.

He shared our banquets. Our purest dreams were never hidden from him; he knew our songs. . . . He often talked with us of those future times when nations, laying aside mutual hatred, will be united as one family. Eagerly did we hearken to those words of the poet. He went to the west, and our blessings accompanied him on the way '."

Many years later, in Paris, Mickiewicz remembered his friends with melancholy thoughts:

" To my Russian friends:
Do you remember me? As often I think
Upon the death, imprisonment and exile of my friends I think of you.
Where are you now? The noble neck of Ryleyev
Which as a brother's I embraced, now,
By the Tsar's command, hangs on the shameful tree.
Cursed be the nation that slays their prophets!
That hand which Bestushev, poet and soldier
Stretched to me; that hand torn from the pen and sword
The Tsar hath harnessed to the convict's barrow,
And to-day it toileth in the mines, chained to a Polish hand."[1]

On the other hand, it cannot be said that the attitude of Poland's magnates to the 1830 insurrection was favourable. This was Adam Mickiewicz's testimony: " Men who have killed the Polish revolution, the Czartoryskis, the Zamoyskis . . . Count Ladislas Zamoyski had related that his friends and he, seeing no better way of forestalling the revolution of 29th November 1830 than by increasing the vigilance of the Russian police, lost in the apartments of the Grand Duke Constantine an anonymous letter which denounced the plans of the conspirators. The Grand Duke did not believe it."[2]

Princess Radziwill told a story of her father, Count Adam Rzewuski, who was aide-de-camp to Field Marshal Diebietch, in command of the Russian army, during the Polish " mutiny " of 1830. When a Russian army corps, under General Rudiger, was cut off and all Russian officers sent to him were caught by the insurgents, it was Rzewuski who finally succeeded, disguised as a pedlar, in making his way through the Polish lines. As a result " Dwernicki, together with Ramorino, another leader of the mutineers, were compelled to seek refuge across the Austrian frontier and to lay down their arms there."[3]

Another aristocrat, Leon Radziwill, also fought on the side of Russia, while his cousin, Alexander Dominic Radziwill, fought with the Poles. The Tsar rewarded the former with the vast domains of the latter, which remained in the possession of this line of the Radziwills up to September 1939. The participation on the side of the Tsar of Rzewuski, Radziwill and others, was probably not accompanied by any feeling of disloyalty towards their own country. In their opinion the national interest of Poland lay in as close a co-operation as possible with Russia. They swore fidelity to the Tsar and felt it

[1] Gardner, pp. 42–44, 45.
[2] Mickiewicz, pp. 152–3.
[3] Radziwill, pp. 1–19.

their duty to stand by their word. This attitude was not new; the last king of Poland, Stanislas August, officially declared Kosciuszko a criminal for having risen against the established authority. The same attitude recurred many times until in 1917 the Russian Revolution turned the Polish aristocrats into enemies of Russia.

After their arrival in France the insurgents set to work to analyse the causes of the continuous defeats of the revolts and to establish a programme of action. After long discussions the programme was ready in December 1836. It was published simultaneously in Polish, English, French and German, and signed by 1,135 Polish officers and soldiers, survivors of the war of 1830–31. This manifesto later became the guide for generations of Polish insurgents.[1] It was a milestone in the history of the peasant question. From this time onwards the problem of Poland's independence was recognised as being closely linked with the peasantry's claims to liberty and land. The Polish patriots came to the conclusion that a programme of this kind offered the only hope of success in any new insurrection against the overwhelming power of Russia, Prussia and Austria. Current among the Polish democrats was a " modernisation " of Cato's warning: " *Ceterum censeo, adscriptionem ad glebam delendam esse.*"

The monopoly of labour possessed by the aristocracy favoured co-operation between the middle classes (consisting of Germans, Jews, some native remnants of the former splendour of the Polish towns, landless nobles, civil servants and professional men) and the peasants. It was obvious that modern industrial production could not be developed while the peasants remained serfs. Workers were lacking and there was no home market for any products which might be manufactured. Freedom for the peasants was thus in the interest of the middle classes.

There were many weak points in the revolutionary movement. The majority of the leaders were nobles and the mass of the peasants were often suspicious of their intentions. Further, the Polish Democratic Society relied on a spontaneous mass movement; they looked upon the oppressed serfs as a powder barrel which would explode when a sufficient number of organised revolutionaries proclaimed a new insurrection with a clear peasant programme. In so doing they overestimated the militancy of the scattered peasants who, moreover, were disillusioned by the failure of previous risings.

The Polish Democratic Society, although formed by the emigrants, had close links with the people at home. Many of its members returned to Poland to co-operate in the movement which sprang up there and to organise the struggle against the occupying Powers. Many of them perished at the gallows in Warsaw, Vilna and in Galicia. Limanowski described one of these revolutionaries, Edward Dembowski, who was afterwards shot during the Cracow revolution in 1846. " He founded in 1842 in Warsaw the *Scientific Review* which, so far as the censorship allowed, spread progressive opinions and fought against reactionaries of all kinds. Soon he was forced to flee and

[1] See Appendix.

went to Poznan, where he became one of the most influential propagandists. He devoted to the Polish revolutionary cause not a part of himself but the whole of his energies. Imprisoned in 1844 by the Prussian government he escaped from prison and came to Galicia, where he worked and conspired with the Mazurian peasants in Tarnow and the Ukrainians in Sambor. . . . Edward Dembowski could be described as a giant, with the face and stature of a fifteen-year-old boy. Watched by the police all over the country, caught, imprisoned, set free, within a space of a fortnight he would instruct conspirators in Poznan, Cracow, Lwow, and still have time to take part in conferences on the banks of the Rhine. He appeared like the will-o'-the-wisp on the moors on a dark night, like the beloved hero of popular legends."[1]

Another leader of the Polish democrats, Simon Konarski, was shot in Vilna in 1838, and a letter he wrote to his mother on the eve of his death was circulated long afterwards in Poland and Lithuania. In Paris in 1835, while editor of " *The North*, a magazine devoted to the liberation of the peoples of North Eastern Europe," he wrote:

> " Does the peasant thief steal treasures? Silver or gold? The wretched father takes a piece of timber from the woods to warm his cold-stiffened children, he carries off a few bundles of corn to feed his wife dying of hunger. That is his crime!
>
> " In no country is there so much arson as in Poland, although in each Diet Polish nobles have imposed increasingly severe laws for incendiaries. Prison, whipping, branding, pillory, chains, even capital punishment, nothing could prevent the criminals. Did Nature create upon earth this peculiar species of monsters, who feel an unconquerable desire to destroy another's property with no benefit at all to themselves? The unfortunate peasant toils by the sweat of his brow with no profit for himself; groaning in misery, cold and hungry, he begs mercy from his master, who replies by beating him. Stricken, in despair, he seizes the torch and takes revenge on the godless master, or on his property. Polish nobles! Learn to love justice, end your oppression, break the rods, acknowledge the peasants as your brothers, let them live free, and arson will disappear and the bells will no more sound the alarm to waken you from your slumber, nor will any blazing fire dazzle your eyes."[2]

In 1844 the Russian authorities discovered a widely organised peasant plot in Central Poland under the leadership of the Catholic priest, Father Sciegenny. He was of peasant origin and was very popular with the serfs. He was in close touch with the emissaries of the Democratic Society and his political ideal was a Poland " free and protected from the arbitrariness of the rich and the autocracy of individual men." The plot flared up prematurely and Father Sciegenny was imprisoned and sentenced to death. No bishop, however, would consent to unfrock him and he was sent to Siberia where he died in 1890, several generations of Polish revolutionaries having previously joined him there.

[1] Limanowski, p. 299.

[2] *Polnoc* (The North), Paris, March 1835. Quoted by Chodzko, p. 11.

The democrats became afraid of further discoveries which would weaken their forces. And, as the signs of the approaching " Spring of Nations " were more and more numerous, they decided to act. They appointed three leaders of the revolution, Dembowski in Austrian Poland, Dombrowski (the son of the Commander of the Polish Legions under Napoleon) in Russian Poland, and Mieroslawski in Prussian Poland.

The time of the insurrection was fixed for the night of 21st and 22nd February 1846. Mieroslawski, however, was arrested by the Prussians and Alcyata, the delegate from the Democratic Society, called off the insurrection. At a time when means of communication were few and slow such a decision could only cause confusion, and Dembowski therefore decided not to submit, but to act on the pre-arranged date, encouraged in this decision by the spirit prevailing in Galicia. The insurrection began according to schedule, a provisional Polish National Government was set up in Cracow, headed by a Cracow lawyer, Tyssowski, and the leaders issued the following proclamation to the people (afterwards reprinted in Paris and London):

> " We are 20 millions—let us rise as one man, and no force on earth can crush our power. We shall enjoy such liberty as never was known on earth. Let us establish a state of society in which every man shall enjoy his share of the fruits of the earth according to his merits and his capacity; in which no exclusive privilege of any kind whatever will be allowed to remain; in which every Pole will find a full guarantee for himself, his wife and his children; in which every man disabled by nature in the use of his bodily or mental functions will find, without humiliation, the unfailing assistance of the whole social body; a state in which those portions of land which hitherto have been merely in the conditional possession of their cultivators, will become their absolute property; in which all rent, socage labour and other similar burdens, entailed upon these lands, will cease without any indemnity to the landlords; and those who will devote themselves in arms to the national cause, will be remunerated by a grant of land from the national domains.
>
> " Poles! From this moment we recognise no distinction among ourselves; brethren, henceforward we are the sons of one mother, our country; of one God who is in Heaven: Let us invoke His support, that He may bless our arms and grant us victory; but to draw down his blessings we must not sully ourselves with intemperance or plunder, we must not disgrace our consecrated arms by using them for oppression or murder of the disarmed dissenter and foreigner; for we do not struggle against the people of foreign nations, but against our common oppressors."[1]

In a separate decree the equality of rights of the Jews with those of the Christians was declared.

The order calling off the revolution reached some parts of the country and not others, and many revolutionaries were undecided whether to rise or not. Those from Russian Poland decided to move towards Cracow, the centre of the revolution. This appears to have been a mistake. The theory of pre-

[1] Manifesto of the Polish National Government, London, 1846.

cipitating a general, regular war prevailed among the revolutionaries, yet they could probably have fought more successfully as guerillas[1] against the overwhelming, well-organised military power of Austria, Russia and Prussia. Guerilla warfare would probably have stimulated the peasant revolution and they might have been able to hold out until the general European revolution, which broke out two years later. It was a simple matter for the regular armies of the occupants to defeat the small groups marching towards Cracow, and for the Austrians to quell the uprising altogether. Those who were captured were sent to the Austrian fortresses of Spielberg and Kufstein; many were executed.

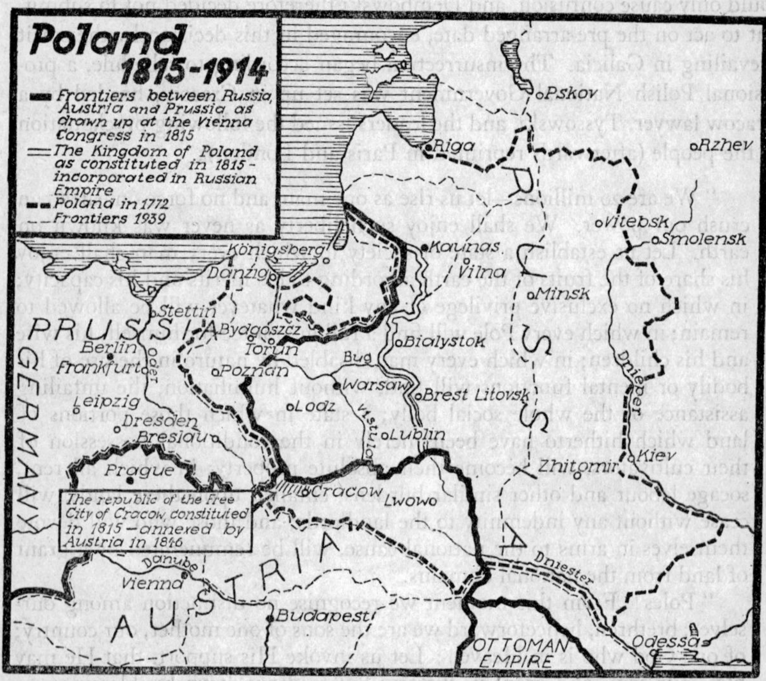

The last act of the abortive Polish insurrection of 1846 took place in Berlin in 1847. The trial of Louis Mieroslawski (the so-called *Riesenprozess*) and other insurgents from Prussian Poland lasted for several months. It was a public trial and aroused great interest all over Germany. The prisoners were accused of harbouring "revolutionary plans with anarchistic and communistic tendencies" and reproached with representing the Polish Democratic Society. On 27th November 1847 Mieroslawski was sentenced to "loss of nobility, confiscation of property and beheading by the axe." Kosinski and six others were given the same sentence, twenty-four were sentenced to life imprisonment, seventeen to twenty years' prison. Mieros-

[1] This method was later adopted in the insurrection of 1863.

lawski's speech for the defence was later printed by German Liberals and distributed throughout the country.[1]

The sentence on Mieroslawski was not carried out because of the tense political situation. A few months later, on 20th March 1848, " The people of Berlin rushed to the Moabit prison, set free the Polish prisoners, put Mieroslawski in a coach decked with the Polish colours, and proceeded to the King's castle. The King, when called upon, came to the balcony in the company of his minister Arnim and greeted the prisoners with the salute ' Long live Poland.' "[2]

Kosinski, the second defendant in the long list of 260 accused, depicted in 1850 the sadness with which the prisoners awaiting punishment contemplated the complete indifference of the Polish landed gentry to their fate. " When we went to prison in February 1846, on account of the abortive insurrection, the conspiracy was not only presented in a most shameful way by our enemies, but even among our countrymen there was not much fellow-feeling for us. On the contrary, reaction grew to such an extent that papers like *The Picture of the National Soul* became popular in the Grand Duchy of Poznan. If our situation were sad in itself, it was really most painful to see our countrymen slinging mud at us, disowning us, declaring us to be madmen. As a consolation to us in prison they sent the message : ' As you make your bed so must you lie on it.' "[3]

The democratic elements of Europe welcomed the 1846 Revolution. In England there were debates in the House of Commons and in 1846 there was a society established for the regeneration of Poland, of which Ernest Jones, the Chartist, was President, and Thomas Singsby Duncombe, the Radical M.P. for Finsbury, a leading member. This society in two successive years presented petitions to the House of Commons in which it demanded the intervention of the British Government in favour of the restoration of Poland's independence.

On the 17th anniversary of the Polish insurrection of 1830 Friedrich Engels declared at a meeting in London that German Democrats were especially interested in the restoration of Poland, as no nation could be free while at the same time oppressing other nations; the liberation of Germany could not be achieved until after the liberation of Poland from German oppression. Poland and Germany, therefore, had common interests and Polish and German Democrats should be able to co-operate in the task of liberating both nations. The restoration of democratic Poland was the first condition for the restoration of democratic Germany.[4]

The Cracow revolution had consequences in Eastern Europe. The Ukrainian revolutionaries, who, like those in Poland, connected the liberation of the serfs with their national emancipation, began to stir themselves. The

[1] L. Mieroslawski, *Verteidigungsrede*, Brunswick, 1847.
[2] Limanowski, *Poles in* 1848, p. 84.
[3] Kosinski, p. 1.
[4] Misko, p. 15.

movement was quickly suppressed, however, by Tsarist authorities. Among those arrested in Kiev was the Ukrainian poet Shevtchenko.

* * *

The defeat of 1846 by no means discouraged the Polish Liberals from their activities. Two years later Mickiewicz and others organised a new Polish legion in Italy to help in the struggle developing against Austria, the common enemy of Poland and Italy. Before marching from Rome the legionaries published their articles of faith (mainly the work of Mickiewicz), the more important of which were as follows:

> "God's words, manifested in the Gospels. Law of nations, domestic and social law. . . . Each member of the Nation is a citizen; each citizen equal before the law and authorities. . . . To Israel, the elder brother, respect, brotherhood, help on his way, eternal and earthly welfare. Equal right in all. To the comrade of life—the woman: Fraternity, citizenship, equal rights in all. To every Slav, living in Poland, brotherhood, citizenship, equal rights in all. To each family, soil for the household under protection of the community; to each community, common soil for use under the protection of the state. . . . Political and friendly help from Poland for the brother Czechs and the peoples related to the Czechs as well as to the brother Russians and the peoples related to the Russians; Christian help for every nation as fellow-creatures."

The German revolution of 1848 provided a favourable opportunity for those in the Prussian part of Poland. Public opinion, however, was divided and a considerable difference of views existed between the Deputation of the townsmen of Poznan and the Democrats. According to Limanowski, "The Deputation of Poznan in the persons of Mielzynski, Raczynski and others, had in mind the provincial, local interest above all. The revolutionary committee on the other hand put the greatest weight on a war for the independence of the whole of Poland. In the Deputation one part was for the complete independence of the Grand Duchy of Poznan, linked by a personal union with the Prussian Monarchy, the other, only for autonomy."[1]

The peasants adopted a passive attitude; serfdom had been abolished in Prussian Poland in 1827 and some of the peasants, remembering the past, feared a return to slavery if Poland again became independent. Under these conditions no armed struggle could be successful although Poznan was for a short time in the hands of the Polish Democrats. In 1920 Field Marshal von Hindenburg recalled the following event which took place during his childhood: "In the year 1848 the rising in Poland had its repercussions on the province of Posen. My father went out with his regiment to suppress this movement. For a time the Poles actually got control of the city. They ordained that every house should be illuminated to celebrate the entrance of

[1] Limanowski, *Polish Democracy*, pp. 370–1.

their leader, Mieroslawski. My mother was in no position to resist this decree. She retired to a back room and, sitting on my cot, consoled herself with the thought that the birthday of the 'Prince of Prussia' fell on that very day."[1]

Mieroslawski later fought with German and Italian Liberals, and acted in turn as Commander-in-Chief of the revolutionary armies in Baden, Bavaria and Sicily; he was also Commander of the Polish insurrection in 1863.

Other Poles took part in the Vienna revolution, and the first to be shot there, together with Blum, the deputy to the Frankfurt Parliament, was Jelowicki, one of the insurgents of 1830. Cracow and Lwow rose after Vienna, and although these towns were at once bombarded and the revolts suppressed, the year 1848 brought one most important change for the majority of the Polish people in Galicia—the abolition of serfdom by the Austrian Government on 17th April 1848. "All praedial labour and other compulsory duties of the peasants performed in the former state of serfdom are abolished against compensation at a cost to the government which will be fixed in the future," declared the Government decree. After the suppression of the revolution this compensation was fixed so as to reimburse the aristocrats at the expense of the people. Right up to the twentieth century Galicia remained one of the most backward parts of Europe.

The Austrian Monarchy had a more difficult task in crushing the revolution in Hungary. Many Poles were in the ranks of the Hungarian revolutionary army, and some of them held leading positions. This served as an excuse for the Austrian Emperor to ask the Tsar to intervene. On 8th May 1849 Tsar Nicholas I declared that "in Hungary and Transylvania the forces of the Austrian Government, divided by reason of carrying on the war on many fronts, could not until now quell the rebellion. The insurrection, strengthened by the influx of our Polish mutineers of 1831 and by reinforcements of exiles and vagabonds from other countries, takes on a more and more threatening form. In such unhappy circumstances, the most illustrious Emperor of Austria asked for our help against the common enemy; we would not refuse the help."[2]

The Russian army was commanded by Prince Paskevitch, who had taken part in the quelling of the Polish insurrection of 1830–31. Under him was Count Rzewuski, a Pole who at that time had also fought with the Russians. Princess Radziwill wrote that in 1848 he was "selected to convey to the town of Moscow the news of the final victory of the Russian troops." She also wrote that Rzewuski's relative, Count Raczynski, was Prussian Ambassador in Madrid.[3]

Count Raczynski, who was Privy Councillor of the King of Prussia and one of the leading members of the Polish landed aristocracy in Prussian-occupied Poland, defined his attitude to the events of 1848 as follows: "It seems that there is being seriously considered in Frankfurt the suggestion of offering the crown to my king. I am trembling. Could my king have

[1] Hindenburg, p. 7. [2] Marx, Engels, Liebknecht, p. 28.
[3] Radziwill, pp. 16–17.

become the instrument of a revolutionary and anarchic assembly? . . . The king is only awaiting a favourable occasion to break with the demagogues and to rally around the policy of resistance of Austria and Russia. I have confidence in the prudent and loyal views of the Austrian Cabinet . . . Be it God's wish that they soon finish with Kossuth."[1]

When Kossuth went into exile after the defeat of the Hungarian revolt, Stanislas Worcell, who became the leader of the Polish Democratic Society in 1849, introduced him to British audiences whom they addressed jointly on numerous occasions. After Worcell's death in 1857 Alexander Herzen, the Russian Liberal, wrote an appreciation of him:

> "Worcell was a holy man; I use this word advisedly, as it best explains his outstanding character. The whole existence of this man was a boundless act of devotion, of complete self-abnegation, of incessant work. Everything which strikes us in the legends of the Saints we find again in him, feature by feature, but with greater love and with a more human element. Born in wealthy circumstances, in the bosom of the Polish aristocracy, he died poor and democratic. He discarded his titles and gave up his fortune when his country was broken. . . . He had one of those single-minded natures . . . which, dominated by a single great thought, by a great and single aim, can achieve the calmness of absolute resolution, an indestructible tranquillity, and consequently gentleness as well as inflexible will. Such were for the most part the martyrs of science, the heroes of religion, at the time of the Renaissance and the Reformation. . . . It was the way of Worcell. It was the way of one of his friends of whom he was passionately fond, Joseph Mazzini. Nine years ago, a few days after the February Revolution (1848), Worcell said to Lamartine, or rather to the French Republic: 'To every call of the peoples, in the armies of struggle and misfortune, Poland is the first to answer "Present"; for she sees in each struggle for liberty a struggle for Poland. She is also present now. . . .' The Polish emigration with Worcell as its outpost remained in fact almost under arms. They were 'Present.' But there was no call. The peoples were sleeping. The order of Warsaw reigned over Europe. The faithful soldier fell by his sentry-box, and the heavy wheels of reaction passed over his body."[2]

Another Pole, Prince Czartoryski, was also active in England. As former Minister of Foreign Affairs (in Russia) he thought that diplomatic action offered the best hope. At the beginning of the Crimean War he offered his services to the British Government, promising that if the Polish question should be raised by the war and Austria be unwilling that Galicia be involved, Russian Poland would rise alone if it were declared independent, and would be a decisive force on the side of the allies. He guaranteed that Galicia and Posen would remain quiet.[3]

[1] Adhemar d'Antioche, pp. 55–56.

[2] *L'étoile polaire*, London, 10th February 1857.

[3] Czartoryski, Vol. II, p. 357.

No evidence is to be found, however, that Czartoryski had any democratic backing. The Polish Democrats were unequivocally against him. Mickiewicz considered him a traitor to the Polish cause, and a friend of Pilsudski's early days said that the Polish Democratic Society had to protect former insurgents of 1830–1 " from the agents of Prince Czartoryski, who did their best to put them in uniforms and send them to the battlefields in Portugal, Algeria and Egypt."[1]

Prince Czartoryski's political counterpart in France, General Rybicki, offered Poland's services to Napoleon III. The Polish Democratic Society countered this step by a declaration, signed by Worcell and others, which said that " at all calamitous epochs for the liberties and rights of a nation, every one of them had its renegades, among these it is that Poland numbers her ex-chief-commander Rybicki. To him belongs the opprobrium he recently drew upon himself, but which in no manner falls upon the Polish nation or the body of her exiled children, as the nation who first inscribed upon her banners that noble motto: ' For our and your liberty,' and never betrayed her word, has since, at several epochs fought for her liberty and that of others, and still fight under the banner of the fraternity of peoples—but under that of oppression—for her slavery and that of others—never."[2]

Lelewel said of Polish leaders, such as Czartoryski and Rybicki, that " they never had either the courage or the will to improve the conditions of the people who could thus have realised that they were fighting for their own welfare. . . . (They) roamed about the world instead of arousing the forces at home, and for foreign conquerors they created servile legions. . . . The best material for the restoration of Poland is on her own soil, in her own forces, and all people who rise for their own liberty are natural allies of Poland. She will not lay claim to support, but to brotherly love: only by this latter will nations be able to help one another."[3]

For these reasons, and also because of the lack of support in Western Europe, the Democrats concentrated their work after 1848 on Polish territory. They emphasised more than ever their identity with the people. A contemporary verse illustrated this attitude:

> " Like peasants, brethren, let us dress
> If you wish the people to lead.
> Our love alone does not express
> Enough. To dress like them we need.[4]

Outward signs of a personal approach to the peasants became numerous. Even such pastimes as dances were affected. The Polonaise, the dance of the aristocracy with its proud solemnity and dignified bearing, gave place to country dances, to the quick, vigorous tempo of the Mazurka, Krakowiak or Kolomyjka. The campaign against illiteracy was carried into the serfs' hovels by the wives and daughters of democratic nobles.

[1] Yodko-Narkiewicz, p. 14. [2] *Reynolds' Newspaper*, London, 13th December, 1852.
[3] Lelewel, p. 538. [4] Soboleski, p. 43.

Religious differences disappeared in the unity of national feeling. The Jewish youth of both sexes took part in patriotic demonstrations during church services. Efforts were made to approach the Lithuanian, Latvian, White-Russian and Ukrainian peoples and to arouse their national consciousness.[1]

Under the unrestrained Tsarist terror, open political activity was confined to demonstrations in churches against the oppressive régime. Revolutionary feeling grew in proportion to the intensity of the terror and, as in the period before 1830, the whole country became riddled with secret societies. In the army Russian-Polish revolutionary committees were formed which were later to lead the armed struggle.

* * *

The Democratic Society, later called the " Red " party, was preparing the insurrection, and its General Staff included Ludwik Zwierzdowski, an officer of the Russian General Staff, Jan Dombrowski, later a hero of the Paris Commune, and Stanislas Bobrowski (Joseph Conrad's maternal uncle).[2]

The Agricultural Society, the other organised body of public opinion, was opposed to the revolt and believed in a gradual increase of national liberty for the Poles within the Russian Empire. The leader of the Society, which was later called the " White " party, was the Marquis Wielopolski, head of the civil administration of the Russian part of Poland.

A French writer gave the following portrait of Wielopolski: " He was perhaps one of the most interesting and significant characters . . . a great landowner, his estates reaching into all parts of Poland, devoted to Russia, not out of servility or out of self-interest, but out of a passion for vengeance against the West.

". . . This aristocrat had nothing but scorn, not to say hatred, for the conspirators and the democratic propagandists who were already organised, and for the party which he was soon to denounce as 'the party of social disorder, the dregs of all classes, bad priests, young demagogues, ruined landowners, farmers in debt, flunkeys, communists.' . . . The Polish nobility will doubtless rather march with the Russians at the head of Slav civilisation, which is young and vigorous."[3]

It is not surprising that Wielopolski decided to suppress the insurrection at its inception. W. Smith O'Brien, in a lecture held in Dublin in July 1863, gave an account of the developments in Poland, saying that " the Grand Duke Constantine . . . listened to the counsel of a renegade Pole, the Marquis Wielopolski, and consented to share with him the responsibility of carrying into effect a scheme for removing from Poland all persons who were considered dangerous by the Russian police. This was to be effected by such a

[1] Limanowski, *Insurrection of 1863–4*, p. 78.

[2] Stefan Zeromski, the Polish writer, called Bobrowski, a "dauntless fighter, conspirator and emissary." (*Wiadomosci Literackie* (The Literary News), Warsaw, 17th August 1924.) Conrad's father was also a member of the Democratic Party (Morf, p. 39.)

[3] Mazade, pp. 117, 190.

change in the law of conscription as allowed the Russian functionaries to select as a recruit any person in the country whom they might wish to expatriate except the highest class of the nobility and the agricultural peasantry." The British Ambassador to Russia described the conscription as " a simple plan by a clean sweep of the revolutionary youth of Poland to kidnap the opposition and to carry it off to Siberia or the Caucasus."[1]

The conscription, called proscription in Poland, was a heavy blow to the Democratic Party. Military service at that time lasted fifteen years, and submission to conscription would have meant a loss of thousands of young men of value to the insurrection. On the night of 14th and 15th January 1863, when the Russian police came to take the recruits, they had to arrest their fathers or younger brothers. The proscripted conspirators had fled into the woods.

The democrats were in a difficult position. They were not yet prepared for an insurrection. The peasants, the main body on which they counted, were not roused. Moreover, the Russian revolutionaries urged a postponement of the rising as they were not ready to co-operate effectively. However, the insurrection was begun and they had to act accordingly.

The Revolutionary Committee of the Democratic Party issued a manifesto on 22nd January 1863, proclaiming the insurrection and declaring " all sons of Poland, irrespective of religion and family, origin and rank, free and equal citizens of the country." The manifesto implied the liberation of the peasants and equality of rights for everyone. Out of a population of about five million persons, only 10,000 badly armed, ill-clothed, inexperienced insurgents joined the struggle, though they managed to harass the armies of the Russian Empire for almost eighteen months.

The Polish insurgents had learned their lesson of the years 1830–31 and 1846–48. It was generally accepted by them that if victory was to be gained against the overwhelming odds, it could only be by guerilla warfare in conjunction with the rising of the serfs, and by spreading simultaneously the revolutionary war into Russia. In a military sense they were better off than before, as Mieroslawski, the hero of 1846–48, had organised a Polish military academy in Northern Italy, where many revolutionaries had studied.

The mass of the peasants were still inactive, though many groups joined the struggle and even fought independently under their own leaders or under the command of priests of lower rank. There were signs that the peasants were losing their mistrust of the revolutionary nobles and were beginning to understand that they were fighting not for the old monarchical Poland of serfdom, but for a genuinely democratic society. However, there were also cases where the " peasants, suspecting the insurrection of aristocratic aims, presented on many occasions a hostile attitude and sometimes threw themselves on the insurgents and bound them, but in those places where they knew what they were fighting for they helped the revolutionaries."[2]

[1] Seton-Watson, p. 432.
[2] Limanowski, *Insurrection of 1863–4*, p. 101.

In March 1864 the insurrection spread into Lithuania; even in Russia, on the borders of the Volga, a rising was prepared but was prematurely discovered. The government became alarmed and granted to the serfs in the so-called Northern Provinces, that is Lithuania, Latvia and Estonia, exclusive property in the land they held. This measure was later extended to other parts of Russia. The hunting of armed detachments of insurgents was fruitless, although many casualties were caused among them. When faced with a concentration of Russian troops they disappeared among the peasantry, only to reappear strengthened by new volunteers. The Russian government saw no solution but to remove the central cause for unrest; on 2nd March 1864 serfdom was abolished throughout Russia (including Poland). The serfs were confirmed in their property rights over the land on which they worked, and the landowners were indemnified by state securities.

From that date onwards it was difficult for the insurgents to count on the mass support of the peasants, or on the spreading of the revolution into Russia. Although the liberation of the peasants was by no means all gain, it meant a very great deal to them. The insurrection lost its dynamic force, and began to drift slowly towards defeat, particularly after the capture and execution of its leader, Romuald Traugutt.

The insurgents, except on rare occasions, did not have the support of the landed aristocracy.

> " The behaviour of the majority of the gentry towards the insurrection was shocking. If they had not been afraid they would even have been ready to help the Russian government to capture the insurgents. They sowed despondency, spread defeatism among the leaders of the insurrection. . . . All the members of the Galician White Committee, an organisation of the gentry, with the exception of Prince Sapieha and some others, declared themselves against the insurrection. One of them, Alexander Dzieduszycki (later Regent of Galicia), declared that ' Galicia had to think only of alms for the barefooted, the naked and the hungry, who would flee from the (Polish-Russian) kingdom ' . . . the enormous concentrations of Russian troops, a reign of terror, the gentry's fear and shrinking from all action and the approaching winter, all this very much aggravated the difficulties of the insurgents. Driven from the manors of the nobles, they found asylum with the poor gentry and in the hovels of the peasants. Without the protection and the help of the peasants they would not have been able to survive the winter; billeted in hamlets, disguised as peasants, they awaited the coming of spring."[1]

In February 1863, a few days after the outbreak of the revolution, Count Lubienski proposed an armistice between the Russians and the Poles. He stated that the partisan war, started in Poland against Russia, was a great misfortune and a grave danger to the two countries; that he had reasons to believe that the revolution was not aiming at the independence of Poland, but wanted on the Vistula, as elsewhere, a hotbed of discontent which could

[1] Limanowski, *Insurrection of 1863–4*, pp. 115 and 172.

always produce new recruits and which could spread into Russia; that it wanted, not a Free Poland, but a revolutionary Russia, for that country offered vast resources to socialism.

"In the middle of the storms which were brewing in Europe Russia boasted of the perfect calm and profound peace in her vast states. This prestige has disappeared. Several years ago the most powerful states in the world, France and England, helped by Piedmont and Turkey, launched their attacks against the rocks of Sebastopol, and were unable to do any serious harm to Russia. At the present time the greatness of the Empire is threatened by a handful of young men, unarmed, unpaid, undisciplined, without uniform. . . . And that is not all. If the revolution triumphs on the banks of the Vistula it will necessarily spread to the banks of the Neva. If the pestilence coming from the West is not stopped by the vitality of Catholic Poland, it will spread without difficulty into Russia. The crime is a recent foreign importation into Poland and serves only to sully the last pages of her history, which are the purest among those of all the nations of the world. The revolution must be put down in Russia with the utmost energy, and that cannot be done except with the co-operation of the Emperor and the Poles." He recommended, therefore, that the Polish provinces should be governed by Poles who recognised Russia's sovereignty.[1]

A similar attitude has been expressed by another Polish magnate, Count Roger Raczynski, who declared that the former Tsars wanted to be rulers rather than oppressors of Poland, and wished their successors to be so in fact, thus fulfilling their "noble duties" and also satisfying their legitimate ambition.[2]

The insurrection had a profound effect in Europe. Britain, France, Sweden, Denmark, Holland, Spain, Portugal, Turkey and Turin all sent notes to the Tsar dealing with the Polish question. Louis Napoleon tried to persuade the Russian Government that conciliatory measures towards Poland would be in their own interest, and the fear of a new revolution in Hungary and Venice caused Austria to do the same. Prince Bismarck, on the other hand, took a different view and, summing up the Prussian attitude in Parliament, said that the movement in Poland, according to evidence in his hands, was prepared with the help of Mazzini and conducted with the co-operation of Mieroslawski, and that it also enjoyed the support of revolutionary elements in all countries. He, therefore, rejected the idea of non-intervention, considering that the Emperor Alexander would be a much more pleasing neighbour for Prussia than the Poland of Mieroslawski, which would devote itself to subversive propaganda.[3]

The Polish insurrection did indeed enjoy the support of many European democrats. In 1868 there was published in Cracow an incomplete list of 4,000 insurgents who had perished either during the insurrection, or later, at the gallows, in exile or in Siberia. Fighting for what they considered to be their

[1] Lubienski, pp. 3–17.
[2] Raczynski, pp. 40–41.
[3] Bismarck, Vol. II, pp. 58–69.

common cause, those who fell included the Russian officer Bezdishkin and the Russian soldier Bondarew, the Polish Count Mycielski and the Kossack Konkow, the Hungarian Count Otto Esterhazy (former cavalry officer of 1848) and the Austrian Baron Benedeck, the Englishman Anderson (whose brother was shot in 1830–31 as an insurgent) and the French Count Young de Blankenheim, the German Jew Posner (former officer of Garibaldi) and the Prussian officer Sprung (who went over to the insurrection from active service), the Swiss Caplazzi, the Ukrainian Kondradenko, the Italian Becchi (former officer of Garibaldi), the Lithuanian Galenaitys, and many others.

After the collapse of the insurrection a French delegation came to London, and at a meeting called in September 1864 to protest against the cruel suppression of the Polish revolution, it was decided to found the " International Working Men's Association " (i.e. the first Socialist International).

According to Jean Jaurès, the European working classes at that time found in the Polish problem an illustration of the fact that isolation was the primary cause of their helplessness; he stated that the International Association was a direct outcome of the meetings on behalf of Poland.[1] Karl Kautsky also regarded Poland as the midwife of the International, and said that the demonstrations in favour of Poland were the first actions of Western European workers since 1848 in which they showed a spirit of international unity.[2]

The Polish insurrection resounded even in America, where many former insurgents found refuge; some of them took part in the Civil War, and two of them, Karge and Krzyzanowski, fighting on the side of the Northern States, attained the rank of general.

The last echoes of the insurrection of 1863–64 were heard in 1871 at the barricades of the Paris Commune, in which the generals Dombrowski and Wroblewski and other Poles took part.

In his history of the Commune, Lissagaray stated that the command of some of the most important positions was entrusted to Wroblewski, whom he praised as " one of the best officers of the Polish insurrection, young and adept in military science, brave, methodical and shrewd, turning everybody and everything to account. An excellent chief for young troops." Wroblewski later escaped to London, where he became a member of the Council of the Socialist International. His views were similar to those of the young Pilsudski, with whose policy in the Polish Socialist Party he agreed. Dombrowski was killed in action and Lissagaray also described a touching scene during his funeral, when soldiers, one after the other, came to place a last kiss on the brow of their fallen commander.[3]

References

Adhemar d'Antioche, Comte, *Le comte Raczynski et le Marquis de Valdegamas*. Paris, 1880.

Alison, Sir Archibald, *The War in Poland*, 1830–31. London, 1863.

Bain, R. N., *Encyclopædia Britannica*, XIth edition.

[1] Jaurès, Vol. X, p. 143.
[2] Kautsky, *Neue Zeit*, 1896, Part II.
[3] Lissagaray, pp. 214, 348.

Bismarck, Prince, *Speeches*, edited by W. Boehm. Stuttgart, 1890.
Bruckner, A., *Geschichte der polnischen Literatur*. Leipzig, 1901.
Chodzko, L., *Zywoty* (The lives of outstanding Poles). Paris, 1859.
Czartoryski, Prince Adam, *Memoirs of*, edited by A. Gielgud. London, 1888.
Gardner, Monica, A. Mickiewicz. London, 1911.
Grabiec, J., *Historja, etc.* (The History of the Polish Nation). Cracow, 1909.
Haiman, M., *Polacy, etc.* (Poles in America). Chicago, 1930.
Hindenburg, Marshal von, *Out of My Life*. London, 1920.
Jaurès, Jean, *Histoire Socialiste*. Paris, 1905.
Kalinka, Rev. I., *Czasy, etc.* (The Times of Stanislas August Pomiatowski). Poznan, 1867.
Kautsky, Karl, *Finis Polonia?*, *Neue Zeit*. Stuttgart, 1896.
Korzon, T., *Historja* (History of Poland). Cracow, 1908.
Kosinski, W., *Kwestja, etc.* (The Polish Question in 1846). Poznan, 1850.
Kosmowski, S., *Czasy, etc.* (The Times of Stanislas August). Poznan, 1867.
Lelewel, J., *Geschichte Polens*. Leipzig, 1846.
Limanowski, B., *Historja, etc.* (The History of Polish Democracy after the Partitions). Zurich, 1901.
Limanowski, B., *Udzial, etc.* (The Participation of Poles in the Revolutionary Movement of 1848). London, 1897.
Limanowski, B., *Powstanie, etc.* (The National Insurrection of 1863–4). Lwow, 1889.
Lissagaray, *The History of the Commune of* 1871. London, 1902.
Lubienski, Comte E., *L'Armistice entre les Russes et les Poles*. Leipzig, 1863.
Marx, Engels, Liebknecht, *Odbudowa, etc.* (The Restoration of Poland). Cracow–New York, 1910.
Mazade, Charles de, *La Pologne Contemporaine*. Paris, 1863.
Mickiewicz, A., *La Tribune des Peuples*, ed. by his son W. Mickiewicz. Paris, 1907.
Mieroslawski, L., *Verteidigungsrede*. Brunswick, 1847.
Misko, M., *Marx, etc.* (Marx and Engels on the Polish Question). Kiev, 1934.
Morawski, C. M., *Poglad, etc.* (A view on the Opposition of the Magnates). Cracow, 1908.
Morf, J., *The Polish Heritage of J. Conrad*. London, 1930.
Narkiewicz, Yodko, and Simon Dickstein, *Polski, etc.* (The Polish Utopian Socialism). Cracow, 1904.
Raczynski, Count Roger, *Mémoires sur la Pologne*. Berlin–Posen, 1863.
Radziwill, Catherine, *My Recollections*. London, 1906.
Seton-Watson, R. W., *Britain in Europe*, 1789–1914. Cambridge, 1937.
Soboleski, P., *Poets and Poetry of Poland*. Milwaukee, Wisconsin, 1929.
Tokarz, W., *Dezyderaty* (The Desiderata of the Galician Gentry). Cracow, 1908.
Whitton, F. E., *A History of Poland*. London, 1917.

B[illegible], Prince, *Speeches*, edited by W. [illegible], Brussels, 18[illegible].
[illegible], A., *[illegible]*, [illegible], 1901.
[illegible], L., [illegible] (The Baron of [illegible]), Paris, 18[illegible].
C[illegible], Prince Adam, *Memoirs*, edited by [illegible], London, 1888.
Gardner, Monica, *[illegible]*, London, 19[illegible].
[illegible] (The [illegible] of the Polish [illegible]), Cracow, 19[illegible].
H[illegible], M., *[illegible] Poles in America*, Chicago, 19[illegible].
H[illegible], M. [illegible], *[illegible] Life*, London, 1920.
[illegible], Paris, 190[illegible].
K[illegible], (The Times of [illegible] August Poniatowski), Poznań, 18[illegible].
[illegible], *The [illegible]*, [illegible], 18[illegible].
[illegible], *[illegible]*, Cracow, 18[illegible].
[illegible] (The Polish [illegible] in 18[illegible]), Poznań, 18[illegible].
[illegible] (The Times of Stanislas August), Poznań, 18[illegible].
[illegible], *[illegible] Poland*, [illegible], 19[illegible].
[illegible] (The [illegible] of Polish [illegible] and the [illegible]), [illegible], 19[illegible].
[illegible], B., [illegible] (The Participation of Poles in the Revolutionary [illegible]), [illegible], 19[illegible].
[illegible], (The National [illegible] of 18[illegible]), [illegible].
[illegible], *The History of [illegible]*, London, 18[illegible].
[illegible], [illegible], 18[illegible].
[illegible] (The Restoration of Poland), Cracow, [illegible] 1910.
[illegible], *[illegible] Contemporaine*, Paris, 18[illegible].
[illegible], *[illegible] des [illegible]*, [illegible], Paris, 18[illegible].
M[illegible], A., *[illegible]*, [illegible].
[illegible], Chicago, 19[illegible].
[illegible] (The Opinion of [illegible]), [illegible].
[illegible], *The Polish Heritage of [illegible]*, London, 19[illegible].
[illegible] (The Polish [illegible]), [illegible], 19[illegible].
[illegible], Louis [illegible], *[illegible]*, 18[illegible].
R[illegible], *[illegible] Recollections*, London, 18[illegible].
[illegible], *[illegible]*, Cambridge, 19[illegible].
[illegible], Milwaukee, Wisconsin, 19[illegible].
[illegible] (The [illegible]), [illegible].
W[illegible], *[illegible]*, London, 19[illegible].

Part Two

THE TRANSITIONAL PERIOD

"WE will not cease our struggle with only half our aims achieved and having restored only part of those rights due to all dwellers upon Polish soil. To our principles belong the future and victory. We may fall, our enemies may prevail for a time for they have on their side the egoists and the misguided people and those who do not think, but the principles in which we believe will not fail. In their name the struggle will begin again over our graves and will be renewed until the equality of rights due to all mankind is guaranteed."

(*From a proclamation of the Polish Democratic Society in Paris, 17th March 1832*).

Chapter III

MODERN DEVELOPMENT

THE insurrection of 1863 closed the last chapter in Poland's feudal history. The liberation of the serfs created conditions favourable to industrial production, which had been almost non-existent in the first half of the nineteenth century, and which was developed on different lines in each of the three parts of Poland occupied by Austria, Prussia and Russia.

Prussian and Austrian Poland were incorporated into areas whose general development was superior to the backward conditions of the occupied Polish territories. Consequently, in spite of the great demand for industrial machinery and products, which arose as an indirect result of the emancipation of the serfs, native industry could not be developed on a considerable scale since the areas were served by German and Austrian industry and trade. The Polish provinces annexed to Germany and Austria remained, therefore, the most backward parts of these countries, serving as their agrarian "hinterland."

In Russian Poland the situation was different. In spite of the mercantilist policy inaugurated by Peter the Great, the development of Russian industry until the liberation of the serfs remained at the stage which had been reached by the industries of England and the Low Countries two centuries earlier. The abolition of serfdom gave both Russia and Congress Poland the same favourable start. But the proximity of Germany and Austria and the fact that Russian Poland was the most westerly part of the Russian Empire and, therefore, the artery for transit trade between these countries, created a situation totally different from that which prevailed in the Prussian and Austrian parts of Poland; thus the Congress Kingdom became one of the most industrialised and most progressive parts of the Russian Empire.

After the Congress of Vienna, Czartoryski's government had brought into the country foreign craftsmen, especially textile specialists from Germany, and even industrialists from Western Europe, such as Coqueril and Fraget. At that time Lodz, the future Polish textile centre, had been founded by the immigration of thousands of German families who were granted free sites for building, exemption from taxes for a time, and other favourable conditions. An important German group has survived to the present time. Some of the former craftsmen, like Geyer, Biedermann and Scheibler, later became large factory owners, employing up to 10,000 workers. Because of the peculiar feudal development of Poland and the lack of a Polish-Christian middle class, the textile industrialists of Lodz were chiefly of German or Jewish origin.

Other measures had included the introduction of Chambers of Commerce, hitherto unknown, and provided for the raising of mortgages. The state-owned Polish National Bank, which had been founded in 1828, engaged in a great variety of business—deposits, the issue of government and private bonds, mortgage loans, and the financing of industry. Yet all these measures failed to stimulate industrial development, for the whole country was cramped by serfdom. In 1857 there were 13,000 factories in Russian Poland, with 56,000 workers, i.e. an average of only 4–5 workers per factory, and the textile industry, in spite of the stimulus of the Crimean War and the blockade of Russia, was still operated by manual labour and not by power.

The abolition of serfdom at once destroyed the feudal system of husbandry, and all branches of human activity were brought into a money economy. The landowner now had to pay for labour, the agricultural worker obtained money to spend, and the peasants, now free from bondage, became both the customers and the source of labour supply of which industry was so much in need. A period of prosperity dawned in Russian Poland.

The following figures illustrate her rapid economic progress:[1]

*Production of coal in million pouds.**

1860	... ...	3.6
1870	... ...	13.8
1880	... ...	78.4
1890	... ...	150.8

Production of pig-iron in million pouds.

1860	... ...	0.7
1870	... ...	1.3
1880	... ...	2.4
1890	... ...	7.4

Number in thousands of spindles in the cotton industry.

1863	... ...	116.2
1870	... ...	289.5
1880	... ...	600.0

Total value of production in million rubles.

		Cotton Industry		Wool Industry	Linen Industry	Industry Total
1860	...	8.1		4.3	1.2	50.0 (1864)
1870	...	10.2		4.0	1.2	63.9
1880	...	33.0		22.0	5.0	171.8
1890	...	47.6	(1891)	35.5	6.5	240.0

* 1 poud = approx. 36 lbs.

[1] Luxemburg, p. 23; Koszutski, p. 250.

The counterpart to the development of industry was the concentration of labour in larger units and an increase in the number of workers. In 1850 there were 50,000 industrial workers in all, while in 1900 there were 300,000 workers in the larger industrial undertakings alone.

The abolition of serfdom and the rise of industrial methods of production completely changed the social structure. The large mass of landless or small land-owning nobles were drawn into the productive process as professional men, merchants, manual and non-manual workers. As in other countries, but to a lesser degree, feudal distinctions began to disappear, and to be replaced by differentiation according to wealth. The new industrialists, merchants and others, rose in the social scale to the level of the old aristocracy, while poorer nobles, who could not afford to pay wages to agricultural workers, had to sell their estates and sank into the middle class.

In the feudal period the small nobility, the middle class and the serfs had organised and fought in the insurrections. In the industrial period the poorer nobles did not exist as a distinct section of the community; they were beginning to disappear among the new classes of society, although the old feeling of superiority to the professional man, the business man or the worker, and, of course, the peasant, was preserved to some extent even up to the present day. The relatively prosperous economic conditions caused those who benefited from them to feel less antipathy towards the Powers who were occupying Poland, and, since it was most probable that the restoration of independence would affect the European *status quo*, not only the landed aristocracy, but also upper sections of the middle class, who had hitherto been actively interested in the revolutionary movement, shunned the idea of taking any action against the occupying Powers. It was the intelligentsia and the industrial workers who carried on the tradition of the struggle for independence.

Active collaboration with the occupying Powers varied both in kind and degree in the three parts of Poland. The majority of the big Polish landowners were of Lithuanian or Ukrainian origin and their biggest estates were mainly situated in the East and South East and not in ethnographic Poland. Consequently they could consider themselves the peers of the grand dukes and lesser dukes of St. Petersburg and Vienna; but in Berlin they were poor in comparison with the East Prussian junkers and were the Cinderellas of the German court. They were admitted to the highest posts in Austria, and virtually ruled that monarchy together with the Austrian and Hungarian barons.

* * *

In 1861 the Galician Diet had adopted the following address to the Emperor of Austria: " Without fear of being disloyal to our national idea, and with faith in the mission of Austria and trusting in the decisive changes which your Imperial words expressed as your definite aim, we declare from the depths of our hearts that we stand and will stand by you, Your Majesty."[1] After the insurrection of 1863 the leader of the Galician Conservative Party, Popiel, wrote to Prince George Lubomirski: "We must dissociate ourselves from this last insurrection, declare and condemn it as pernicious, and get rid of the men who stood at its helm or supported it."[2]

The Austrian Monarchy, beaten in Lombardy in 1859 and crushed at Sadowa in the Prussian war in 1866, needed reorganisation, and strengthening by the admission to the Government of non-German-speaking peoples. Socially, the nearest were the Polish barons of Galicia, and they were the first, and practically the only ones, to be accepted on fully equal terms in Vienna. According to Professor Alison Phillips, "The Poles in Galicia, or at least those who carried political weight, were and are a dominant aristocracy, and their ideals could only be realised at the expense and in the teeth of the opposition of the mass of the Ruthenians (Ukrainians) whose sympathies were naturally attracted to their brethren across the Russian border. To the Austrian Government their support has been invaluable."[3] There was hardly an Austrian Government between 1860 and 1914 which did not include a Polish Minister. In 1914, at the outbreak of war the following Poles occupied important posts in Austria: Bilinski, Minister of Finance of the Dual Monarchy; Zaleski, Finance Minister of Austria; Tarnowski, Ambassador in Sofia; Pomiankowski, Ambassador in Constantinople; Szeptycki, Military Attaché in Rome; Adamkiewicz, Chief of the Austrian Intelligence Service in Serbia; the army included generals Baczynski, Beck-Rzykowski (Chief of General Staff), Grzesicki, Przyborski, Zielinski and others. It also happened that the Russian Minister in Vienna in 1914, Szebeko, was of Polish extraction.

Count Potocki and Count Badeni were each Prime Minister for a long time, and many of the Ministers of Finance were Poles. Bilinski, who was also Minister for Bosnia and Herzegovina, was one of the main authors of the ultimatum to Serbia in 1914.[4] Wickham Steed has stated that the annexation of Bosnia and Herzegovina was first conceived by the Foreign Minister, Count Goluchowski, who was also a Pole.[5]

In return for their co-operation the Polish barons obtained autonomy for Galicia; the post of Minister for Galicia in the Vienna Government and that of the Regent of Galicia were reserved for their nominees. The magnates had also, as a result of the electoral system,[6] a stable majority in the autonomous parliament. Professor Dyboski wrote that "loyalty to the Church of Rome and to the Austrian state were its fundamental principles; it abhorred all dreams of national revolution as well as radical social changes."[7]

[1] Daszynski, Memoirs, Vol. 1, p. 17.
[2] Lipinski, p. 2.
[3] Phillips, p. 215.
[4] Temperley, Vol. IV, p. 69.
[5] Steed, p. 240.
[6] The electorate was divided according to income and social classes with equal parliamentary representation. The proportions were: one deputy per 60 landowners or per 4,000 industrial entrepreneurs, 12,000 country dwellers or 70,000 inhabitants of towns. (Drage, p. 103.)
[7] Dyboski, p. 239.

The chief aim of the Austrian Government towards their largest province was to keep Galicia as an agricultural market for the products of Austro-Hungarian industry. This aim suited the large landowners of Galicia who feared a rise in the price of labour if the country were industrialised. The results were the preservation of an abundant reserve of agricultural workers and abject poverty among the population of Galicia, living in worse conditions than existed anywhere else within the Austrian Empire.

The autocratic policy of the Galician nobles caused most suffering amongst the former serfs, whether Poles or Ukrainians. The reform of 1848 had given them liberty and the soil upon which they worked, but the resulting burden of debt and heavy taxes turned them into life holders of over-mortgaged property.[1] The peasants were evicted from time to time, and the small lots of land were bought up by neighbouring landowners. In addition, the natural increase of population, the lack of any industry able to absorb it, and the old custom of dividing the land among all the heirs, greatly impoverished the peasants, who formed three-quarters of the population of Galicia.

> " All the faults of the *ancien régime* of Poland," wrote Limanowski, " multiplied by the 100-years-old Austrian policy of stagnation, have up till now distinguished Galicia. . . . People live on potatoes.[2] They suffer from unremitting hunger, lose their vitality and are unable to resist disease in its mildest forms. Mr. Szczepanowski (a leading Galician industrialist who violently attacked the policy of the Galician rulers) calculates an average of 50,000 who die of hunger every year in Galicia. The average expectation of life of the Galicians (27 years for men and 28½ years for women) is about six years less than that of Czechs and thirteen years less than that of the English. The population is underfed and therefore physically weak. Of all the provinces of Austria, Galicia produces the highest percentage of men unfit for military service: out of 1,000 conscripts there are no more than 115 who are well built, healthy and strong enough to bear all the burdens of the soldier. . . . The Galician agriculturalist produces forty per cent less than the agriculturist of the Polish Kingdom (Russian Poland) and of Hungary."[3]

The aristocrats lived on a grand scale, entertaining strangers to Galicia in the old luxurious manner of the Polish and Russian aristocracy. Mr. Szczepanowski, for instance, relates a story about a member of a deputation from the Austrian Parliament, who came to Galicia in a special train, went to Lancut in a procession of forty coaches and was afterwards entertained on a lavish scale in the French restaurant at the Lwow Exhibition: " Now," he said, " I know what it means to be a Polish magnate and what Poland is!"[4]

Generosity towards foreigners of the same rank and extreme niggardliness towards their own people were the characteristics of these pillars of the Austrian Monarchy. Besides large estates, they inherited from the feudal past

[1] Limanowski, p. 122.
[2] Galicia was at that time a large grain exporter.
[3] Limanowski, p. 90.
[4] Szczepanowski, Vol. I, p. 265.

another privilege, which was not abolished in 1848, namely, a monopoly of the production of beer and spirits; no one could produce spirits except the owners of former serf-estates (the so-called tabular properties). At the end of the nineteenth century forty per cent of all Austrian breweries and distilleries were in Galicia, with the result that out of all sentences for drunkenness in Austria, Galicia's share in 1890 was 91 per cent. Galicia also held the record for another form of malpractice, namely, usury; sentences for offences against the usury laws were 81 per cent of the Austrian total. Only about 4 per cent of the Galician population, the lowest percentage of the whole Empire, paid any income tax (the figure for the province of Lower Austria was 36 per cent).[1]

Industrialists were scorned politically, and spurned socially, and economically all possible barriers were raised against the development of industry by the united front of Austro-Polish landed magnates. Here, as well as in other branches of human activity, the situation was changed only a few years before the outbreak of the war of 1914–18.

According to the census of 1910 there were in Galicia 4,096 so-called larger industrial enterprises, employing 102,000 workers (an average of about 25 workers per enterprise), of which 2,300 (56 per cent) with 85,000 workers were using steam power. The great majority of industrial workers were recruited from amongst the peasantry who would agree to almost any wages and conditions. According to the law, the working day was 11 hours, but this limit was exceeded almost everywhere. In the building trade it was 14 hours, in flour mills 15 hours, and in saw mills 16 hours. Factory buildings were poor, unhygienic and frequently endangered by fire. In spite of this, Galicia had only one fire brigade to 78,000 inhabitants and 1,371 houses, whereas the corresponding figures in Bohemia and Moravia were 3,000 inhabitants and 367 houses. The Galician figures for schools and police were also low. The differences seem to have been caused by the fact that after the liberation of the serfs, the two communities, the village and the manor, were separated and the peasants had to bear alone the cost of the village administration. In 1900–10, on the average, only about 10–30 per cent of industrial enterprises had to be insured against accidents, although the accident rate in Galicia was high. In spite of these conditions the Galician workers were said to be capable, industrious and honest, and when the Canadian system of boring was introduced in the Galician oil industry, it was found that the trained Galician workers were equal to the Canadians. In the oil industry there appeared for the first time in Galicia signs of an intelligentsia of manual workers. It was stated that, in spite of poverty, insufficient education and their despised social status, the working class had more consciousness of citizenship than most other classes.[2]

The last available figures show that 32 per cent of the land in Galicia (2.5 million out of a total of 7.8 million hectares) belonged to five thousand

[1] Rocznik, etc. (Statistical Yearbook of Galicia) 1900–10.

[2] Limanowski, pp. 110–13.

people, while more than five million peasants owned the remaining land.

When the Polish peasants, driven by poverty, found refuge in the United States, the contrasts of backward Galicia with progressive America had serious repercussions on their national consciousness. In Galicia they were despised and treated as inferior; in the United States, on the other hand, the peasants, whose fathers and forefathers had for centuries been trained to submission and servility, began for the first time to feel like free human beings. A desire for quick assimilation was the natural result.[1]

The Polish emigrants were welcomed as industrious and dexterous workers, and, poor and submissive as they were, they were ready to accept even the hardest labour and were pleased with the lowest positions. " Polish emigrants, poor and ignorant, adapt themselves quickly to a new culture which seems superior to their own since they never came into contact with higher forms of Polish culture."[2]

A large number turned to agriculture in order to appease their age-long hunger for land. The peasant saw in the possession of land a sign of social superiority, and the heritage of the serf mentality probably explains, to some extent, their very strong attachment to the soil. The authors of an extensive work on the Polish peasantry wrote, for instance, that

> " in the consciousness of the peasant who pays absurd prices for a piece of land there is no equivalence possible between land and any other economic value; they are incommensurable with each other. Land is an unique value, and no sum of money can be too large to pay for it; if there is bargaining and hesitation, it is only because the buyer hopes to get, elsewhere or at another moment, more land for the same money, not because he would rather turn the money into something else. And if later the interest on his capital is hardly 1 per cent, he does not complain if only his general income, that is the interest and his work, is sufficient to give him a living. He does not count his work, or rather he does not associate the interest on his capital and the product of his work, because his work is due to the land, and he is glad that he can work on his own land, not elsewhere. How strong and one-sided the land hunger can be is proved by some examples of emigration to Brazil. Peasants who had twenty morgs of cultivated land sold it and emigrated, because they were to get there, at a cheap price, forty morgs of land, although not cultivated. So the mere difference of size between their actual and their future farm was a sufficient motive to overcome the attachment to their country and the fear of the unknown, to lead them to undertake a journey of two months and incalculable hardship afterwards."[3]

* * *

A similar situation to that which existed in Galicia developed in Prussian-occupied Poland. Prince Antoni Radziwill, who married a niece of Frederick

[1] Panek, p. 28. [2] Daszynska-Golinska, p. 21.
[3] Thomas, Vol. I, pp. 190–1.

the Great, became the first Regent of the Grand Duchy of Poznan, after it was annexed by Prussia. He had been a commander of the Magdeburg garrison and his chief-of-staff was the future Field Marshal von Moltke, who remained a close friend of the Radziwill family.[1] Many others also accepted high positions in Prussia. The Bishop of Poznan, Stablewski, declared: " We feel ourselves to be Prussian subjects; we have recognised unconditionally the existing legal situation of the State "[2] (i.e. of Posnania as a part of Germany).

The general reasons for Polish co-operation were indicated by Count Mycielski: " A Pole, whatever his class, is fanatically attached to his tragic country, his language, religion and customs. This is a noble virtue of which one should not complain, just as every honest person holds in high esteem those Alsatians, who remained faithful to Germany, in spite of belonging to France for centuries. The love of the Poles for their country is by no means irreconcilable with the political *status quo*. The best servants and the firmest supporters of the Crown have been recruited from amongst the Austrian Poles, with whom we share a common outlook. We have listened long enough to false friends and we have made unfortunate as well as unwise attempts to regain our independence with arms. We have realised that this is not possible and we have had more than enough of pulling chestnuts out of the fire for others."[3]

Living conditions were much better in German Poland than in other parts of Poland, owing to the higher degree of industrialisation in Germany and to the fact that serfdom there had ceased to exist in 1827. It was not abolished under pressure as it was in Austrian and Russian Poland, and was therefore carried out in a more orderly manner. From 1827 for a period of about thirty years, the peasants every year received allotments which were sufficient for existence as well as for a gradual indemnification of the landowners, while landless peasants became absorbed into the rising industries (especially in Upper Silesia and later in the Ruhr area). At the end of the nineteenth century the German Government tried to carry through, by legal means, a complete assimilation of the annexed Polish territories. The plan was to uproot the Polish element from the land. These efforts succeeded to the extent of buying out the Polish aristocrats—hence the pre-1939 situation in Western Poland where there was a number of German estates but no settlements of German peasants—but failed, on the other hand, with regard to the Polish peasantry. As a result of the German drive the peasants gained national consciousness and, favoured by economic prosperity, even began to buy land; thus the peasants proved to be a more effective bulwark against the German invasion of the land than the large landowners.[4]

The situation in Russian Poland was similar to that of Austrian and Prussian Poland. The National Democratic Party under the leadership of Roman Dmowski declared: " The present state and situation of our nation

[1] Radziwill, p. 65.
[2] Lipinski, p. 3.
[3] Mycielski, pp. 4–6.
[4] Dyboski, p. 220.

does not present any conditions for armed or diplomatic action for the sake of independence, nor even for any immediate preparation for such action . . . therefore, the National Democratic Party takes as the starting point for its activity the existing conditions and the juridical system of the state."[1] Roman Dmowski himself held that the period of insurrections and of armed struggles for independence was thenceforward closed. The Polish question did not present itself even to Polish public men as an international question with the reconstitution of the Polish state for its immediate object. "There is taking shape a totally different conception of the Polish cause. It is to be henceforward the struggle for existence, the struggle for justice, for the maintenance of national individuality, and for the affirmation of the personality of the Polish nation in each of the three Partitioning States."[2]

Other Polish politicians went still further:

> "Is it possible," wrote Count Lubienski, "for Poles to regain some time in the future the independence of their country which, within its ethnographic boundaries, is inhabited by 15 million Poles? Obviously, no calculations can be based on such uncertain assumptions and the fate of 15 million persons cannot be made dependent on them. It is necessary, therefore, to give up all dreams and political ambitions and replace them by action for the improvement of the well-being of Poles in those countries into which they have been incorporated. They can do so by becoming faithful subjects of their monarchs and useful members of the communities in which they have to live, preserving, however, their attachment to the Polish nation. . . . It seems to me that in the relations between Russians and Poles the Russians should themselves aim at making it possible for the Poles to exist under Russian rule; they should, it seems to me, even in the Russian interest, try to attract that quite numerous section of educated Poles to work for the common end, for the further increase of the power and glory of Russia. . . . The Poles do not give up hope that such a solution of the Polish question in Russia, which would make possible moral and material well-being in accordance with justice and human dignity, will sooner or later be reached. Their hope in that respect is based on their unshakable belief in the monarchs, who, in caring for the happiness of the many millions of their subjects, aim at the happiness and glory of Russia; and who would, by the solution of the Polish problem, undoubtedly increase the glory and true greatness of the Empire."[3]

The co-operation of the Polish pro-Russian element with the government of St. Petersburg was particularly strong in the economic sphere. The British Consul-General in Warsaw pointed out that in the opinion of Warsaw and Moscow manufacturers, they should unite in their efforts against the British in Central Asia and Persia and eliminate those (German) manufacturers on the bank of the Vistula who were "Russian subjects only *de jure*."[4]

The "National Review," published under the auspices of the Polish National Democratic Party (led by R. Dmowski) demanded in 1908 the

[1] Lipinski, p. 7.
[2] Dmowski, p. 68.
[3] Lubienski, pp. 99–104.
[4] Foreign Office, Annual Series, 1893, No. 1183, p. 5.

extension of the Polish Kingdom to East Prussia and declared that in this instance Polish interests were identical with those of the Russian nation. (" In this struggle of international antagonisms it will probably be possible to find a common point of view, so long sought, but until now without success, by the best representatives of both nations."[1])

The identification of Poland's interests with those of Russia served as a basis for the support of Russian and the re-emergence of Polish imperialism. A National Democratic publication noted, for instance: " We are Poles, and we want Poland for ourselves, we want her, if it is not possible otherwise, even at the expense of the liberty and progress of other nations, at the expense of civilisation and social justice. . . . The old-time patriots and democrats, who for many years have become used to the idea of the national struggle being a struggle for liberty, and of the Polish cause being the cause of all the oppressed, even the cause of all peoples, will recognise the necessity of a struggle against foreign occupants, but they cannot consent to the idea that the national cause should require the use of force against other nations, or that it should be necessary to force upon others something against their own will."[2]

The Polish Club in the Russian Duma, like the Polish Club in the Austrian Parliament,[3] voted, in most cases, with the majority, often supporting the Tsarist Government against the Russian liberal opposition.

* * * * * * *

Socialist circles had already existed among the exiled insurgents of 1830 and 1863. No evidence, however, is available as to the existence of organised Socialists in ethnographical Poland before 1880, when the Socialist Party " Proletariat," directed by Louis Warynski and based on Marxist principles, was started. In 1884 the " Proletariat " concluded a working alliance with the Russian Party " Narodna Wolja " (The People's Will). After the assassination of Tsar Alexander II in 1881, which was organised by the " Narodna Wolja," and the liquidation of that party (in consequence of which Joseph Pilsudski and his brother were sent to Siberia for five years, although they were innocent), came the turn in the fortunes of the Polish " Proletariat." In 1885 several hundred members of the party were arrested and some of them hanged in the Warsaw citadel, which was built for the insurgents of 1830–1; Warynski was sentenced to sixteen years' imprisonment and sent to the Schlusselburg fortress, where he died three years later. The political attitude of the " Proletariat " can be gauged from the report of a speech made at a meeting in Geneva on the fiftieth anniversary of the 1830 insurrection, by Dr. Casimir Dluski. Dluski was the brother-in-law of Madame Curie, under whose guardianship the great scientist spent her first years in Paris. " Between

[1] *Przeglad Narodowy* (The National Review). Warsaw, May 1908, pp. 618–21.
[2] *Przeglad Wszechpolski* (The Pan-Polish Review). Lwow, October 1901 and May 1902.
[3] Phillips, p. 215.

Marie and Casimir Dluski a fraternal affection had been formed which was to last out their lives."[1] Dluski later built a sanatorium for consumptives in the Tatra Mountains, where he sometimes used to hide fugitive Russian revolutionaries.

He said that Kosciuszko's insurrection failed because of the opposition of the gentry who cared only for the interests of their own caste. He pointed out that the insurrection of 1830 had done nothing for the people, and had also failed as a result of the egoism of the propertied classes; and finally that the insurrection of 1863 had neither the power nor the opportunity to remove the influence of these class interests. He declared that patriotism in Poland was only a mask to cover the egoistic aims of the gentry and the bourgeoisie, and demanded that this should cease. The new conditions in Poland led to the emergence of Capitalism, which gave rise to Socialism, its inevitable counterpart; and that in view of the peculiar history of the Polish nation, the task of the Socialists in Poland should be above all to explain the separate interests of the working classes, and the true significance of the slogans so skilfully employed in Poland to the detriment of the masses. Dluski concluded that the watchword of the Socialists in Poland ought to be " Down with patriotism. Long live the International."[2]

At the same meeting in Geneva a letter was read which was received from the Socialist International and signed by Marx, Engels and others. The letter said that the cry " Long live Poland," which resounded in the nineteenth century in Western Europe, was not only an expression of sympathy and respect for the militant patriots of Poland, crushed by brutal force; it was also a solemn greeting to the nation whose insurrections, so unfortunate for itself, had always barred the way to counter-revolution, and whose best sons had carried on the struggle unceasingly, fighting everywhere under the banner of the revolution of the peoples. On the other hand, since the partition of Poland was confirmed by the Holy Alliance, and by the domination of the Tsar over all the governments of Europe, then the cry " Long live Poland " signified: " Death to the Holy Alliance, and death to partisans of the armed forces of Russia, Prussia and Austria."[3]

The Social Democratic Party of Poland and Lithuania (SDKPL), founded in 1893, became the political heir of the " Proletariat." This party, like its predecessors, considered that Socialism was the primary aim to be achieved, and that national freedom could only be gained if the governments of the occupying powers were overthrown by revolution. They laid more stress, therefore, on Socialist propaganda and international co-operation with other Socialist parties than on the struggle for national liberty.

The national struggle was not very popular amongst the peasants, or among the first generation of industrial workers who were largely recruited from them; the era of serfdom was still fresh in their memories and they were afraid of losing the advantages gained in the nineteenth century, if

[1] Curie, pp. 102–8. [2] *Rownosc* (Equality). Geneva, November 1880.
[3] K. Marx, F. Engels, W. Liebknecht, pp. 152–4.

Poland became independent again. Ignacy Daszynski, the famous Socialist rebel of the Viennese Parliament, and a close friend of Joseph Pilsudski, gave another reason for this prejudice:

> " We understand very well why it is so," he wrote. " The National Democrats, clericals and ' compromisers ' have so besmirched the word ' nation,' have so well succeeded in making of it an universal antidote to Socialism, and a cover for hypocrisy and gendarme methods, that many comrades spit upon the infamy of such chauvinism and will not hear anything about the ' nation.' . . . The upper classes, not being able any longer to live by exploitation alone, nor by squeezing out the peasants and workers, and having no forces on which to build an independent state, begin to cultivate political blackmail. I do not mean, of course, by the use of this word to brand and insult personally each member of the upper classes in Poland. But I condemn as blackmail the wholesale propaganda of ' patriotism ' which at the same time declares criminal or mad those who would prepare the people for the struggle for independence.
>
> " . . . No wonder that the worker, exploited and deceived, clenched his fists at this despicable and cowardly ' patriotism ' of the gentry. No wonder, too, that during the revolution (of 1905), when they carried in processions the White Eagle, the coat of arms of the Polish State, some of the workers shouted after it ' White goose!' "[1]

Although the Social Democrats laid stress mainly on Socialist action, it cannot be said that they were without national aspirations. They considered that Poland could regain her independence in the event of a Socialist revolution in Russia, Germany and Austria. One of their leaders, Julian Karski-Marchlewski, brother of a contemporary Chancellor of Cracow University, wrote that

> " Where the nobility hopes to gain some advantage, it hangs up its national sentiment on the peg and turns into a nauseous sycophant, humiliates itself, degrades itself. . . . (The nobility) refused to recognise any national feeling in the common people, the large mass of agricultural proletariat—peasants gaining a livelihood entirely from their land are very rare in Poland. Yet if there had not been this sentiment in them the Polish nation would have ceased to exist a long time ago, for the Russian and Prussian Governments would soon have suppressed the national resistance of the gentry. In reality, this proletariat has extraordinarily strong national feelings, against which a Bismarck and a Hurko (Russian governor of Warsaw) have hammered in vain. There is this consolation, that a ruling class can throw itself away, can lose its national consciousness, but a people—never."[2]

The leaders of the SDKPL put into practice their ideas of international co-operation. Rosa Luxemburg became a member of the German Socialist

[1] Daszynski, Policy, pp. 28, 89, 97.

[2] *Neue Zeit*, Stuttgart, 1898, Vol. II, p. 815.

movement and was killed together with Karl Liebknecht in 1919 in Berlin; Felix Dzierzynski played an active part in the Russian revolution and became the chairman of the Commission on Counter-espionage and Counter-revolution. In 1918 the SDKPL made propaganda in favour of the nationalisation of landed property, which ran counter to the wishes of the peasants, and later it participated in the foundation of the Communist Party of Poland.

Another section of Socialists founded in 1892 the Polish Socialist Party (PPS), in the creation of which the historian Limanowski played a large part. At the outset this party stressed the necessity of both national and social freedom. Some of its leaders underlined the national aspect and considered the Socialist propaganda of the party a weapon by which to gain independence without prejudicing the future economic and social system of Poland; others gave equal importance to both aspects of the party's programme, being convinced that, in any case, Poland could become independent only in the event of a Socialist victory; others again had more in common with the Social Democrats. The policy of the PPS was, therefore, more flexible than that of the SDKPL and appealed to other classes as well as the industrial workers. The first party congress was held in Vilno in the summer of 1893, and it was decided to publish a party organ, *Robotnik* (Workman), which, to escape the censorship, would have to be secretly printed and circulated. The nominal editor of the paper was Strozecki, whilst Pilsudski was responsible for its technical production. After the arrest of Strozecki and others, Pilsudski, Wojciechowski[1] and Malinowski became leaders of the party, and from 1894 to 1900 Pilsudski was responsible for the contents of the party's organ. In view of the important role Pilsudski was later to play in Polish affairs, it may be useful to quote extracts from some of the articles which appeared in *Robotnik*.

In an article which appeared in October 1894, Pilsudski described how " the industrialists of Bialystok (an important textile centre) were so touched that the Tsar passed through their town that they sent him a large deputation bearing bread and salt. The gendarmes did not wait long before admitting the deputation to the Tsar, who was afraid to look his subjects in the face. Finally the deputation had the pleasure of kissing his majesty's feet, and were then immediately ordered to clear out." Six months later Pilsudski reviled both the higher clergy and the upper classes for their subservience to Russia:

> " The higher Catholic clergy take part in a dinner given by Hurko . . . the archbishop Popiel confirms the oath of fidelity to the new Tsar in Russian, and Father Dudkievicz in Dombrowa implores his parishioners from the pulpit not to learn to read, because then they would be able to get to know the contents of the Socialist pamphlets and so forth. This is the Polish clergy, the ally of Tsarist rule in our country and the faithful

[1] President of Poland 1922–26, deposed by Pilsudski's *coup d'état*. I. Moscicki, President of Poland from 1926 till September 1939, was once also a leading member of the PPS.

defender of our exploiters. One would have thought that a despotic government, especially a foreign one, would meet decisive opposition from our propertied classes. But where? To-day the capitalists are concerned only with the possibility of unhampered exploitation, for which they would even go to the length of kissing the devil's tail, and as for the Tsar! In return for so many outrages committed by the government, for the trampling under foot of the most sacred human rights, for the thousands of people murdered or exiled—their representatives went to the tomb of Alexander III to lay on it a wreath of silver and gold weighing a poud." (May 1895.)

In an article written two years later, he outlined his political ideals:

"The people's Republic, which we will build after throwing off the Muscovite yoke, will be a Republic of brotherhood and community, where for all human beings the door to happiness and liberty will be open wide and where human welfare will stand before everything. Instead of the right of property, we will introduce another right—'all is for all'; instead of a government we will declare liberty for everyone without restrictions, which come from authorities, and without compulsion; instead of a multitude of duties which are now imposed by the State, we will acknowledge only one duty—that of fraternity and mutual help. The acquisition of such a Republic is the ultimate aim and chief task of the working class. It is our leading principle, our ideal." (April 1897.)

The vague, anarchic and revolutionary contents of the last article seem to convey the impression that Pilsudski's violent opposition to the existing order overshadowed his constructive programme for changing the existing conditions. It may be said that this article suggests that there was already evident in embryo that philosophy which Pilsudski, together with Mussolini and politicians of the Left akin to them, embraced years later.

References

Curie, Eve, *Madame Curie*. London, 1938.

Daszynski, J., *Pamietniki* (Memoirs). Warsaw, 1923.

Daszynski, J., *Polityka Proletarjatu* (The Policy of the Proletariat). Warsaw, 1907.

Daszynska-Golinska, Z., *Rozwoj, etc.* (Economic Development in Polish Territories). Warsaw, 1914.

Dmowski, R. *La Question Polonaise*, Paris, 1909, quoted by Ralph Butler, *The New Eastern Europe*. London, 1919.

Drage, Geoffrey, *Austria-Hungary*. London, 1909.

Dyboski, R., *Outlines of Polish History*. London, 1931.

Koszutski, S., *Rozwoj, etc.* (The Economic Development of the Polish Kingdom). Warsaw, 1905.

Limanowski, B., *Galicia*. Lwow, 1892.

Lipinski, W., *Walka Zbrojna* (The Armed Struggle for the Independence of Poland). Warsaw, 1935.

Lubienski, T., Wentworth, *Kwestja, etc.* (The Polish Question in Russia). Cracow, 1898.

Luxemburg, Rosa, *Die Industrielle Entwicklung Polens*. Leipzig, 1898.

Marx, Engels, Liebknecht, *Odbudowa*, etc. (The Restoration of Poland). Cracow–New York, 1910.
Mycielski, J. von, *Offener Brief eines Polen an die deutschen Einwohner der ehemaligen polnischen Landesteile*. Posen, 1892.
Panek, P., *Emigracja Polska* (Polish Emigration to the U.S.A.). Lwow, 1898.
Phillips, W. Alison, *Poland*. London, 1915.
Radziwill, Catherine, *My Recollections*. London, 1906.
Steed, H. Wickham, *The Hapsburg Monarchy*. London, 1919.
Szczepanowski, S., *Pisma* (Works). Lwow, 1903.
Temperley, H. W. V., *History of the Peace Conference of Paris*, London, 1920–24.
Thomas, W. I., and F. Znaniecki, *The Polish Peasant in Europe and America*. Boston, 1918.

Chapter IV

THE WAR OF 1914–18

As Socialist action and propaganda had achieved little, Pilsudski and others came to pin their hopes on war rather than revolution as the lever which might send the Russian Empire to its doom. Accordingly when the Russo-Japanese war was declared, Pilsudski went to Tokio to propose to the Japanese military authorities that Poland should be armed behind Russia's back. (Roman Dmowski, on the other hand, tried to persuade the Japanese government that Pilsudski in no way represented Poland.) Pilsudski also visited a number of Polish notables in Poland, Lithuania, Ukraine and Russia and tried to incite them to action, pointing out the fate of those hundreds of thousands of helpless people whom the Russians would slaughter for their own selfish aims in the war against Japan. Everywhere he met with the same excuses and objections. In one place he was even denounced to the police.[1]

The unsuccessful attempts to organise insurrection in the rear of embattled Russia, the defeat of the Russian revolution and the split which divided the PPS and which put him in the minority (the majority favoured a policy similar to that of the SDKPL), prompted Pilsudski to seek allies in Austrian Poland. There he found full support for his activities, mainly military in character. In Galicia there were already in being some semi-military organisations; they were gymnastic societies (Sokols) under the leadership of the future General Haller, and Rifle Societies, consisting of conservative elements under the leadership of the future generals Neugebauer and Januszajtis. Pilsudski's contribution was the creation of a new organisation, consisting of Socialist workers and called the Union of Riflemen. During the Balkan war these societies recognised the authority of a common committee, and in view of an impending new war which might involve Russia, speeded up their programme of military training. The societies were non-political in form, though most of them had definite political leanings, and of course depended, to a certain extent, on official Austrian sanction and support. The future General Sikorski was at that time organising student circles for military training and afterwards allied himself with the military organisation of Pilsudski. It was in this military movement in Galicia that nearly all those who later became leaders of the Polish army, including

[1] Sieroszewski, pp. 36–7.

generals Sosnkowski, Rydz-Smigly,[1] Kukiel, Skladkowski and others, received their initial training.

To what extent the Austrian General Staff exercised control over these Polish activities is not clear. Pilsudski referred vaguely to his co-operation with the General Staff, in his account of a bitter controversy with his one-time friend, Daszynski, when the latter opposed Pilsudski's dictatorial tendencies in 1929–30:

> " M. Daszynski says that ' Pilsudski entered at that time into close contact with the General Staff of Austria-Hungary, and used to have conferences with Austrian military leaders in Lwow and Przemysl. He considered it necessary to confide in me continually the burden of these conversations.' So far as the former statement is concerned, it is true, though not the whole truth. The latter statement, however, is completely false. I have never spoken with M. Daszynski on this question, not considering it correct to confide these matters to him. Above all, I was bound by mutual promises not to speak to anyone else about these conversations, and I am not accustomed to breaking my word. . . . Political tension increased, and the likelihood of war drew ever nearer. About Christmas 1912 there were moments so critical that the staff of the first Austrian corps in Cracow advised me not to leave my home because at any moment the order might come to begin preparations for mobilisation, and then, according to our agreement, I had the right to order the concentration of all groups of riflemen at the agreed place at Wadowice."[2]

There is no doubt that Pilsudski and his friends, as well as the Austrian General Staff (probably with the knowledge of the German Government), prepared for war against Russia. Each party pursued its separate aims. Pilsudski counted on a general upheaval and the establishment of a Polish state, or at least on the union of Russian Poland with Austrian Poland, under an autonomous régime; Austria relied on the possible advantages to be derived from the fact that she would be able to appeal to the Russian Poles to join the Polish legions, which were under her command. When the war broke out, a flood of solemn manifestos and other forms of propaganda descended on Poland; the following leaflet, which appeared immediately after the outbreak of war, is an example:

> " Poles,
>
> In Warsaw a National Government has been formed. The duty of all Poles is to rally solidly behind it. Citizen Joseph Pilsudski has been

[1] Later Smigly-Rydz; the proper order of the two names developed in Poland, in the years before 1939, into a sort of touchstone of one's political views. His surname was Rydz (which means " Mushroom "), but he later added to this the nickname of Smigly (which means " Dashing ") which had been bestowed on him by the Austro-Polish legions of 1914–18. After Pilsudski's death Rydz-Smigly was recognised by the Government party as the late Marshal's political heir and the " deciding factor " in Polish politics. When Rydz-Smigly was promoted Marshal in the autumn of 1936, the official spokesmen began to call him Smigly-Rydz, while the opposition adhered stubbornly to the previous order of Rydz-Smigly. *The Times* referred to him as Rydz-Smigly up to October 21st 1936, but on November 10th and subsequently as Smigly-Rydz.

[2] Pilsudski, pp. 30–6.

appointed commander of the Polish armed forces and his orders must be obeyed by all.

Warsaw, 3rd August, 1914. THE NATIONAL GOVERNMENT."[1]

These statements were fictitious. There was no such government in Warsaw in 1914, nor even any important political group supporting the Central Powers.

On 6th August Pilsudski issued a proclamation to the Polish population of Russian Poland:

> "The decisive hour has struck. Poland ceases to be a slave and will alone determine her fate; she will build her future by throwing the weight of her armed forces into the balance. Groups of the Polish army have already crossed the soil of the Polish Kingdom, restoring it to its real owner—the Polish people—who caused it to become fruitful and rich. They take possession of it in the name of the Supreme Authority of the National Government. To the whole nation we bring release from its chains, and to every class the right to develop freely. At present the whole nation should rally round the National Government. Only traitors will remain apart, and for those we shall have no mercy.
>
> Commander-in-Chief of the Polish Army,
>
> J. PILSUDSKI."[2]

The Supreme Command of the German and Austro-Hungarian armies also issued a proclamation which ran as follows:

> "The moment of liberation from the Muscovite yoke is near. The allied armies of Germany and Austria-Hungary will shortly cross the frontiers of the Polish Kingdom. The Muscovites are already falling back. Their cruel domination over you, which has lasted for hundreds of years, is crumbling. We come to you as friends. Have confidence in us.
>
> "We bring you liberty and independence for which your forefathers suffered so much. Let Eastern barbarism fall before Western civilisation, which is common to both of us.
>
> "Rise in memory of your past, which is so great and full of glory. Unite with the allied Powers. With united forces we shall expel the Asiatic hordes from the frontiers of Poland."[3]

The Polish Club in the Austrian Parliament declared that the hour had struck for which three generations of the Polish people had shed their blood in vain in a terrible and hopeless struggle with the Russian invaders; and that Austria, in defence of the liberty of her peoples, was sending to Polish soil a mighty army against the Russian oppressors. In that great hour the Polish Club, conscious of its responsibility, considered it a "holy duty" to direct the thought and action of the nation.

> "The Virtuous Emperor of this State, under whose just and wise government a part of our nation for half a century was able to develop Polish national forces, is entering the struggle for the highest ideals of

[1] Kumaniecki, p. 12 [2] Kumaniecki, p. 12. [3] Kumaniecki, p. 25.

human culture, and looks upon the Polish nation as a proven defender of these ideals. . . . Under Polish command and in close alliance with the Supreme Command of the Austrian and Hungarian army, the Polish legions will go into battle so that, in this greatest of wars, they should make a contribution worthy of the Polish nation which will be a pledge for a better future. Submit with confidence and complete faith to the leadership of the Polish Club . . . cast aside your doubts, pluck from your hearts evil thoughts, and drawing strength through unity, have the courage to sacrifice both life and property for our motherland."[1]

Not everybody shared the views of the Polish Club. On 28th September, 1914, the Chief of the Austrian General Staff, Conrad von Hoetzendorf, wrote to the Austrian War Minister, von Krobatin: " The Polish legion is really cannon-fodder. We accepted it mainly from political motives. Besides, Pilsudski's legion is giving very good service to our First Army."[2] And twenty years later Professor Kutrzeba declared that the legionaries died thinking of Poland, of which they were to " dream in their grave " according to one of their popular songs; they died with the doubt in their hearts that they were sacrificing their lives in vain.[3]

As the war went on and the hold of German and Austrian armies over the occupied area of Russian Poland grew stronger, the plans of the Central Powers became clearer. Mobilisation for the armed forces within occupied areas during war was at variance with the principles of International Law as laid down at the Hague Conference of 1907; and, besides, conscription of a willing population would give better results than the compulsory incorporation of millions of Poles into the German and Austrian armies. It was, therefore, decided to create an Independent Polish Kingdom, under the protection of, and allied with, the Central Powers. In order to avoid dissension between the Austrian and German Governments, since there was considerable difference of opinion as to who should administer the occupied areas, Austria desiring Warsaw, against Germany's wish, which prevailed,[4] it was agreed to set up the Polish state in the occupied part of Russian Poland only. On 5th November 1916, the following manifesto was published simultaneously in Berlin and Vienna:

" His Majesty the German Emperor and His Majesty the Austrian Emperor and Apostolic King of Hungary, sustained by their firm confidence in the final victory of their arms, and guided by the wish to lead to a happy future the Polish districts which by their brave armies were snatched with heavy sacrifices from Russian power, have agreed to form from these districts an independent state with an hereditary monarchy and a Constitution. The more precise regulation of the frontiers of the Kingdom of Poland remains reserved. In union with both the Allied Powers the new Kingdom will find the guarantees, which it desires for the free development of its strength. In its own Army the glorious traditions of the

[1] Kumaniecki, pp. 16–17.
[2] Hoetzendorf, Vol. IV, p. 878.
[3] Kutrzeba, p. 38.
[4] Hoetzendorf, Vol. IV, p. 479–81.

Polish Army of former times and the memory of our brave Polish fellow-combatants in the great war of the present time will continue to live. Its organisation, training and command will be regulated by mutual agreement." (*The Times*, 6th November 1916.)

In conjunction with this manifesto, generals von Beseler and von Kuk, German and Austrian commanders of the occupied areas of Russian Poland, published a proclamation which read:

> " The struggle with Russia has not yet ended; in this struggle you must also participate. Stand therefore by our side as volunteers and help us to crown our victory against your oppressor. Your brothers in the Polish legions fought with us courageously and gloriously; follow in their footsteps and enlist in the new formations which, united with the legions, will constitute the Polish army, which will provide strong support for your new state, and will secure its safety both within and without."[1]

A Provisional Council of State (with Pilsudski as military member) was formed, but the response of the Polish population was negligible; only a few thousand men enlisted in the new army.

The Russian revolution of March 1917 brought a fundamental change in the situation. The Polish legions were no longer prepared to fight the Russians and, in order to eliminate undesirable elements, an oath of allegiance to the German and Austrian Emperors was demanded of them, after they had been transferred from Austrian to German command. They refused to comply and were sent to internment camps; Pilsudski and Sosnkowski were imprisoned in the Magdeburg fortress, from which they were released by the German revolution on 10th November 1918. Other democratic elements, under the leadership of the Polish Socialist Party, formed the illegal Polish Military organisation (P.O.W.) which, commanded by the future Marshal Smigly-Rydz, organised sabotage in the rear of the German and Austrian armies. Some legionaries, under the command of General Haller and others, continued to fight on the side of Austria and Germany. The Provisional Council of State, which was succeeded in September 1917 by the Council of Regency, and the Polish Club in the Vienna Parliament and its representatives in the Austrian Government, continued their co-operation with the Central Powers until their defeat.

On 3rd June 1918, at a time when the Allies had already declared their intention of creating an independent Polish State, the following " strictly confidential " memorandum of the Polish Parliamentary Club in Vienna was addressed to the Austrian Government:

> " As a logical consequence of the historical situation, the first day of the war between our Monarchy and the Russian Empire witnessed a spontaneous community of interests, a tacit agreement, between Austria and her Polish inhabitants. The Monarchy was determined to prosecute

[1] Kumaniecki, p. 50.

the war, thrust upon it by Russia, and in the event of victory always intended to annex the kingdom of Poland, which had been created by the Congress of Vienna and was in Russian hands. At the same time the Poles of Galicia promulgated the idea of uniting this kingdom of Poland with Galicia to form an independent kingdom under the Hapsburg Monarchy. . . . The Polish Club, with the people behind it, reassert their unchanging attachment and gratitude to the most noble Emperor, and will remain faithful and steadfast to this tacit agreement of August 1914. We are ready in the spirit of these sentiments to influence the people further, if the most worthy government consider it of value."[1]

Another document throwing light on the policy of the Polish Club was a letter from the Chairman of the Union of National-German parties,[2] Dr. Waldner, to the Austro-Polish Minister, von Twardowski:

"Parliament, 20th June 1918.

"Your Excellency,

"I beg to draw attention to the fact that the Union of National-German parties is always ready to discuss with the Hon. representatives of the Polish Club the whole range of the Polish question, and to consider everything that could contribute to the furtherance of German-Polish community of interests in the present and in the future. Such a conference would, in our opinion, only be successful if the Hon. Members of the Polish Club would take part in the discussion with the will to create, with the German parties, a clear majority in Parliament to implement the requirements of the state in the present crisis. At the same time, the Hon. Members of the Polish Club should consider taking a firm stand against the subversive machinations and dangerous plans of the Czechs and Southern Slavs, and warding off, in conjunction with the deputies of the Union and of the Christian-Social Association, any attacks by the Czechs and Southern Slavs. (Signed) Dr. WALDNER."[3]

The meeting took place and M. Twardowski afterwards drew up the following draft of the agreement:

"In the face of the immense dangers which are threatening, in an ever-increasing degree, the existence of the Austrian State, a discussion took place between the German and Polish members of both houses of Parliament, and the conviction was expressed that their close political co-operation was in the common interest for the preservation of the present structure of this country.

"For the immediate and urgent tasks of the allied policy a speedy solution is required of the Polish question on Austro-Polish lines to safeguard all political, military and economic interests; a solution which corresponds in equal proportion to the interests of both Central Powers.

[1] Bilinski, Vol. II, p. 412.

[2] The political programme of these parties was in favour of the closest co-operation with Germany. In recent times they constituted one of the sources of the Nazi movement in Austria.

[3] Bilinski, Vol. II, p. 431.

" With regard to the existing conflict between the Poles and Ruthenians (Ukrainians) concerning the partition of Galicia and national autonomy in Eastern Galicia, it has been agreed that the said German parties' respective unions will offer their services in settling the controversy.

" With these reservations, it was agreed on the other hand that the Polish parties should declare their readiness to support the Germans against the efforts of the Czechs to set up a Czechoslovak state, as expressed in the declaration of 30th May 1917, and against those of the Slovenes who aim to set up a Yugoslav State."[1]

* * *

According to the German Minister, Erzberger, " The wishes of the Polish population in Prussia were modest; they aimed in general at the recognition of equal rights for the Polish and German languages, and in particular for the inclusion of Polish in religious instruction. The law of expropriation which was directed against the Poles and the prohibition of settlement had naturally to be abolished. I was in close contact with several influential Polish leaders; there were numerous conferences with them. . . . However, in 1918, the Polish Club in the Reichstag finally voted against the granting of new war credits, an action which was most deeply regretted by the more right-wing Poles."[2]

Thus it seems that the Vienna Poles were the only organised group which supported the Central Powers to the end of the war.

The reasons behind the policy of Germany towards Poland were frankly explained after the end of the war by Field-Marshal von Hindenburg and General von Ludendorff. Hindenburg revealed that Poland was one of the first political problems with which he was concerned after he assumed control of operations. The German Government viewed with disfavour the prospect of a unified Poland; Austria-Hungary, on the other hand, hoped for this solution, in the belief that a Catholic Poland would be permanently bound to the Dual Monarchy. In order not to exacerbate German and Austrian differences German General Headquarters originally intended to remain passive on the Polish question. In the opinion of the German Governor of Warsaw, however, an announcement of the creation of a Polish Kingdom might result in a reinforcement of German armies by Polish troops, amounting to one million men on the introduction of general military service. Hindenburg, therefore, reconsidered his attitude, assuming that " a victorious Germany would be able in any case to settle the Polish question after the peace." But the decision to set up a Polish State, as announced in the Manifesto of the German and Austrian Emperors, was delayed because the German Government thought for some time that there were possibilities of a separate peace with Russia.

[1] Bilinski, Vol. II, pp. 431–2.

[2] Erzberger, pp. 171–2.

" The conclusion of the whole business was that these hopes of a separate peace with Russia broke down, that the manifesto was published in the early days of November, and that the recruiting of Polish volunteers to which it referred was entirely without results."[1]

Similar reasons for the policy of the Central Powers towards Poland were given by General von Ludendorff. He mentioned that when he became Quarter-Master General he found that there was an agreement in existence which bound Germany and Austria-Hungary to establish an independent kingdom of Poland, with an hereditary monarchy,[2] a constitutional government and a national army under a single command, which was to be entrusted to Germany. This new Poland was to be accepted as a member of the alliance of the two empires, and its foreign policy was to be conducted accordingly. The two Central Powers mutually guaranteed their existing Polish possessions, and provided for frontier adjustments, at the expense of Russian Poland, which would have to be made for the greater security of their territory. Such claims were to be limited to strictly military necessities.[3]

* * *

The Russian policy towards Poland developed on similar lines to those of Germany and Austria. On 14th August 1914, the Grand Duke Nicholas, as Commander-in-Chief of the Russian Army, issued a manifesto to the Poles, in which he said that, a century and a half previously, the living flesh of Poland had been torn to pieces, but her soul did not die. She had lived in the hope that the time would come for the resurrection of Poland as a state and its fraternal reconciliation with Great Russia. " The Russian Army," he continued, " brings the joyful tidings of this reconciliation. May the frontiers which have cut the Polish nation into pieces be effaced. May the Polish nation be reunited as one body under the sceptre of the Russian Emperor. Under this sceptre Poland will be reborn, free in her faith, her language and in self-government."[4]

Of this proclamation Dmowski stated that it was " beautifully written," but with regard to its contents he understood that Russia could not say more at the time. It contained the principal object for which Poles would fight with all their might—the unity of Polish territories.[5]

In answer to the Duke's manifesto, four political parties, under the

[1] Hindenburg, pp. 222–4.

[2] There were close connections between the Hapsburg family and certain Polish aristocratic families. Two daughters of the Archduke Charles Stephan were married to Poles, one to Charles Radziwill, the other to A. O. Czartoryski. The Germans planned, however, to reintroduce the King of Saxony's family on the Polish throne.

[3] Ludendorff, Vol. I, p. 395, Vol. II, p. 441.

[4] Kumaniecki, p. 27.

[5] Dmowski, p. 155.

leadership of the National Democratic Party, published the following declaration. (*The Times*, 25th September 1914.):

> "The representatives of the undersigned political parties assembled on August 16th in Warsaw welcome the proclamation to the Poles of His Imperial Highness, the Supreme Commander of the Russian Armies, as an act of the greatest historical weight, and believe firmly that after the end of the war the promises expressed in the proclamation will be realised, and that the dreams of our fathers and forefathers will be fulfilled; that the body of Poland rent to pieces a century and a half ago, will be reunited and that the frontiers which have divided the Polish nation will vanish. The blood of her sons shed in the common struggle against Germany will constitute equally a sacrifice offered on the altar of the resurrected fatherland.
>
> THE NATIONAL DEMOCRATIC PARTY.
> THE POLISH PROGRESSIVE PARTY.
> THE PARTY OF REALISTIC POLICY.
> THE POLISH PROGRESSIVE UNION."

In addition to the above declaration, sixty-nine Polish leading political personalities[1] addressed a letter to the Grand Duke Nicholas, in which they said:

> "Deeply moved by the proclamation of Your Imperial Highness, who announces to us that the gallant Russian Army, unsheathing its sword in the defence of the Slavs, fights also for the holy cause of our nation, the restoration of a united Poland, the unity of all her torn pieces under the sceptre of His Imperial Majesty, the undersigned representatives of Polish political parties and social groups firmly believe that the blood of Poland's sons shed together with the blood of Russia's sons in the struggle with the common enemy will constitute the greatest guarantee of a new life in peace and friendship for the two Slavonic nations.
>
> "On this historic day of the proclamation so important for the Polish nation we are full of an ardent desire for the victory of the Russian army, which is under the most illustrious command of Your Imperial Highness, and we are awaiting its complete triumph on the battlefield.
>
> "We beg Your Imperial Highness to place at the feet of His Majesty the Emperor these wishes and our sentiments of loyalty as Russian subjects."

To implement the above declarations a Polish Legion was formed and subsequently fought with the Russians.

The first revolutionary government of Russia upheld the policy of the Tsarist government towards Poland, later replacing it by a declaration promising autonomy; after the Bolshevik Revolution the Soviet Government

[1] Among others, R. Dmowski, W. Grabski (later Polish Prime Minister during the war with Soviet Russia in 1920), Prince Lubomirski, Count S. Lubienski and Count M. Zamoyski (later Polish Ambassador in Paris and candidate of the right-wing parties to the Presidency of Poland in 1922).

developed this policy still further, declaring its wish to see an independent Polish State.

In a proclamation to the Poles in April 1917, the Kerenski government stated that the Polish State, united with Russia in a free military alliance, would form a bulwark against the Central Powers' drive towards the Slavonic peoples. The Russian Constitutional Assembly would ultimately confirm the new " brotherly union," and would also give its consent to the territorial change in the Russian State, necessary for the formation of a free Poland out of her still divided parts.[1]

In the autumn of 1917, even a few days before the Bolshevik Revolution, the Russian Government still maintained its ambiguous attitude towards the Polish question. The first point in the instructions issued by the Central Executive Committee of Soviets to their representative for the Paris Conference of the Allies on War Aims (20th October 1917) proposed the evacuation of Russia by the German troops and autonomy for Poland, Lithuania and the Lettish provinces.[2]

In December 1917 the Bolshevik Government declared that " from the fact that the occupied territories belonged to the former Russian Empire the Russian Government draws no conclusion which would impose any constitutional obligation on the population of these regions in relation to the Russian Republic. The old frontiers of the former Russian Empire . . . have vanished with Tsarism. The new frontiers of the fraternal union of peoples of the Russian Republic and the peoples which desire to remain outside its borders must be defined by a free resolution of the peoples concerned."[3]

The Bolsheviks seem to have been the first of all the political groups amongst the belligerents, apart from the Poles, to refer to the possibility of Poland's independence (and not only autonomy) and to the Polish people's right to self-determination.

* * *

The Western Powers, allied with Russia, supported the Russian solution of the Polish question, and when, after the publication of the manifestos of the German and Austrian Emperors, the Russian Government protested against the infringement of international law, M. Briand and Mr. Asquith, on 16th November 1916, sent a telegram to M. Stuermer, Prime Minister of Russia, expressing satisfaction that the Russian Government placed on record the breach of international law and of international conventions committed by Germany and by Austria-Hungary, and protested against the pretension of these powers to create a new State in a territory at the moment occupied by them, and to raise an army from the population of these regions. They were gratified to see that Russia, who at the very outset of the war gave to the peoples dwelling in all the Polish lands assurances of autonomy, had solemnly renewed that decision.

[1] Kumaniecki, p. 67. [2] Scott, p. 167. [3] Bunyan, p. 494.

In January 1917 the Allied Powers defined their general war aims, in answer to a request from President Wilson; they declared that victory should bring the restitution of provinces formerly torn from the Allies by force or against the wish of their inhabitants, the liberation of the Italians, as also of the Slavs, Rumanians and Czecho-Slovaks from foreign domination, and the expulsion from Europe of the Ottoman Empire.[1] Six months later, in June 1917, in reply to a note of the first Russian revolutionary government regarding allied war aims and their revision, the British Government made a further declaration dealing more specifically with the case of Poland: "In the proclamation to the Russian people enclosed in the note it is said 'that Free Russia does not propose to dominate other peoples or to take from them their national patrimony, or forcibly to occupy foreign territory.' In this sentiment the British Government heartily concur. They did not enter upon this war as a war of conquest, and they are not continuing it for any such object. Their purpose at the outset was to defend the existence of their country and to enforce respect for international engagements. To those objects has now been added that of liberating populations oppressed by alien tyranny. They heartily rejoice, therefore, that Free Russia has announced her intention of liberating Poland, not only the Poland ruled by the old Russian autocracy, but equally that within the dominion of the Germanic Empires. In this enterprise the British Democracy wishes Russia God-speed. Beyond everything we must seek for such a settlement as will secure the happiness and contentment of the peoples and take away all legitimate causes of future war."

After the Bolshevik Revolution, on 5th January 1918, Mr. Lloyd George stated: "We shall be proud to fight to the end side by side with the new democracy of Russia, so will America and so will France and Italy, but if the present rulers of Russia take action which is independent of their allies, we have no means of intervening to arrest the catastrophe which is assuredly befalling their country. Russia can only be saved by her own people. We believe, however, that an independent Poland comprising all those genuinely Polish elements who desire to form part of it is an urgent necessity for the stability of Western Europe."

This statement followed the declaration of the Soviet Government of December 1917, and was the first explicit reference made by the Western Powers to the independence of Poland. Three days later, President Wilson in his speech to Congress on the Fourteen Points, devoted Point Thirteen to Poland: "An independent Polish State should be erected which should include the territories inhabited by indisputably Polish populations, which should be assured a free and secure access to the sea, and whose political and economic independence and integrity should be guaranteed by international covenant."

On 25th October 1918, the German Foreign Minister, Solf, accepted the Thirteenth Point, saying that "with regard to the future Polish State I would

[1] Temperley, Vol. 1, p. 172. According to Temperley the term "Slavs" was not intended to include the Poles.

declare that the German Government has frankly and sincerely accepted the programme of the President of the United States. This programme is founded on a peace of justice and reconciliation and does not desire to give rise to fresh antagonisms and wars."[1] The emergence of an independent Poland thus became only a matter of time.

* * *

Those Polish political parties which had accepted the manifesto of the Grand Duke Nicholas in August 1914, formed the Polish National Committee for co-operation with the Russian Government. After the Russian revolution of March 1917, the Committee transferred its headquarters to Paris. In September 1918 France and Great Britain recognised the Committee, which was headed by Roman Dmowski, as the supreme Polish authority. The United States did the same in November 1918. Paderewski was the Committee's representative in the U.S.A., Count Sobienski in London, Piltz in Paris, Skirmunt in Italy; they all later became either ministers or ambassadors of the Polish Republic.

A leading article in the *Manchester Guardian* of 7th December 1917 severely criticised the Allies' step, saying that the British Foreign Office " came to a momentous choice between Polish parties and policies in profound ignorance of the fundamental facts. It had, on its own confession, no reliable information about M. Lednitsky and his policy, yet it decided against them. M. Lednitsky is not an unknown or obscure individual. He is the foremost Pole in Russia, and represents the Liberal element in Polish politics. As soon as the Revolution broke out the Provisional Government (at that time a coalition, including such moderates as Milyukoff and Gutchkoff), with the hearty approval of the Poles in Russia, charged M. Lednitsky with Polish affairs. M. Lednitsky has throughout the Revolution represented the mind of Liberal Poles. His Polish policy was both Liberal and moderate. . . . For what does M. Dmowsky stand? For Jingoism and reaction. He is the leader of reaction in Poland and the Father of modern Polish anti-Semitism. All his associations with Russia before the war were reactionary, and it would never have occurred to a Liberal Russia to accept him as the spokesman of Poland. . . . Our Foreign Office knew nothing ' reliable ' of M. Lednitsky and identified itself with M. Dmowsky. In doing so it broke on the Polish question with Liberal Russia and with the Polish Progressives. And all this it did, apparently, in sheer ignorance, and only after it had plunged did it start to ask for information."

General Haller, who continued to fight on the side of the Central Powers after Pilsudski's imprisonment, leading some detachments of Polish legionaries, went over to the Bolsheviks after the peace of Brest-Litovsk, having realised the duplicity of the Central Powers. Eventually General Haller,

[1] Scott, pp. 106, 230, 437.

with the major part of the second brigade of the Polish legions, joined the Polish troops of General Dowbor, who was previously a supporter of Kornilow's abortive *coup d'état* against the Kerenski government. Later he took part in the Allied campaign against the Bolsheviks at Murmansk, whence he was transferred to France in the autumn of 1918.

In May 1917 the French Government permitted the organisation of Polish detachments on French territory; in 1914 Polish volunteers had been attached to the Foreign Legion. In June 1917 President Poincaré issued a decree saying that " for the duration of the war an autonomous Polish army will be created in France, which will fight under the Polish flag and under the supreme command of the French."[1]

In July 1918 the Polish army numbered 10,000 soldiers, mostly Polish-Americans, and in October 1918, General Haller was appointed Commander-in-Chief by the Polish National Committee.

The nucleus of a political and military organisation for Poland had been formed under Allied auspices.

* * *

Thus, the Polish parties of the " Left " and " Centre " during 1914–18 were on the side of the Central Powers; those of the " Right " were pro-Russian, and therefore on the side of the Allied Powers. There was no " extreme right wing " party at that time in Poland. The political attitude of the Social Democratic Party of Poland and Lithuania (the " extreme left wing " party) was defined in an article which appeared in the *Polish Review*, edited by A. Zaleski, the future Foreign Minister, for the pro-Pilsudski Polish Information Committee. The article, written in January 1918, was entitled " The Bolsheviks and Poland " and included the following remarks:

> " . . . Poland means the Polish masses. They only are the sovereigns, and they must be appealed to in their entirety. . . . The restoration of Poland should be accomplished in conditions conducive to the westward spread of the proletarian power established on the Neva. This is no interference in the internal affairs of Poland; though the voice is that of the Soviet, the hand is that of the Polish Socialists, comrades with them in the previous struggles against Tsardom, comrades with them in the present fight against the European Imperialism. . . . Polish Socialism realised at the outset that the Polish masses alone could gain freedom for their country by gaining it for themselves in a common fight, supported by their German, Austrian and Russian comrades against their own Imperialists. . . . The hope of the Polish masses for success grows stronger with every increase of power of the Bolsheviks in Russia and with every succeeding manifestation of the coming mass movement throughout Europe. It will be fully realised

[1] Lipinski, p. 426.

on the day when a pact is made between victorious Russian, British, French, German, Central European, Italian and Polish Socialist Democracy and their democratic friends and followers." (*The Polish Review*, London, January 1918.)

* * *

The documents of the 1914–18 war show that neither Pilsudski nor Dmowski, nor any of the statesmen of Russia, Germany and Austria, France or Britain thought of an independent Poland until the fall of Tsardom; that Polish political parties on either side of the front supported both by word and deed—with the possible exception of the Social Democrats—the policy of the particular power with which they had already been connected during the long period of peace which preceded the war; that all the Polish legions which fought on various fronts, sometimes against each other, were working, in spite of the assurances of some of their leaders and in spite of their patriotic fervour, in reality for the victory of the Central Powers or of Tsarist Russia.

Poland gained her independence, as did Hungary, Czechoslovakia, Finland and the Baltic States, only as a result of the Russian revolution, the victory of the Allied Powers and the revolutions in Berlin and Vienna; it would appear, therefore, that none of the Polish political groups could, on the basis of its record in 1914–18, justly claim the right to represent the people of Poland, even if it were thought that a democratic form of government should be rejected on the grounds of the alleged " immaturity " of the Polish people.

Pilsudski wrote in 1931: " There is no doubt that at the outbreak of war in 1914 the Poles and Poland were in a state of complete prostration. There is, indeed, the undeniable fact that everywhere in Russian, German and Austrian Poland, the Poles did as they were bidden by each occupying authority, that is, they sacrificed freely and unconditionally their lives and property because the war required it. This fact is so true and incontrovertible that it is with genuine disgust that one sees or hears it denied by those who glorify themselves, and themselves only, in their accounts of all they have done. . . . Many people in Poland, without any reason or justification, tell fairy-tales and live perpetually in a world of make-believe. They make me think of some miserable creature, trampled underfoot by others, who would like to make himself out to be a giant in stature."[1]

This statement might have been applied with equal force to Pilsudski himself, and particularly to his pro-Fascist followers.[2]

[1] Pilsudski, pp. 7–9.

[2] Mr. Fiala stated that the Polish legions of Austria formed two brigades, altogether 30,000 men. In 1935, according to official evidence, there were about 15,000 of them left. " Is it not therefore interesting to learn that the League of Polish Legionaries has 250,000 members who make a great song of their doings?" (*La Pologne d'aujourd'hui*, p. 34).

References

Bilinski, Leon, *Wspomnienia, etc.* (Memoirs and Documents). Warsaw, 1925.

Bunyan, J., and H. H. Fisher, *The Bolshevik Revolution*, Stanford University. California, 1934.

Dmowski, R., *Obdudowanie, etc.* (Polish Policy and the Restoration of the State). Warsaw, 1926.

Erzberger, M., *Erlebnisse im Weltkrieg*. Stuttgart, 1920.

Fiala, M., *La Pologne d'aujourd'hui*. Paris, 1936.

Hindenburg, Marshal von, *Out of My Life*. London, 1920.

Hoetzendorf, Conrad von, *Aus meiner Dienstzeit*. Vienna, 1923.

Kumaniecki, K. W., *Odbudowa, etc.* (The Restoration of the Polish State. Documents). Warsaw-Cracow, 1924.

Kutrzeba, S., *Odbudowanie, etc.* (Poland Restored). Warsaw, 1935.

Lipinski, W., *Walka Zbrojna* (The Armed Struggle for the Independence of Poland). Warsaw, 1935.

Ludendorff, General, *My War Memories*, 1914–18. London, 1920.

Pilsudski, J., *Poprawki*, etc. (Historical Corrections). Warsaw, 1931.

Rose, W. J., *Poland*. London, 1939.

Scott, J. B., edited by, *Official Statements of War Aims and Peace Proposals*. Washington, 1921.

Sieroszewski, W., *J. Pilsudski, Zamosc*. 1921.

Temperley, H. W. V., *The Peace Conference of Paris*. London, 1920–24.

Chapter V

NATIONAL MINORITIES

WHEN Poland first began to play a part in the history of Europe, it was a small country covering the major part of what was later to become Prussian-occupied Poland. In the eleventh century King Boleslaw I extended the dominions of Poland by conquering Silesia and Cracow; in addition, he was recognised as sovereign of Pomerania. Two centuries later Casimir the Great united so-called Red Ruthenia (which was later Eastern Galicia) with Poland. The most important event, however, in Poland's territorial development, was the extension of Poland's influence over the Lithuanian Empire, which included territories that stretched from the Baltic to the Black Sea and included the present Baltic States, White Russia and most of the Ukraine.

In 1325 King Wladyslaw Lokietek of Poland concluded a treaty of alliance with the Lithuanian Prince Gedymin; this *rapprochement* developed into a personal union of the two States in 1384, when King Jagiello of Lithuania married Jadwiga, daughter of the Hungarian King Louis d'Anjou. The union was formally confirmed by Polish and Lithuanian barons after the victorious battle against the Teutonic Knights at Grunwald in 1410. Separate state institutions, such as the diets and executives, were maintained until 1569, when Lithuania ceded to Poland the greater part of the Ukraine, Kiev included, and the two states formed one legislative and administrative entity. The new state comprised Great Poland, i.e. territories extending eastwards from Poznan to Warsaw (including also, though only formally, what is at present East Prussia); Little Poland, i.e. territories from Cracow to Kiev; and Lithuania, i.e. territories embracing the modern Baltic States and White Russia (Brest-Litovsk, Minsk, Smolensk and Vitebsk included). On the whole these lands remained intact from the sixteenth century until the Partitions of the eighteenth century, under the sovereignty of the "King of Poland, Grand Duke of Lithuania, Ruthenia, Prussia, etc."

The expansion of Poland towards the east, which was signified in 1596 by the choice of Warsaw instead of Cracow as capital of the Empire, greatly strengthened the backward economic and political development of Poland proper. From the sixteenth century onwards the bonds which linked Poland with western and southern Europe, so apparent during the Renaissance, were weakened and the Lithuanian and Ukrainian "princelings" assumed a leading role in the country. Poland's culture and civilisation were at a higher level than those of the eastern provinces, and soon the Lithuanian and Ukrainian barons adopted Polish habits. At first they remained conscious of their origin (*gente Ruthenus natione Polonus*), but by the eighteenth century most of the magnates in the eastern part of the Empire considered themselves Poles and very often did not even understand the language of their serfs. This process went on parallel with the assimilation of German and later also of Russian culture by some of the Polish aristocratic families. Besides those formed by the magnates, there were other isolated Polish linguistic areas in the Ukraine, Lithuania, and White Russia, especially in the towns; for instance, Lwow, which played an important part in the fifteenth and sixteenth centuries as a trade centre and was a key-point on the transit route for the export of grain via Danzig, became partly Polish.

The peasantry beyond the Bug and Niemen spoke either Russian (and White Russian) or Lithuanian,[1] and two-thirds of the area of the Polish-Lithuanian Kingdom was inhabited, not by Poles, but by other peoples. Ethnographical Poland covered about eighty thousand square miles (coinciding with what is still inhabited by peoples speaking the Polish language), including the whole of the future Russian Poland, the Prussian province of Posen, about half of the province of Pomerania, a part of Silesia, and about one-half of Austrian Poland.[2]

That part of Poland which Austria took over in 1772 and named Galicia,[3] contained in the east a strong Ukrainian group. Like the Polish people, the Ukrainians were torn away from their main national centres, which came under Russian rule. According to L. Wasilewski, who was to be the first Foreign Minister of independent Poland, the Ukrainian territories in the Austrian State (without Hungary) embraced north-western Bukovina, eastern Galicia, and a narrow strip of land along the Carpathian Mountains to Nowy Sacz and Nowy Targ (in western Galicia).[4] In 1857 the Poles constituted about 45 per cent of the Galician population, Ukrainians 45 per cent, and Jews 10 per cent; in 1910 the proportions were respectively 47, 42, and 11 per cent. In 1880, 52 per cent of the Galician population declared Polish and 43 per cent Ukrainian, to be their native tongue, while in 1910 the proportions were respectively 59 and 40 per cent (the Jews considered themselves increasingly as being of Polish nationality).[5]

In 1902 out of two and a half million hectares of land owned by proprietors of estates of more than five hundred hectares, only half a million were situated in western Galicia. This is attributable to the fact that the oppression of the Ukrainian serfs could not be carried out effectively, and the latter were able to leave their paternal allotments without the consent of the master and

[1] Lelewel, p. 491.
[2] Eversley, pp. 15–17.
[3] A distortion of the name Halicz. The independent Grand Duchy of Halicz was incorporated under the name of Red Ruthenia into Poland in 1340.
[4] Wasilewski, p. 11. Father of the writer W. Wasilewska, who was one of the founders of the Union of Polish Patriots in Moscow in 1943.
[5] The Statistical Yearbook of Galicia, 1913.

to live as free men among the Cossacks on the banks of the Dnieper. The landowner usually enclosed into his estate the plots of land left by the serfs and, consequently, the landed estates in eastern Galicia were larger than in the west.

The Ukrainian population in Galicia consisted mainly of peasants and of a small middle class, which began to emerge after the liberation of the serfs in 1848. For social and also for religious reasons (Austrians and Poles professed the Roman Catholic faith, while the Ukrainians were Uniats) the Poles had a much stronger position in Vienna, with the result that the Polish-Galician magnates obtained practically a monopoly of the administration.

The opposition of the Ukrainian population, which sometimes took the form of political assassinations, strengthened the tendencies of the Galician magnates towards closer co-operation with Austria. The Vienna Government skilfully handled the situation, using the Polish-Ruthenian (Ukrainian) enmity as a valuable weapon in their policy of "divide and rule". The Ukrainian peasants, oppressed like the Polish peasants, agitated against the landowners for political and economic rights. At Vienna and Lwow the Ukrainians demanded greater representation in the Austrian Reichsrat and the Galician Diet, and equal rights for their language in both education and administration. The struggle became more intense when others became interested in the outcome. As Germany drew away from Russia and into closer relations with the Dual Monarchy, the theory was evolved that the partition of Russia was necessary to the security of the Central Powers. From this partition there was to emerge a Ukrainian State upheld by Austrian guarantee.[1]

This Ukrainian programme met with vigorous opposition from the Galician members of the Austrian Government and was shelved in favour of the project of a Polish State under Austro-German protection. At the beginning of the war of 1914–18 a large part of the Ukrainian population openly welcomed the Russian armies; the Grand Duke Frederick, Commander-in-Chief of the Austro-Hungarian armies, gave his explanation of their feelings in a letter to the Emperor Francis Joseph:

> From the time of annexation of Galicia and Bukovina by the Monarchy up to the present, the Polish element has exercised an almost unlimited supremacy over the other nationalities resident in these provinces on account of its old culture, influential nobility and large estates; it had almost a monopoly of all categories of civil service posts. Resistance to this supremacy by the Ruthenians, whose national consciousness developed relatively late, has been almost completely unsuccessful for want of any kind of political power. Most of the Ruthenian population, therefore, were convinced that further efforts were useless. They listened to foreign agitators, who spread among them the belief that they belonged to Russia by race, language and religion, and were illegally oppressed by the Poles

[1] Fisher, p. 44; Steed, pp. 289–92.

and the Imperial Government. . . . Consequently, at the beginning of the war the Ruthenian population was divided into two hostile parties, of which one did not hesitate to support the invading enemy in every possible way."[1]

In the immediate post-war period the Ukrainian national movement became a prey to chauvinism and hatred against Poland. In the treaty of Brest-Litovsk, signed with Germany and Austria on 8th February 1918, the Ukrainian leader, Petliura, claimed and obtained a large area of the territory between the rivers Bug and Vistula, which was in fact inhabited by a Polish population. (The Soviet delegation at the Brest-Litovsk conference did not, however, recognise the treaty with Petliura. In September 1939 the Soviet authorities occupied part of this territory, but later withdrew their troops.) Petliura accepted the land as compensation for the Galician Ukraine, which he resigned in favour of Austria. It was in protest against this treaty that General Haller went over with the Second Brigade of the Polish legions to the Bolsheviks.

The White-Russian and Lithuanian territories, included in the Union of Poland and Lithuania, did not belong to the Polish Kingdom which was created at the Congress of Vienna in 1815. The situation here was similar in almost all respects to the position in the Ukraine. The Poles, or rather those Lithuanians and White-Russians who had become Polish in both language and customs, formed the aristocracy and upper classes; the serfs and lower classes were partly White-Russian and partly Ukrainian.

The Jewish question differed from the other national problems. The first geographical descriptions of Poland were made by Jewish travellers from the large empire of the Khasars on the banks of the lower Don, who settled in Poland, in the tenth century, when the Khasar empire ceased to exist; thus the first Jews in Poland were of eastern extraction. In the eleventh century the persecution of Jews in Bohemia brought a number of them to Poland; and in the fourteenth and fifteenth centuries those driven from Spain and Germany found hospitality on Polish soil; this was the period of Polish liberalism and religious tolerance, when religious minorities from all over Europe found refuge in Poland.

Until the nineteenth century the Jews in Poland were forced to live in isolation in ghettoes. Their history falls into two sections owing to the changed conditions of Poland after the sixteenth century.

The Church in the Middle Ages forbade the lending of money for interest, and this prohibition seems to have been strictly observed in Poland. Economic developments nevertheless compelled the introduction of money-lending and the Polish sovereigns favoured the immigration of Jews who were able to serve as an intermediary between the lender and the borrower. For the expansion of trade between the fourteenth and sixteenth centuries the services of Jewish bankers were almost indispensable. Besides being bankers, the Jews

[1] Bilinski, Vol. II, pp. 395–7.

played an important part in developing trade, but owing to their separation in ghettoes this was a secondary role.

In the period of feudal reaction the barons found that some of the Jews were useful collaborators in the organisation of their landed estates and grain export trade. The Jews became managers of estates and agents of the large landowners. The fact that the Jews occupied an intermediate position between master and serf served to foster the religious prejudice of the serfs against the Jews; the latter were also allowed to keep inns and shops on the estate and the peasants were not permitted to buy elsewhere. The anti-semitism, which thus developed, was particularly strong in the Ukraine, White-Russia and Lithuania, because there the Polish nobles usually lived far away from their estates and left the management entirely to their Jewish agents. The great majority of the Jews, however, lived in ghettoes in towns which were then on the decline, and religious prejudice was made worse by economic rivalry in conditions of rapidly diminishing trade.

With the development of a democratic movement in Poland the position of the Jews was fundamentally changed. The compulsory separation in ghettoes disappeared and Jews began to take an active part in the political life of the country. They were concerned in all the insurrections, in which they sometimes occupied leading positions. The development of factories and other industrial activities transformed the social structure of the Jews together with that of the Christians. As their entry into any occupation other than commerce had been banned for centuries some of them soon became influential in sections of industry, trade and banking. Others were absorbed as workers, especially in the cotton industry of Lodz, and the engineering and building industries of Warsaw. A large number, however, owing to the country's backward economy, remained where they had been so long, in the depressed lower middle class.

The traditional attitude of the Polish insurgents towards equality of national minorities was bequeathed to their heirs, the liberal and socialist parties. In 1916, at the Third Conference of Nationalities held in Switzerland, Polish democratic organisations sent a declaration to the effect that they did not seek the incorporation into the future Poland of any nationality against its will; that the rights of national minorities should be scrupulously respected; that people of non-Polish nationality within the jurisdiction of Poland should enjoy all civil rights; and that they adhered strictly to the principle of religious liberty, which they would like to see extended to every state.[1]

In October 1917, when Kerenski's government was in power, the Polish Democratic Congress representing all shades of Polish political opinion in Russia, was held in Moscow and passed a resolution expressing the hope that all classes of the population would participate in the work of organising the Polish State. The Congress also expressed the hope that the Polish State would be based on democratic forms of organisation, since only a truly

[1] Harley, p. 242.

democratic constitution could ensure for Poland stability and progress. The Congress sent greetings to the rising Ukrainian State, and expressed its firm conviction that the Ukraine, as well as Poland, possessed the necessary qualifications for independent existence. The Congress was hopeful that the two nations would base their future relations on principles of justice and on mutual confidence, and would do their best to restrain the chauvinistic currents which were harming relations between the two neighbours. The Congress further expressed the hope that the political independence of the Lithuanian and White Russian nations would develop on the basis of the self-determination of nations, and that the bonds uniting these two countries with Poland would result either in a renewal of the previous union on modern lines or in the most cordial neighbourly relations. The Congress took the view that all national minorities in all States ought to have national and cultural autonomy.[1]

On the other hand, Polish reactionary groups were opposed to the policy of equal rights for national minorities. M. Zdziechowski, professor at Cracow University and later the candidate of Marshal Pilsudski for the Presidency of Poland in 1926, wrote that, in his opinion, the mere idea of a Polish-Ukrainian agreement was an illusion because a separate Ukrainian nationality existed only in imagination.[2]

An article in the "National Gazette," the organ of the National Democratic Party of Dmowski, read as follows:

"What exactly are the Ruthenians and Lithuanians? Are they nations in the modern sense of the word? This question must be answered in the negative. Have these peoples a future, are they able to create new, individual forms of culture of high value and to reach the degree of evolution of other European nations? The answer is again negative. Who benefits by the Lithuanian or Ruthenian movement? It is weakening the Poles and thus is serving above all the enemies of the Polish people; it is therefore a crime for a Pole to co-operate with them."[3]

Another paper of the same party published in 1913: "The question of the existence of ritual murders aroused the general interest of the public, which will not allow itself to be terrorised by the cries of the Jewish press. The *Slowo* (The Word), it is true, expressed the opinion that a Catholic is not allowed to believe in the legend of ritual murder, in view of the declaration of the Holy See on this question, but the arguments of the *Slowo* have been proved to be baseless."[4]

Public opinion in Western Europe assumed that the independent Poland which was to emerge from the war of 1914–18, in view of her 150-year-old struggle for a democratic way of life, would have to be true to that tradition. It was in this firm belief that Joseph Conrad wrote: "It is historically unthinkable that the Poland of the future, with its sacred tradition of freedom and its

[1] *The Polish Review*. London, January 1918.
[2] *Gazeta Narodowa* (The National Gazette). Lwow, 11th August 1911.
[3] *The National Gazette*. 25th August 1911.
[4] *Przeglad Narodowy* (The National Review). Lwow, December 1912.

hereditary sense of respect for the rights of individuals and States, should seek its prosperity in aggressive action or immoral violence against that part of its once fellow-citizens, who are Ruthenians or Lithuanians."[1]

These hopes were not to be fulfilled.

REFERENCES

Bilinski, L., *Wspomnienia*, etc. (Memoirs and Documents). Warsaw, 1925.
Conrad, J., *Notes on Life and Letters*. London–Toronto, 1921.
Eversley, Lord, *The Partitions of Poland*. London, 1915.
Fisher, H. H., *America and the New Poland*. New York, 1928.
Harley, J. H., *Poland Past and Present*. London, 1917.
Lelewel, J., *Geschichte Polens*. Leipzig, 1846.
Steed, H. Wickham, *The Hapsburg Monarchy*. London, 1919.
Wasilewski, L., *Ukraina*, etc. (The Ukraine and the Ukrainian Question). Cracow, 1911.

[1] Conrad, p. 177.

Part Three

POLAND INDEPENDENT

"Princes and lords may flourish or may fade,
A breath can make them, as a breath has made;
But a bold peasantry, their country's pride,
When once destroyed can never be supplied."

OLIVER GOLDSMITH.

Chapter VI

THE RESTORATION OF POLAND

IT may be useful at this stage to summarise the main problems which confronted Poland on the eve of the restoration of her independence and which were the result of her backward social and political development.

(1) Serfdom survived in Poland until the nineteenth century. This had an important bearing on the relations between the peasants, who formed the great majority of the population, and other social classes, particularly the former barons. Memories of serfdom were fresh and the cleavage which existed (and still exists) between these classes, and which was more noticeable because of the numerical weakness of the middle classes, was much greater in Eastern Europe (including Prussia) than in Western Europe, where serfdom had disappeared some centuries earlier. To some extent, the "Prussian spirit" may even be regarded as a rudimentary survival of the psychology of master and serf. Arrogance and megalomania on the part of barons could be found in Prussia, in Poland, as well as in other east European countries; these characteristics were combined with indifference to the living conditions of the people, the self-assumed right to speak on behalf of the whole country, and contempt for the idea of parliamentary representation. The leaning to dictatorial forms of government was thus latent in certain sections of the Polish population.

(2) The custom of dividing land proportionally amongst all heirs, regardless of sex and seniority, was practised in those areas of Europe in which serfdom survived up to the eighteenth and nineteenth centuries. In Western Europe the free peasant could move from his native village and emigrate or settle in towns, and so it became the custom in those areas to leave intact the freehold land or estate, and the title attached to it, both of which passed to the eldest son. The east European peasant was not allowed to leave his native soil for this would have meant a loss to the estate owner of free labour and property. As a result, agricultural land was overcrowded and the property of the individual peasant family gradually declined in size. The absence of opportunities for industrial employment and his inability to make use of modern methods of cultivation contributed to the poverty of the peasant.

(3) The self-sufficiency of the feudal village, coupled with the prohibition of the serf's becoming a free worker, impeded the development of industry

in Central and Eastern Europe. Factories were established only with the help of the State and of State-owned banks (and foreign capital) and the hold of the State on economic life was never entirely relaxed. This "Mercantilist" policy and the so-called *Banques d'Affaires* which developed out of it and which were also present to a lesser extent in Western Europe, created favourable conditions for the development of monopolies.

(4) Property belonging to the insurgents of the nineteenth century was confiscated and given either to Russians or to Poles in reward for their services in quelling the rebellions. Consequently, the landed estates in Russian Poland in 1918 belonged either to those who had actively co-operated with the invaders, or to those who had taken no part in the struggle against them. It should be noted that the titles 'baron,' 'count' or 'prince,' assumed by Polish magnates, were of foreign origin. Bernard Connor observed: "Tho' the Poles in their own country have no Honorary Titles above a Gentleman, yet several have been known to have usurped them when they were travelling into France, Germany and Italy."[1] According to Prof. Bruckner, princes and counts originated after the fall of Poland.[2]

(5) Those Poles who co-operated with the three occupying powers became accustomed to thinking in terms of imperial aggrandisement. For example, Mr. Wickham Steed has stated that the annexation of Bosnia and Herzegovina, which was one of the immediate preliminaries to the outbreak of the war in 1914, was prepared by the Austrian Foreign Minister and Polish aristocrat, Goluchowski: "As has been stated, the idea of annexation was mooted by Count Goluchowski, during the Emperor Francis Joseph's visit to St. Petersburg in April 1897. Russia negatived the suggestion and the matter dropped. Some nine years later, in the summer of 1906, Count Goluchowski again broached the subject in conversation with the Russian Ambassador in Vienna, Prince Urussoff, who once more deprecated the idea."[3] Two years later Bosnia and Herzegovina were annexed by Austria. In spite of the fact that Poland herself had been a victim of aggression, there were bound to be dangerous external complications if statesmen bred in the imperialistic schools of Germany, Austria and Russia were to govern the new Poland.

Similarly, the internal peace of Poland would be endangered by the advent to power of politicians like Roman Dmowski or General Haller. Dmowski wrote: "I have never been a preacher of liberal humanitarian principles. I never belonged to any of the international organisations founded for increasing the happiness of mankind."[4] And General Haller, according to Sir Robert Donald, looked forward to the realisation of Dmowski's conception of Greater Poland: "In discussing the future with him at a manor house in the Corridor, he said: 'There are five great countries in Europe—England, France, Germany, Italy and Poland, but the greatest of the five is Poland.' General Haller has strong views on many of the Eastern problems—

[1] Connor, p. 174.
[2] Bruckner: *Geschichte der Polnischen Literatur*, p. 35.
[3] Steed, p. 240.
[4] Dmowski p. 139.

take his view, for instance, of Minorities. He thinks that minority treaties are a mistake, a crime. He declares that a man who belongs to a minority of any sort is only half a citizen. . . . If he had his way he would wipe out all minority treaties and thereby solve the minority problem."[1]

(6) A considerable proportion of the lower middle classes consisted of impoverished descendants of the gentry. They retained some feeling of superiority over their fellow-citizen of " common " origin, as well as many other feudal characteristics of the gentry. According to Professor Lord of Harvard University, the American member of the Inter-Allied Commission to Poland in 1919, the majority of the Szlachta (nobility) in pre-Partition Poland belonged to that impoverished aristocracy which had either no land at all or only enough to make a bare living. " Poverty-stricken, ragged, and dirty, living like peasants or worse, but still filled with all the pride of their caste, and eager to vent it on all occasions, these people excited the derision of every foreigner, and were, indeed, one of the most unique spectacles to be seen in Poland. Hundreds of thousands of them lived at the courts of the magnates, serving the latter in their militia, in the administration of their estates, or even in menial capacities. It was a point of honour and almost a matter of necessity for every great ' Lord ' in Poland to have hosts of such ' clients ' at his disposal, and their services were extremely useful. For it was from this class that the magnates recruited those hordes of tattered and drunken ' citizens ' who swarmed into every Dietine, ready to acclaim ' whatever the Lord Hetman (or the Lord Palatine) wishes ' and quick to use their swords in case of opposition. . . . It was the magnates who ruined Poland, and the ' barefoot Szlachta ' who formed their constant and efficacious instrument."[2]

Many of the descendants of the small gentry participated whole-heartedly, and often sacrificed their lives, in the struggles of the nineteenth century. Some of them later joined the Socialist movement out of disgust with the new industrial profiteers or from aristocratic scorn for the ever-growing wealth of the *nouveaux-riches*. Doomed to a miserable life in the semi-feudal conditions of Poland, unfortunately situated between the industrialists and the workers, they sought the support of the latter, but never lost hope of ascending into the ranks of the former. For some of them, the restoration of Poland's independence would have solved the difficult problems arising from their economic and social conditions. Since the only people who had not made any subservient agreement with the occupying powers were the Socialist workers, they turned to Socialism. Nevertheless, a considerable number retained their former outlook and continued the activities, which sometimes bordered on hooliganism, of the eighteenth century Szlachta. Ninian Hill's description of Polish patriotism applies particularly well to this class:

> " Poland suffered from a lamentable lack of true patriotism. Patriotism of a false and spurious character she had enough of and to spare. There

[1] Donald, pp. 250–1.
[2] Lord, *The Second Partition*, pp. 28–29.

was much patriotism founded on pride and vanity, and altogether wanting in loyalty and obedience to the voice of the nation, speaking through constitutional channels. It boasted in liberty which sank into licence. A patriotism which is not founded on ordinary wisdom and virtue, but moves at the impulse of ignorant prejudice and sentiment, even though it leads to heroic deeds, is far from being a blessing; on the contrary, it presents a most insidious danger which, because of its plausibility, is the more difficult to expose and crush. True patriotism has little in common with the blatant chauvinism of the demagogue, whose stock-in-trade consists of vulgar self-conceit, and ignorant contempt for whatever transcends the distorted conceptions of his narrow mind."[1]

Adam Mickiewicz's Gerwazy, a small noble in the service of an aristocrat, is perhaps a typical representative of that class, whose superstitions and prejudices are still alive to-day:

"... came towards her the astonished
And sour Gerwazy. 'I know all' ... he said.
The judge has spoken of this liberty.
But yet I do not understand what this
Can have to do with serfs. I fear me lest
'Tis something German. Liberty indeed
Is not a thing for peasants, but for nobles.
'Tis true that we from Adam all descend;
But I have heard that peasants come from Ham,
The Jews from Japhet, we nobility
From Shem, and thus as elders rule o'er both;
Yet otherwise the parish priest now teaches.
He says that it has been so formerly,
And in the ancient dispensation; but
When Christ our Lord, though He from Kings descended
Was born among the Jews in peasants' stable,
He levelled all ranks, and made them agree
And so thus let it be, if it may not
Be otherwise."[2]

(7) Polish democratic opinion was organised in the Peasant and Socialist Parties. The Peasant Party also included professional and middle-class people of "common" origin, and the Socialist Party, in addition to the workers, included professional and middle-class people of "noble" origin. The Peasant Party stood for political democracy, agrarian reform and peasant ownership of land. The Socialist parties were divided into two groups, the Social Democratic Party of Poland and Lithuania (S.D.K.P.L.) and the Polish Socialist Party (P.P.S.).

The S.D.K.P.L. advocated socialist revolution, nationalisation of land and industrial property and a European union of socialist states. The P.P.S. was made up of the right "nationalist" wing which was led

[1] Hill, p. 70. [2] Mickiewicz, pp. 247–8.

by Pilsudski, and the left "socialist" wing, which was led by Daszynski and Moraczewski. In its view any future independent Poland could not avoid being socialist, and therefore the struggle for independence was synonymous with the struggle for Socialism. It was to the leaders of the Polish Socialist Party that the Russian Socialist (Menshevik) leader Plekhanov directed his criticism: "The most honourable Polish comrade is convinced that Russian Social Democracy, on account of the backward conditions in our country, will not be able, even in a constitutional Russia, to exercise any serious influence on our social life. But we do not share this opinion of the very honourable Polish comrade, because according to us he argues more from the influence of sentiment than on the basis of hard political judgment. We, for our part, do not want to indulge in prophecies, either about ourselves or about the Polish socialists. However agreeable to us it would be to pronounce our conviction that the latter will immediately become the government of Independent Poland, we nevertheless think that on this point also it would be more cautious to say: *Qui vivra verra.*" (*Vorwaerts*, Berlin, 23rd July 1896.)

The descendants of the Szlachta played an important role in the P.P.S.; most of them ceased to be members of that party soon after the establishment of independence, although their influence still lingered on. Among these leaders was Joseph Pilsudski, of whom it is told that in November 1918, "when former colleagues addressed him as 'Comrade' he took them up shortly in memorable words: 'I have travelled with you in the same train as far as the station Poland, but there I left the train. Now I'm a comrade no longer!'"[1] Other ex-members of the P.P.S. in the course of time became leaders of the dictatorial parties and governments between 1926 and 1939.

(8) It was obvious that the foreign policy of the new Poland ought to be directed towards establishing and maintaining peaceful relations with her neighbours, since her geographical position and historical development had placed Poland between two homogeneous national blocs—Germany at least three, and Russia four times as strong as the Polish ethnic group of 20–25 million persons. Such indeed was the advice given by the British and American members of the Inter-Allied Commission to Poland in 1919. Sir Esmé Howard (later Lord Howard of Penrith) considered that Poland was destined to be a factor of the greatest importance in the political structure of Europe. Her geographical position would enable her to act as a bridge between the east and west, between Slav and Teuton, between Latin and Slav, provided she did not allow herself to be carried away by the recurring waves of ultra-national feeling, and resisted the temptation to super-patriotic megalomania which had made certain nations a danger to their neighbours and to themselves. "The truth is that Poland's best prospect of surviving to play the great part which is her due lies in the realisation that, having no natural frontiers (except to the south) her best frontiers are to be found in the goodwill of her neighbours. In this she may become a beacon light to us all and teach Europe a lesson which indeed it badly needs."[2]

[1] Rose, p. 59.

[2] Howard, p. 312.

Similar views were expressed by other Allied statesmen[1] as well as by non-political representatives of the Polish professional classes. The philologist A. Bruckner wrote that " the attractive power of a nation, its foreign influences, were not created by its political power, by military preponderance, nor by economic riches, but by culture, morale, education and art."[2] A. Zaleski, who later became Foreign Minister, thought likewise that military and political power was not the essence of true greatness and spiritual supremacy meant far more than the supremacy of the sword.[3]

The internal situation also demanded a peaceful policy. The retarded economic development of Poland, the agrarian problem in particular, and the reconstruction of industry after the ravages of war required all the energies of her people. However, it was to be otherwise. The Allied Powers, fearing world revolution,[4] decided on the policy of establishing a *cordon sanitaire* against the advance of Bolshevism, in which Poland was to play a great part. The encouragement of Polish reaction by the victorious Allied Powers and the weakness of Polish democracy decided the direction of the foreign and domestic policies of Poland at the outset of her independent life.

Four days before the Armistice, on 7th November 1918, amid a general movement of German and Austrian soldiers in Poland to set up revolutionary councils, the Polish Socialist Party and the Peasant Parties formed a Provisional Government in Lublin. This was the gist of its proclamation:

The Polish State, embracing all territories inhabited by the Polish people, with its own coastline was to constitute the Polish People's Republic, whose first president would be elected by the Constitutional Assembly, which was itself to be elected within two months. Complete political and civil equality was to be accorded to all citizens of Poland, without distinction as to origin, religion or race. They were to enjoy freedom of conscience, of press, speech, meeting, and demonstration, freedom of association, freedom to organise trade-unions and strikes, as from the date of the proclamation. All entailed estates, all forests, whether private or previously government-owned, were to be the property of the State; the eight-hour working day was to be introduced into trade and industry. The Provisional Government also declared its intention of proposing to the Constitutional Assembly projects for the following

[1] Lord, *Some Problems of the Peace Conference*, pp. 153, 158.

[2] Bruckner, *History of Polish Culture*, Vol. II, p. 377.

[3] Zaleski, p. 13.

[4] It may perhaps be recalled that the " Red Peril " at this time, just as later during the Nazi period, was often successfully used as a propaganda weapon against progressive political measures as well as to eliminate statesmen and politicians. Mr. Lloyd George related, for instance, that Philip Kerr (later the Marquess of Lothian) was particularly helpful to him in his difficulties with Russian entanglements. It was not fair, however, to characterise Kerr as pro-Bolshevik, as did some of both Kerr's and Mr. Lloyd George's friends, just because he was as strongly opposed as Mr. Lloyd George to the intervention of Allied forces in the internal affairs of Russia. So energetic were his protests that a prominent Allied diplomat sent a warning to the latter that Kerr was " the Bolshevik head centre in Western Europe." (Lloyd George, p. 264.) Many democrats and Socialists in Poland, including Pilsudski, were at one time or other accused of Bolshevik sympathies, or of being the " agents " of Soviet Russia.

social reforms: Complete expropriation and abolition of the larger and middle-sized landed estates of more than about 500 acres, and their restoration to the peasants under State control; nationalisation of mines, oil, transport, and other branches of industry where possible; participation of the workers in the administration of those industries which could not yet be nationalised; laws for the protection of labour, unemployment insurance, sick benefit and old-age pensions; confiscation of capital amassed during the war by illegal speculation in basic necessities and army contracts; introduction of compulsory, free, undenominational education.[1]

The proclamation was signed by Moraczewski, Daszynski, Rydz-Smigly and Thugutt amongst others. Daszynski was to act as Prime Minister.

On the same day the Provisional Government recognised Joseph Pilsudski as leader of the Polish armed forces, and Rydz-Smigly was to act as his deputy.

According to Sieroszewski, the Lublin Government had the confidence of the masses of peasants and workers. They were ready to wait peacefully for the promised reforms. Poland, therefore, avoided Communist manifestations, which were spreading round her to the east and west like a sea of flame.[2] The Government also had the confidence of the councils of soldiers of the German and Austrian army groups, which were occupying Poland. There is no doubt that this government could have maintained its power, could have introduced the urgently-needed social reforms and organised the Polish State on a solid democratic basis. The First Government of Independent Poland had no revolutionary programme, apart from its radical measures for agriculture. Nevertheless it lasted only a few weeks.

The German revolution of 9th November 1918 opened the gates of the Magdeburg prison, and Pilsudski arrived in Warsaw the next day. There he accepted the title of supreme commander of the Polish Army from the hands of the Council of Regency, which had been set up by Germany and Austria a year before. The Council had been overthrown four days earlier by the Daszynski Government, yet Daszynski recognised Pilsudski as temporary head of the Polish State and accepted from him the mission to form a new government. He did not succeed, and it was Moraczewski, a leader of the P.P.S. and close friend of Pilsudski,[3] who formed the second Polish Government. This Government began to lay the foundations of Poland by passing a suffrage law and fixing the elections to the first Constitutional Assembly for January 1919. The elections, however, did not take place then.

The Allied Powers had previously recognised the Polish National Committee in France as the official authority of Poland.[4] The committee con-

[1] Kumaniecki, p. 131.

[2] Sieroszewski, p. 105.

[3] He left the P.P.S. in 1930 when the party went into opposition against the Pilsudski régime. In 1936, at the height of the period of friendship of Poland with Nazi Germany, Moraczewski reasserted his democratic views and strongly declared his solidarity with the Spanish Republic.

[4] When Dluski, the brother-in-law of Madame Curie, came to Paris as representative of Polish democrats, including Pilsudski, he was not admitted to the Peace Conference.

sisted mainly of Poles of Tsarist-Russian orientation. Neither France, Britain nor the U.S.A. recognised the first two Polish Governments which held power in Poland and which, without doubt, were representative of the majority of the Polish people. This situation was paradoxical: one government, unrepresentative and absentee, was recognised diplomatically; the genuine home government was not recognised—mainly because of French opposition.

Poland at that time was represented in Paris and London by Dmowski, the leader of the N.D. Party. According to an American observer at the Peace Conference, Dmowski was politically an opportunist, a reactionary and an anti-semite. How and why he was taken at that time by the Quai d'Orsay as the true and only delegate of Poland, it would be hard to say. The new ideas that were shaking the world were something to be opposed. Dmowski, subtle, polished, and imperialist, appeared to the Quai d'Orsay as a man to be encouraged. He was put forward by a body of emigrés, while in Poland itself Pilsudski governed with the aid of the Socialists. Socialism, of course, was taken to mean Bolshevism, and for a long time Dmowski, in spite of, or rather because of, his associations with the late Tsar, his dislike of agrarian reform, and his antipathy to the Jews, was supported by the Quai d'Orsay as against Pilsudski, who was regarded as dangerously advanced. Needless to say, Dmowski made the greatest territorial claims for Poland, and he inoculated M. Pichon, the French Foreign Minister, with his ideas. M. Pichon was horrified at the thought of having a soldier like Pilsudski, with socialist leanings, at the head of a nation. This brought another clear division in the Peace Conference; France ranged herself with Dmowski against the British Foreign Office and Mr. Wilson.[1]

In London, on the other hand, there was a strong dislike of the Dmowski group,

> " which perhaps, unfortunately, but owing to the circumstances over which the Polish people had little or no control, had taken upon itself the representation of Polish interests in the Allied countries and had been more or less formally recognised as the representative of the new Polish State that was to be. The Polish National Committee was considered to be working in the interests of the reactionary forces in Poland rather than of the great masses of the Polish people, and there was a feeling that if Poland were assisted with the supplies she required after the Germans had evacuated the country, this would be bolstering up a reactionary government, and might be contrary to the interests of the Polish population as a whole and even contrary to their desires. In fact the prevailing opinion at the time seemed to be that to do anything the Polish Committee asked for would be to fasten upon Poland a *régime* of wicked landlords who spent most of their time in riotous living, and establish there a Chauvinist Government whose object was to acquire territories inhabited by non-Polish populations. At the same time there was undoubtedly a strong desire to see Poland re-established as a united independent country,

[1] Huddleston, pp. 42–4.

both from the point of view of righting an old injustice and of establishing a buffer between Germany and Russia, and a bulwark against the Bolshevik invasion from the East."[1]

According to Sir Esmé Howard, Mr. Balfour, then Foreign Secretary, pointed out to Paderewski, when he came to London, in what an unfortunate position Poland would be placed unless she could appear united at the Paris Conference table. In taking leave of Paderewski, whom he knew intimately, Mr. Balfour emphasised this point and said: "It is your task. I want you to go to Poland to unite Polish hearts."[2]

Moraczewski's government ceased to exist a fortnight after Paderewski's arrival in Danzig, on board the British cruiser "Concord," on Christmas Day, 1918. "The propertied classes, lacking faith in the Socialists, were unwilling to support the loans which the government offered, or to pay the taxes which it attempted to levy. There were unmistakable intimations that the Allies would do nothing for Poland in the way of military supplies or financial support unless a more representative government were established which included the Conservative as well as the Socialist party. . . . Under these circumstances, a compromise was made by which the Moraczewski Cabinet resigned and Paderewski became Premier and Foreign Minister."[3]

The events of the fortnight between Paderewski's arrival and the overthrow of the democratic government have not yet been disclosed. Lord Howard threw some light upon it when describing the first encounter between Paderewski and Pilsudski; he quotes Paderewski's biographer, Rom Landau: "When both men rose after the long conversation, Paderewski knew that no understanding was possible, and not merely because of the differences of political opinions. It was as though two planets had tried to revolve in the same orbit."[4]

All the same, the two men were reconciled barely twenty-four hours afterwards. "The same evening on his return home feeling discouraged, Paderewski was informed that Prince Sapieha and some friends were preparing a *coup d'état* against the Pilsudski Government. Paderewski, however, would have nothing to do with it and left immediately for Cracow. Whatever happened he was not going to assist in creating a breach in Poland instead of a union of hearts. The next night in Cracow he was aroused from his bed at 3 a.m. by General Szeptycki, Pilsudski's right-hand man, and told that the *coup d'état* had failed, that its authors were in prison and that Pilsudski invited him to return to Warsaw and form a Cabinet as Prime Minister."[5]

It is evident that Paderewski knew of the preparation of the *coup d'état*; but he did not inform the existing Government, and he went away from Warsaw for the night of 4th and 5th January 1919. It is probable, in view of his later policy, that Pilsudski also knew. The whole affair ended in Prince

[1] Howard, pp. 649–52.
[2] Howard, p. 324.
[3] Fisher, pp. 122–3.
[4] Howard, pp. 326–7.
[5] Howard, ibidem.

Sapieha's being released from prison; he even became Polish ambassador in London; and the Moraczewski Government was dismissed from office. Paderewski became Prime Minister and Pilsudski retained the office of Head of the State.

Paderewski, according to his biographer, looked upon Dmowski as the legitimate head of Polish affairs in the western world during all the years of his political activity. No vital decision was reached, no change of policy affected, without an exchange of lengthy telegrams between the two men.[1] Although the Paderewski Government was formally a coalition government, the N.D. Party under the leadership of Dmowski was the dominating element. Professor Namier says that the National Democrats who had the full support of the French Government, tried to proscribe their political opponents among the Conservatives and moderates, and to reduce the radical left to a decorative place in a predominantly National Democratic Government.[2]

Thus, Allied pressure and the readiness of Polish democratic parties to follow Pilsudski's leadership[3] brought about the defeat of the Moraczewski Government, which embraced not only Socialists and Democrats, but all that was progressive in Poland, with the exception of the Communists. The Allies had not recognised the two previous Polish Governments; Paderewski's Government, however, was recognised *de jure* by the U.S.A. on 22nd January, and by Great Britain on 26th February 1919.

M. Bilinski, former Austrian Minister of Finance and co-author of the ultimatum to Serbia in 1914, became Finance Minister in Paderewski's Government. He lived in Vienna and was called to Warsaw by telegram. These were his views about Paderewski: "On the same day as I presented myself to Pilsudski, I presented myself to the Prime Minister, M. Paderewski and to his wife, because, as is well known, Madame Paderewska governed in reality in the name of her husband or through his intermediary. . . . M. Paderewski gave the impression of an artist of genius, of an excellent patriot and a naïve, political child, all combined in one person. . . . To my amazement, they lived in the Royal Castle, in which ante-chambers were full of military guards, civil servants, secretaries and military adjutants, just as round the monarch or the head of a state! Even at the Emperor Francis Joseph's court it was not so pompous, and at Pilsudski's it was almost modest."[4]

Behind Paderewski all the various Polish officials of the former Russian, German and Austrian empires got a grip on the young Republic and determined its policy. Some of them had been pro-Russian and anti-German in the past, others pro-German and anti-Russian. In 1919 they seem to have agreed on an anti-German and anti-Russian policy. A similar development took place in other Eastern and South-Eastern European countries, and territorial claims and counter-claims well nigh wrecked the peace, for which the peoples had prayed during four years of war.

[1] Landau, p. 134. [2] Temperley, Vol. IV, p. 103.

[3] Mr. Lloyd George stated: "John Morley once said to me that 'there is no worse Jingo than a Jacobin turned Jingo.' This doctrine was applicable to Pilsudski." (p. 308).

[4] Bilinski, Vol. II, p. 205.

Mr. Lloyd George drew a vivid picture of the situation:

"The emancipated races of Southern Europe were at each other's throats in their avidity to secure choice bits of the carcasses of dead Empires. Pole and Czech were fighting over Teschen. The Poles and Ukrainians had both pounced on Galicia, whilst Rumanians and Serbs were tearing up Hungary and Austria. Poles and Lithuanians had their fangs on the same cities and forests.

". . . No one gave more trouble than the Poles. Having once upon a time been the most formidable military power in Central Europe—when Prussia was a starveling Duchy—there were few provinces in a vast area inhabited by a variety of races that Poland could not claim as being historically her inheritance of which she had been reft. Drunk with the new wine of liberty supplied to her by the Allies, she fancied herself once more the resistless mistress of Central Europe. Self-determination did not suit her ambitions. She coveted Galicia, the Ukraine, Lithuania and parts of White Russia. A vote of the inhabitants would have emphatically repudiated her domination. So the right of all peoples to select their nationhood was promptly thrown over by her leaders. They claimed that these various races belonged to the Poles through the conquering arm of her ancestors. Like the old Norman baron, who, when he was asked for the title to his lands, unsheathed his sword, Poland flourished the sword of her warrior kings, which had rusted in their tombs for centuries."[1]

In the same context Lloyd George repeats a statement he made in a discussion with Paderewski during the Paris Peace Conference:

"We won freedom for nations that had not the slightest hope of it. Czechoslovakia, Poland and others. Nations that have won their freedom at the expense of the blood of Italians and Frenchmen and Englishmen and Americans. And we have the greatest trouble in the world to keep them from annexing the territory of other nations and imposing upon other nations the very tyranny which they have themselves endured for centuries. You know, I belong to a small nation, and therefore I have great sympathy with all oppressed nationalities, and it fills me with despair the way in which I have seen small nations, before they have hardly leaped into the light of freedom, beginning to oppress other races than their own. They are more imperialistic, believe me, than either England and France, than certainly the United States. It fills me with despair as a man who has fought all his life for little nations."[2]

Mr. Gibbons, an American observer in Paris in 1919, considered that the ungenerous attitude of the Poles towards their neighbours had been one of the most disheartening phenomena of the aftermath of the World War. One would have thought that they, having suffered so much at the hands of their masters, would instinctively refrain from playing the detested role themselves. But as soon as they had a chance they demonstrated how well they had learned to employ the brutal methods of their own conquerors. As

[1] Lloyd George, pp. 306–12. [2] Lloyd George, p. 998.

Russians and Germans had acted towards Poles, so Poles proceeded to act towards Lithuanians and Ukrainians. Ever since the Poles found that they were to receive back their freedom, their territorial appetite has known no bounds, and indulgence has not modified it. Each successive triumph in getting a strip of territory from a neighbour was followed by new demands. A study of the frontiers already assigned to Poland but still disputed could not fail to make one pessimistic about the chances of a durable peace in Eastern and Central Europe. The Poles have made enemies of all their neighbours: Czechoslovaks, Ukrainians and Lithuanians, as well as Germans and Russians.[1]

In April 1919 General Haller's army came from France to Poland. This army comprised, in July 1918, only 10,000 men who had hardly been to the front. Its real organisation began after the Armistice. By an agreement with the French Government Haller's army was placed under the political authority of the Polish National Committee of Dmowski. In spite of the ending of hostilities, the Polish prisoners of war of the former German and Austrian armies in France and in Italy were sent to Haller's army and were not allowed to go home. The newly-formed army was organised chiefly during February and March 1919, the demobilised French infantry troops transferring the whole of their military equipment and uniforms to the new Polish detachments.[2] By April 1919, Haller had 100,000 men at his command.

The problem of the transportation of the army to Poland gave rise not only to dissensions amongst the Allies themselves but also to complications with Germany. According to Lord Howard, this question caused much discussion at the Peace Conference, the Polish National Committee being fervently in favour of it, while Pilsudski was dubious. The means of transport and the route to be taken were also hotly debated between the French and British authorities.[3] The Allies finally decided to demand the consent of Germany to transport Haller's army via Danzig to Poland. Germany categorically refused and would not yield to diplomatic pressure. Finally, the army was brought by train through Germany to Poland. According to Lloyd George, the army, which was ready for war when it arrived, was immediately marched into Galicia, ostensibly to drive off the Bolsheviks, but in reality to conquer the country and annex it to Poland. The Supreme Council sent a message to General Haller ordering his withdrawal. He did not take the slightest notice. Subsequently, he pretended that he had not received the telegram in time to act upon its instructions. Whether it was intercepted and held up by Pilsudski's orders, whether it had never been despatched from France, or whether they were all in a conspiracy to ignore it, was never discovered. President Wilson was not anxious to offend his Polish friends by pressing the enquiry too insistently.[4]

After the dissolution of the Austrian Empire the Ukrainians of Eastern Galicia created the West Ukrainian Republic at the same time as Poland

[1] Gibbons, p. 235.
[2] Lipinski, p. 460.
[3] Howard, p. 309.
[4] Lloyd George, p. 312.

became independent. The leaders of the Republic were against its reunion with the Russian Ukraine, partly because of their fear of Bolshevism and partly because of differences arising from the long separation. When fighting broke out between Poles and Ukrainians, the Supreme Council of the Allies despatched a telegram to Paderewski, in April 1919, recalling that, in its note of the 19th March, the Peace Conference had suggested to both the Polish and Ukrainian Governments that a suspension of arms should be arranged in Eastern Galicia, pending the discussion in Paris of an armistice through the mediation of the Allied Governments. It was essential that the Convention for the suspension of arms should contain nothing that would prejudge the nature of the future armistice, and the Allied and Associated Governments could not doubt that in the negotiation for a suspension of arms the Polish Government would act upon this principle. A further telegram was despatched to Pilsudski, in May, stating that the Supreme Council felt it their duty to tell the Polish authorities in the most friendly spirit, but with the most solemn earnestness, that if they were not willing to accept the guidance and decisions of the Peace Conference in the Polish-Ukrainian conflict, the Governments represented in the Council of the principal Allied and Associated Governments would not be justified in furnishing Poland with supplies or assistance any longer. If it was her deliberate purpose to set at nought the counsel proffered by the Conference, its authority could no longer, it was feared, be made serviceable to her.[1]

The Polish Government was not intimidated and occupied the whole of Eastern Galicia. The Western Powers, in spite of their earlier protests, accepted the *fait accompli* on the 25th June 1919. According to H. J. Paton, " the alleged danger that the Bolsheviks were about to advance through Eastern Galicia to join the Bolsheviks of Hungary undoubtedly affected the views of the representatives of the Great Powers."[2] The recognition *de jure* did not follow until March 1923, when the Conference of Ambassadors finally assigned Eastern Galicia to Poland. The legal situation of Galicia during 1919–23 was anomalous. In the Treaty of St. Germain (Art. 91) Austria ceded the whole of Galicia to the Allies. In the Treaty of Sèvres (Art. 1) the Allies offered only Western Galicia to Poland, but the Polish Government refused to sign the Treaty. Thus legally the whole of Galicia was under the sovereignty of the Allied Powers until 1923.

Dmowski's conception of the territorial reconstruction of Poland was known to the Allies from his memorandum, addressed to Lord Balfour in 1917. In the east he was prepared to sacrifice a large portion of the so-called Borderland possessions included in Poland before the Partitions, partly because they were largely inhabited by non-Polish populations, and partly because he wished to leave the door open for a future understanding with Russia. Pilsudski, on the other hand, inherited with the blood of the Eastern Borderland gentry from which he had sprung a vivid sense of the great historical tradition of Poland's imperial union with her eastern neighbour

[1] Temperley, Vol. II, p. 337. [2] Temperley, Vol. VI, p. 246.

Lithuania, and of Poland's civilising mission in the Lithuanian and Ruthenian border countries. His programme was, accordingly, more extensive and ambitious on the eastern than on the western side. Reckoning with the development which Ukrainian, White Ruthenian and Lithuanian national separatism had attained, Pilsudski visualised the constitution of the Eastern Borderlands as a series of small buffer states between Poland and Russia, which would, by the superior civilisation of Poland, gradually be drawn into some sort of federative union with her.[1]

"Two answers were possible," wrote Count A. Skrzynski, Polish Under Secretary of Foreign Affairs in 1919. "The first one was relatively modest in territorial claims, conservative in practice, and founded on the principle that Poland must endeavour to keep on good terms with Russia, whatever form of Government that State might adopt. According to this theory Poland must not advance too far eastward and must not allow any elementary cause of political or national friction to arise between herself and Russia. The other theory, reverting in a way to the ancient traditions of Poland, very audacious, but slightly romantic, aimed at the break-up of Russia into her national components, limiting her to a purely Russian ethnographical territory and surrounding her with a chain of States more or less independent, from the Ukraine in the south, to the Lithuanian and White Russian State in the north. . . . The federalistic conception was represented by Marshal Pilsudski, who was supported in it by the Socialists and by several social elements known under the name of the "Left" and in addition, but obviously for other reasons, by a part of the Polish nobility and large landowners, who, seeing their property submerged by the Bolshevik deluge on those same territories which the federalistic programme embraced, hoped by its realisation to regain them."[2]

This anti-Russian programme of Pilsudski was supported by propaganda in Allied capitals. It was argued that the Poles had fulfilled a high civilising mission in Russia over many years and had taken part as a leading factor in her economic life. Before and even during the war until the emergence of the Bolshevik régime, both the capital and the managerial direction of a great number of big industrial enterprises in Russia were in Polish hands. There was no single department of economic life, it was stated, in which Poles did not play a very important role. The metallurgical industry in the south of Russia was in the hands of Polish managers, as were the railway service and other departments of trade and industry. These Poles, although most of them had returned to Poland, had never lost touch with Russia. In two respects Russia was necessary to Poland; first, as a country possessing great quantities of raw materials; second, as a country where industry was very little developed, and thus a good field for economic influence and a market for the exportation of Polish products. Other countries also needed Russia for the same reasons, and Poland was the natural gateway to the East. It was also suggested that close co-operation between Great Britain and

1 Dyboski, p. 83.

2 Skrzynski, pp. 36–8.

Poland in economic policy in Russia would greatly facilitate the restoration of Russia as an element of economic power and civilisation.[1]

Apart from economic considerations, political arguments also were proposed.

Lenin, an Asiatic monster, it was said, in character and appearance an exact replica of Attila, Genghis Khan and Tamerlane, reigned supreme in Moscow. It was not surprising, therefore, that the liberated peoples of the old Russian Empire turned from the East towards the West, towards Poland. Poland had won her own liberty; it would be her greatest glory if she succeeded in winning that of others. These peoples should look towards Poland and not towards Attila and his successors; for Poland was the new European centre of order and energy, of liberty and justice in the East, the European bulwark against Bolshevism, and the hope of the oppressed. "Therefore, when critics say Denikin has failed and nothing therefore remains save to accept Bolshevism and let it work its will, let us say, Never! . . . Poland to-day is playing the same role as she played in the time of Sobieski. She is defending Europe against the onslaughts of barbarism. Her defence is brave and sure, but she needs British support. If that support be given, not only will Europe be defended against any peril from invasion by a modern Attila, but it will also be possible through Poland and the Baltic States to restore civilisation in Russia, and to rescue the unfortunate Russian peasantry—a peasantry as capable of progress as any in the world—from a brutal Asiatic scourge."[2]

The Polish-Soviet war broke out in due course. During 1919, the newly-formed Polish army, reinforced in the spring of the year by Haller's army from France, was actively extending Poland's frontiers eastwards. Soviet Russia, occupied with domestic war against leaders of counter-revolution in its east, north and south, was not capable of much resistance on her western side; and the Poles succeeded in recovering a considerable belt of their historical eastern border territory. Operations, however, were not very active until, in the spring of 1920, Pilsudski took a decisive step towards the realisation of his federalist conception. An anti-Bolshevik Ukrainian Government having been formed by Ataman Petlura, the aspirations of that Government towards domination of the whole of the Ukrainian South of Russia were recognised by Poland, and an alliance entered into with it, on the understanding that Poland was to retain Eastern Galicia.[3]

Peace negotiations were without result. To the first Russian proposal of 22nd December 1919, the Polish Government made no reply at all. To the second (29th January 1920) the Warsaw Government replied after a delay of two months (27th March 1920) during which both sides prepared for war. Poland had sounded Paris and London before replying. The Quai d'Orsay

[1] *Polish Economic Bulletin*, edited by the Polish Commercial and Financial Agency in London, March-April 1920.

[2] *The New Poland*, London, 15th and 22nd November 1919.

[3] Dyboski, pp. 88–9.

advised against negotiating with the Bolsheviks, and Lloyd George warned against hazardous adventures in the east.

On 26th April 1920, the campaign of Ukrainian liberation began. The Bolsheviks at first offered little resistance and on 7th May the city of Kiev was in Polish hands. Petlura summoned the Ukrainians to defend their liberties, and Pilsudski promised to withdraw his troops as soon as the Ukrainian government was established and ready to assume its functions. The Bolsheviks in their turn called on the Ukrainian peasantry to rise. The Polish-" Petlurist " triumph was short-lived. Russian troops assumed the offensive at the end of May; on 13th June Kiev was abandoned and the retreat of the Polish armies began. Through the month of June the retreat continued, a costly demonstration of Polish unpreparedness. On 10th July the Polish Premier, Grabski, appeared before the Supreme Council in session at Spa and asked for arms, munitions, military instructors and credits. The Council received Grabski's request " very coldly," and Lloyd George intimated that since the Poles had undertaken this adventure against his advice, they must now suffer the consequences. He said, however, that he would intervene if Poland agreed to renounce all ideas of conquest, to withdraw to the Curzon Line, and to accept Allied decision on the pending questions of Danzig and Teschen. At the same time, the Russians would be required to halt 50 kilometres east of the Polish army and a peace conference would be assembled in London to which representatives of Soviet Russia, Poland, Finland, Lithuania, Latvia and Eastern Galicia would be invited. The British Government then sent the Lloyd George proposal to Moscow, but the Bolsheviks declined to enter such a conference and preferred to deal with the Poles alone, whereupon the British and French Premiers threatened to support Poland with all the means at their disposal. " There was great excitement in the west and dire consequences were foretold of a Bolshevik-German alliance."[1]

On 25th July 1920, the Grabski Government resigned; Witos, the peasant leader, became Prime Minister, and Daszynski, the Socialist leader, Deputy-Prime Minister. The change was significant, as the Peasant and Socialist Parties were against the anti-Bolshevik campaign. Grabski's resignation did not take place, however, without pressure from outside. Field-Marshal Sir Henry Wilson noted in his diary on 16th July 1920: " Lloyd George told me he had heard—I don't know how—that the Bolsheviks were going to completely overrun Poland and come up against Germany. We had a meeting of Lloyd George, Millerand, Foch and me. Foch and I said that it was no use pouring in more arms into Poland, unless and until the Poles had a good national Government, fully representative of a united people determined to stand against invasion. Lloyd George asked if Foch would go out to Poland and steady the situation. He replied that that was a matter for M. Millerand. Millerand said he could not agree, unless the conditions put forward by the two Marshals were fulfilled, and I said it would never do to risk the priceless

[1] Fisher, pp. 248–51.

asset of Foch's name in a wild scheme of this sort."[1] Three weeks later Sir Henry wrote: "Winston (Churchill) told me that when he went over to see Lloyd George he found him closeted with Krassin and Kameneff, and he sent out a note to Winston to say, 'I have told them that if they don't stop their advance in Poland I shall order the British Fleet into the Baltic at once.' So he is thinking of declaring war on the Bolsheviks, having thrown away every card in the pack."[2]

On 6th August 1920, at the time when the Soviet armies were approaching Warsaw, *The Times* reported: "It is a terrible truth that once more we stand upon the edge of a crisis fraught with possibilities only less tragic than those that lowered over us in the first week of August six years ago."

On 9th August 1920, the Conference of the Parliamentary Committee of the British Trades Union Congress, the National Executive of the Labour Party and the Parliamentary Labour Party adopted a resolution which said that the Joint Conference felt certain that war was being engineered between the Allied Powers and Soviet Russia on the issue of Poland, and declared that such a war would be an intolerable crime against humanity. It therefore warned the Government that the whole industrial power of the organised workers would be used to defeat that war; and proclaimed that the executive committees of affiliated organisations throughout the country be summoned to hold themselves ready to proceed immediately to London for a national conference, that they be advised to instruct their members to 'down tools' on instructions from that conference, and that a council of action be immediately constituted to take such steps as may be necessary to carry the above decisions into effect.[3]

On 10th August 1920, Lloyd George declared that the Polish attack upon Russia was not justified, in his judgment, and he sincerely regretted that it had been made in spite of the warnings of France and of Britain. But, whatever the mistakes may have been which were committed by a Government in an act of aggression upon another nation, nothing justified a retaliation which went to the extent of wiping out national existence. The Allied Governments made it quite clear that it was a fundamental condition of any Allied support, whether moral or material, that the Polish armies should retire to the ethnographical frontier of Poland.[4]

Meanwhile the Soviet advance was brought to a halt on 15th August and the danger of a European war was averted.

The anti-Bolshevik motives behind Pilsudski's eastern policy were much less important than his territorial ambitions. Pilsudski was against the re-establishment of Tsardom in Russia and no doubt preferred the Bolsheviks to the Whites, knowing that the latter could count on the support of the Allies against Poland's territorial aims. In 1919 when the situation of the

[1] Callwell, Vol. II, p. 253.
[2] Callwell, Vol. II, p. 255.
[3] Coates, p. 337.
[4] D. Lloyd George, The Russo-Polish Situation. Extracts from speeches delivered in London in 1920.

Bolsheviks was critical, Pilsudski, fearing the restoration of Tsardom, concluded an armistice with the Soviet Government. Paradoxically, the armistice was concluded between J. Marchlewski, the former leader of the Social Democratic Party of Poland and Lithuania, as the representative of the Soviet Government, and J. Beck and J. Berner, as the representatives of Pilsudski, the former leader of the Polish Socialist Party.

The Polish campaign of eastward expansion culminated in the seizure of Vilna, the ancient capital of the old Lithuanian Empire.

In November 1918 Lithuania had declared her independence with the restoration, after almost 150 years, of Vilna as her capital. In January 1919, Vilna became the seat of the Lithuanian Soviet Government; three months later it was occupied by Poland, but was lost in July 1920 during the retreat before the Soviet armies. Shortly before the armistice between Poland and the Bolsheviks, an armistice was concluded with Lithuania, and Vilna was placed outside the Polish sphere of occupation. " This naturally produced dissatisfaction among a division of the Polish army recruited almost entirely in the Wilno district, and this division, with General Zeligowski at its head, revolted against the Suwalki agreement and occupied Wilno a few days later. General Zeligowski appointed a provisional government of the province, which he called " Central Lithuania."[1]

According to Mr. Polson-Newman, Poland paid a big price for Vilna, for confidence in Poland waned, and Europe began to wonder whether after all a Polish State was conducive to general peace.

The action of General Zeligowski not only violated the agreement with Lithuania which the Poles had signed, but ignored the authority of the League of Nations and the Commission which it had set up. " The Vilna question by itself is a comparatively small matter, but the situation and character of the dispute is such that it directly or indirectly affects other European problems of first importance, and thereby involves the interests of most of the European Powers. Although the dispute seems interminable and nearly exhausts the patience of statesmen in Western Europe, it has to be treated seriously and as a question with dangerous possibilities. Vilna is to-day one of the danger points of Europe, and it is only necessary to visit this area to realise that there is enough explosive material on these rolling plains to set the whole of Europe ablaze once more."[2]

The aggressive foreign policy of 1918–20 was by no means based on internal strength. Former Russian Poland was devastated by the battles of 1914–18, and in former German and Austrian Poland the situation was not much better. The Soviet campaign brought to light the economic weaknesses of Poland: the army had no reserves, no regular flow of arms and supplies could be provided from a largely devastated industry, and the rout from Kiev was the result.

The " Federalist " programme, which played such a prominent part in Poland's foreign policy between 1918–20, was sponsored mainly by Pilsudski

[1] Dyboski, p. 93.

[2] Polson-Newman, pp. 123–7.

and his friends from the Austro-Polish legions and by the former Austro-Polish politicians of Galicia (as well as by the large estate-owners in the East). They believed in that programme when co-operating with Austria and Germany before 1914 and during the war of 1914–18, and they guided Poland's foreign policy again after 1926, particularly after 1933, on those principles. The foreign policy of Germany and Austria-Hungary before 1918 and that of Nazi Germany after 1933 moved along much the same lines of thought and action.

References

Bilinski, L., *Wspomnienia*, etc., (Memoirs and Documents). Warsaw, 1925.

Bruckner, A., *Geschichte der polnischen Literatur*. Leipzig, 1901.

Bruckner, A., *Dzieje Kultury* (The History of Polish Culture). Cracow, 1931.

Callwell, Sir C. E., *Field-Marshal Sir Henry Wilson*. London, 1927.

Coates, W. P., and Zelda K. Coates. *Armed Intervention in Russia*, 1919–22. London, 1935.

Connor, Bernard. *The History of Poland*. London, 1698.

Dmowski, R., *Polityka*, etc. (The Polish State and the Restoration of the State). Warsaw, 1926.

Donald, Sir Robert, *The Polish Corridor and the Consequences*. London, 1929.

Dyboski, R., *Poland*. London, 1933.

Fisher, H. H., *America and the New Poland*. New York, 1928.

Gibbons, H. A., *Europe Since* 1918. New York, 1923.

Hill, Ninian, *Poland and the Polish Question*. London, 1915.

Howard of Penrith, Lord, *Theatre of Life*. London, 1936.

Huddleston, Sisley, *Peace-Making at Paris*. London, 1919.

Kumaniecki, K. W., *Odbudowa*, etc. (The Restoration of the Polish State. Documents). Warsaw–Cracow, 1924.

Landau, R., *Paderewski*. London, 1934.

Lipinski, W., *Walka Zbrojna* (The Armed Struggle for the Independence of Poland). Warsaw, 1935.

Lloyd George, D., *The Truth About the Peace Treaties*. London, 1938.

Lord, R. H., *The Second Partition of Poland*. Cambridge, Mass., 1915.

Lord, R. H., *Some Problems of the Peace Conference*. Cambridge, Mass., 1920.

Mickiewicz, Adam, *Master Thaddeus*. English translation by Miss M. A. Briggs. London, 1885.

Polson-Newman, E. W., *Britain and the Baltic*. London, 1930.

Rose, W. J., *Poland*. London, 1939.

Sieroszewski, W., *J. Pilsudski*. Zamosc, 1921.

Skrzynski, A., *Poland and Peace*. London, 1923.

Steed, H. Wickham, *The Hapsburg Monarchy*. London, 1919.

Temperley, H. W. V., *History of the Peace Conference of Paris*. London, 1920–24.

Zaleski, A., *Landmarks of Polish History*. London, 1916.

Chapter VII

ECONOMIC POLICY AND THE STANDARD OF LIVING OF THE POPULATION

POLISH economic life was largely destroyed by the war of 1914–18 and its aftermath, and the problems of reconstruction, which were therefore considerable when peace came at the end of 1920, had not been investigated nor had plans been prepared and methods determined for dealing with the economic chaos which prevailed in 1921.

Only the industries of Western Poland were in working order; in the rest of Poland the plants were either destroyed or were carried away to Germany. In former Russian Poland, for instance, out of 459 factories of various sizes only 195 had begun work again at the beginning of 1921. The textile industry, one of the most important, was working with about 30 per cent of its pre-war plant.

The men responsible for determining the economic policy of reconstituted Poland were drawn largely from former officials of Austria-Hungary. They were limited by practice and outlook to the policy they had drafted and executed when in office in an old-established State, and they did not show any initiative in finding a solution for the unprecedented economic situation in the newly-formed State, except by aiming at a spiral of rising prices. It was intended to set industry in motion and to provide employment for the population by large credits to would-be employers, with guaranteed profit margins and prospects of a depreciation of the loans incurred. That short-term policy was successful to a limited degree; it helped to rebuild industrial enterprises and to give employment to some of the population. It did not, however, provide a substitute for a long-term policy of mobilising all, or most, of the economic resources of Poland; indeed, it aggravated in many respects the problems of agricultural and industrial development and considerably weakened the social fabric of Poland.

As in Germany, the inflationary policy, pursued until the end of 1923 in Poland, impoverished the middle classes and brought fortunes to a few. It undermined the class of medium-sized peasants who lost the savings of their lifetime. According to W. J. Rose, thousands of peasants had savings hidden in their " stockings " when the war ended, and they would have put them into land, had not the authorities frowned on the idea.[1] The inflationary policy also quickened the pace of the formation of monopolies. Above all, it introduced into the economic life of Poland the corrupting influence of State help and protection for large private interests.

There are no data available of the movement of prices of goods and services. A few figures may, however, illustrate the degree of inflation.

TABLE I.

The dollar rate in Warsaw (in marks).[2]

	Marks
31st December, 1918	8
,, ,, 1919	110
,, ,, 1920	590
,, ,, 1921	2,922
,, ,, 1922	17,800
,, ,, 1923	6,375,000
27th April, 1924	9,250,000[3]

Although the fall in the internal value of the currency was considerably less than the depreciation of the foreign exchange, the 1923 " hyper-inflationary " rise in prices and the subsequent conversion of marks to zlotys wiped out all existing obligations, whether contracted in marks before 1924 or dated from before 1914 and revalued between 1916–24.

During 1918–24 the Government raised internal loans amounting to thousands of millions of marks and granted during that period credits of equal dimensions to employers and would-be employers. In consequence of the enormous rise in prices, the holders of State securities and of Titles to fixed incomes, lost almost everything, while the debtors of the State and holders of stocks of production and consumption goods gained almost everything. An illustration of this is that out of 1904 joint stock companies existing on 1st January 1925, 997 had been founded between 1921–24.

Inflation is probably the most inequitable method of taxation. Some restriction of personal consumption was no doubt unavoidable in Poland in 1921 as, particularly in the early stages, the output of consumption goods fell considerably short of the personal income and effective demand of the population. Inflation performed that task; in addition, however, it directly redistributed the income and savings of those who trusted the State and who wanted to help in the economic reconstruction, in favour of those who received the help of the State and of State-sponsored institutions. It also

[1] Rose, p. 81.

[2] Until 28th April 1924, the unit of Polish currency was the mark; after that date it was the zloty converted at the rate of 1 zloty to 1,800,000 marks. The mark was established in 1916 by the German-occupying authorities, who set up the Polish State Loan Bank with the monopoly of issuing state currency.

[3] Zdziechowski, pp. 6–7.

destroyed the small private savings of the people; the following table shows the degree of that destruction to have been greater in Poland than elsewhere:

TABLE 2.

Comparison of saving deposits in 1913 and 1927 in certain countries (in millions of dollars).[1]

Country	1913	1927	1913=100
United Kingdom	1,175	1,748	(149)
France	772	579	(75)
Italy	904	1,160	(128)
Czechoslovakia	568	457	(81)
Germany	4,690	1,114	(24)
Austria	600	140	(23)
Poland	602	92	(15)

The Government did everything possible to further the boom which was based on a very liberal credit policy; the bank-rate, for instance, was never raised above 8 per cent. Here is an example which illustrates some results of the inflation. The large textile works at Zyrardow, near Warsaw, came under the administration of the State as the result of a decree of the Moraczewski Government on the 16th December 1918. They were very badly damaged during the war, and the Government, in order to reconstruct them, made several investments at different times, totalling 69 million Polish marks, that is, the equivalent of about 3,034,000 Swiss francs. After the works were restored to private ownership, the owners repaid to the Government in January 1924, the 69 million marks which at that time were worth only 18,800 Swiss francs, that is, 0.6 per cent of the original loans, if measured by a stable currency.[2]

The cut in personal consumption achieved by the inflationary tax, much greater in respect of non-manual than of manual workers, can be gauged from the following figures:

TABLE 3.

Daily real wages and salaries of certain classes of workers and state employees in 1914 and 1921–23 (marks).[3]

	Metal Industry		Textile Industry		Printing Industry	
Date	Skilled Workers	Unskilled Workers	Weavers	Unskilled Workers	Compositors	Printers
Jan. 1914	4.64	2.38	4.32	2.16	4.78	2.08
Jan. 1921	3.33	2.70	3.28	2.52	4.13	2.06
Jan. 1922	3.48	2.82	2.37	1.59	6.27	3.14
Jan. 1923	2.85	2.12	2.26	1.27	5.89	2.94
Oct. 1923	2.49	1.80	1.65	0.84	2.84	1.42

[1] Gruber, p. 121.
[2] Szturm de Sztrem, pp. 16–21.
[3] *International Labour Review*. Geneva. September 1924, p. 395.

State Employees

	Heads of Departments	Higher Grade Clerks	Lower Grade Clerks
Jan. 1914	40.13	11.23	5.33
Jan. 1921	4.85	2.78	2.04
Jan. 1922	7.10	3.91	2.93
Jan. 1923	9.91	5.49	4.13
Oct. 1923	4.73	2.46	1.85

* * *

The creation of a considerable home market for industrial products was the *sine qua non* for the development of industry. For that reason, and from historical, political and social considerations, as well as for the sake of agricultural production itself, the reorganisation of the land tenure was of the utmost importance. Count Skrzynski described the question of land reform at the time:

"Of great account is the fact that Poland is surrounded towards the East and the North by countries which in more or less radical ways have changed their system of land-owning. Soviet Russia solved its agrarian problem by the complete elimination and expropriation of the big landowners. But besides Russia, perhaps in a less violent but equally radical way, an agrarian reform was carried out by the new Baltic countries Esthonia, Latvia, and Lithuania. . . . A clear-minded social politician must see that the Russian agrarian developments and the benefits shared there by the peasant, could not fail to have its effect in the Polish village. Such are the factors which make the agrarian question the centre of all the political, social and economic problems of Poland to-day.

. . . On account of the profound conservatism of the big Empires which divided Poland, and oppressed her during a century and a half, agrarian conditions changed the least and remained relatively as they were at the end of the eighteenth century. Obviously, the evolution of the economic, social and political life had its effect. Here were important changes in landed property; but they were not of such a character as to change the system itself. It remained in the same state as that in which it was left by ancient Poland, more or less feudal.

. . . No doubt remains as to the necessity of land reform for Poland from the point of view of both social and political affairs. Anybody who wants to govern this country must accept the inevitability of land reform, and nobody denies its importance.

. . . The large landed property in the Eastern provinces does not belong either to the White Russians or to the Ukrainians, but to the Poles as a survival of the conditions obtaining in the time of the old Kingdom of Poland. In discussing the agricultural question in Poland one comes to the conclusion that it cannot be solved unless the agricultural colonisation of Poland is directed Eastwards, where there still exist some very large landed properties. But here the Polish colonist meets with the claims of the native population, which also is land-hungry and can justify its claims by pointing to the fact that these lands were always cultivated by their hands."[1]

According to the Census of 1921 the agricultural structure of Poland was as follows:

TABLE 4.

Number and area of agricultural holdings according to size. (In hectares).[2]

	Holdings with an area of hectares.			
	Total	Under 10	10–100	Over 100
Number of holdings (in 000's)...	3,262	2,845	398	19
Total area of holdings (in 000's)	30,341	9,667	7,069	13,589
Percentage of holdings	100.00	87.2	12.2	0.6
Percentage of area	100.00	31.8	23.4	44.8

Thus, small and medium-sized farms, constituting 99.4 per cent of all holdings, possessed 55.2 per cent of agricultural land, while estates of over 100 hectares constituting 0.6 per cent of total holdings, possessed 44.8 of the land. Land reform was regulated by the Acts of the Polish Parliament of 10th July 1919 and 15th July 1920. The law of 1919 stated that the agricultural policy of the Polish Republic should be based on sound peasant farms of different types and acreage, capable of intense production, and based on private ownership. The owners of the land were to be the only persons who would work themselves on the farm. In principle the maximum of land not subjected to expropriation was to vary according to districts, from 60 to 180 hectares (148–444 acres). The lowest figure applied to industrial and suburban districts.

The law of July 1920 placed many of the categories of land subject to expropriation according to the 1919 Act, at the disposal of the then-created Central Land Office. It stated that the following lands came under the Agricultural Reform Acts:

(1) All the surface over 60 hectares of landed estates situated in industrial and suburban districts, as well as all surface over 400 hectares of landed estates situated in certain parts of the former Prussian Poland.

(2) All the surface over 187 hectares of landed estates situated in all other parts of the Polish Republic.[3]

The relatively moderate legislation of 1919 and 1920 was never implemented. The Acts were passed under heavy pressure from the peasant parties, and the large landowners could not effectively counter them amidst the general

[1] Skrzynski, pp. 67–74.
[2] *Concise Statistical Year-book of Poland*, 1930.
[3] Haden Guest, pp. 110–18.

upheaval in Eastern Europe. Dmowski declared in 1919 in the Supreme Council:

> " We are encompassed on all sides by revolutions: the Russian, the Hungarian, the German. We have no army. We had to do what weak animals do who are deprived of claws or talons: we assumed a protective colouring."[1]

The pressure of those who opposed land reform became considerable once the Polish-Russian war came to an end. It was so strong in 1923 as to lead even to the fall of the Witos Government when it attempted to deal with the question. In 1924 land reform was linked up with a capital levy to be paid by industry and agriculture and it still remained inoperative.

At last the Seym took definite action and an Act was passed on 28th December 1925, which modified that of 1920 by restricting the parcellation of estates to two million hectares (about five million acres) annually over a period of ten years. The Act permitted voluntary parcellation, with recourse to expropriation by the State as a last resort, and the principle of fair compensation was admitted. Also the acreage which a landowner could retain was extended beyond that allowed by the former Act, especially in the so-called Eastern Borderlands.[2]

Mr. Malbone W. Graham reported on the controversy which attended the passing of the new bill:

> " While the bill was under consideration by the Senate a great congress of landlords met in Warsaw and, under the auspices of Prince Casimir Lubomirski, formerly minister to the United States, passed resolutions against all land reform. The results of their lobbying and influence in the upper chamber were particularly noticeable in the land exemption provisions and numerous restrictive and reactionary clauses. Under the bill as passed by the Senate, lands scheduled for parcellation but not actually distributed within a given year would not thereafter be subject to distribution; all forced partitioning was postponed until 1927; land alone was to be valued at a computable rate, while buildings and movable property were to be paid for at their ' real ' worth. In short, the effort made by the Senate was to complicate the reform as much as possible and to increase the profits accruing to the proprietors.
>
> " On the return of the demanded bill, the Seym accepted most of the Senate amendments and added new ones exempting forests and historic estates from compulsory partitioning and further taking the sting out of its provisions. As finally passed, 28th December 1925, the bill was, in the opinion of the Christian Nationalist press ' no longer contrary to the constitution or economic life.' This tribute from the arch-representatives of a clerical, monarchist, feudal, land-holding aristocracy was indeed significant! The *Messager Polonais*, representing the government's viewpoint, stressed the non-partisan character of the reform, its high humanitarian import and its value as a measure of national conservation."[3]

[1] Dmowski, p. 365.
[2] Machray, pp. 189, 206.
[3] Graham, pp. 514–15.

In May 1926, however, came Pilsudski's *coup d'état* and even this modified act was not implemented.

The results of the agrarian reforms carried through in Poland as compared with other countries after 1918 were as follows:

TABLE 5.

Percentage of total agricultural land affected by agrarian reforms.[1]

	Percentage
Greece	50.0
Latvia	42.4
Rumania	29.7
Estonia	25.0
Lithuania	17.5
Czechoslovakia	14.1
Hungary	10.0
Poland	6.1

More than two-thirds of the land subdivided was disposed of by the original owner by private sale, rather than by State expropriation. The tendency of the private owner was to dispose of his inferior land, and when he sold it to satisfy the agrarian law it usually passed to a comparatively well-to-do peasant rather than to needy families.[2] It is not possible to say precisely how far the agrarian reform in Poland transformed the structure of land tenure after 1921, as no data are available for a later period. However, taking into account the negligible results of the land reform, the increase in the population and the depression between 1930 and 1939, it may be estimated that the number and proportion of smallholdings in 1939 were substantially the same as in 1921.

The subdivided area came chiefly from the smaller landed proprietors and from estates owned by Germans in Western Poland; the large estates of the Polish barons were in 1939 of almost the same size as in 1919. The dividing up of the German estates in Western Poland, while leaving intact the property of the Polish landowner in the area of the "Eastern Borderlands" made the national question more acute. The German Junkers appealed to their friends in Berlin, while the White Russian and Ukrainian peasants felt still more strongly their relationship with the peasants of Minsk and Kiev.

The legislation dealing with the land reform aimed not only at the division of large estates but also at the abolition of common rights and the consolidation of farms. The custom of dividing peasant property among all heirs had given rise to the "chequerboard," so characteristic in Poland and certain other continental countries, which transformed the Polish countryside literally into a crazy quilt of tiny cultures.

[1] *Royal Institute of International Affairs, World Agriculture,* p. 149.
[2] Buell, p. 205.

"Often single farmers may have sixty strips of land two yards in width scattered several miles apart. Such a system of land tenure—which prevailed in Russia before Soviet collectivisation, and in England more than a hundred and fifty years ago—makes efficient farming impossible. Hours of time are consumed in walking from one strip to another; the use of agricultural machinery is virtually impossible; much land is wasted in boundaries; and countless time and money are spent in law suits over boundaries."[1]

The rate of the abolition of common rights and of the work of farm consolidation increased considerably after Pilsudski's *coup d'état*. Between 1919 and 1926 an area of 257,300 hectares, i.e. an average of 36,800 hectares per annum, was re-allocated. Between 1926 and 1937 the figures were 4,736,400 hectares, i.e. an average of 394,700 hectares per annum, ten times as much as in the previous period. Up to 1926 the abolition of common rights affected 16,500 holdings, i.e. an average of 2,400 per annum; and in the following twelve years 256,400 holdings, i.e. an average of 21,400 per annum, ten times as much as in the previous period, lost the right of cutting wood, grazing animals, and so forth, on the property of the landowner.[2]

The reorganisation of land tenure failed to solve the problems it aimed at; it did not satisfy the demand of the peasants for land, and it did not provide them with farms yielding an income above subsistence level. A well-planned policy of economic development, or even of public works, might perhaps have provided a substitute for an agrarian reform. There is no evidence, however, that any attempts were made to devise new methods of promoting industry and agriculture to raise the income of the population.

In such circumstances the direct intervention of the Government was necessary for the development of industry, its modernisation and the introduction of newly-discovered techniques of production. This intervention took mainly the form of protecting foreign trade and the foundation of Government-owned enterprise in those branches of industry where risk was considerable.

Exports were encouraged and protection granted to home industry; in both cases monopolistic interests were favoured. For instance, the export trade in agricultural products was monopolised by such concerns as the Cattle, Sheep or Hog Exporters' Syndicates, the Bacon Industry Union and the Union of Grain Exporters. Some of these associations had the right to issue export certificates, without which no product could leave the country. Export duties and duty refunds on the export of Polish agricultural products were in force almost exclusively for the benefit of trade organisations and served either to centralise export or to create certain standards of quality for export. The government policy aimed at a "syndicalisation of agricultural export by means of facilities granted to the organised export at the cost of wild, individual foreign trade."[3] Another means of eliminating the small trader was the direct imposition of certain conditions of weight, packing,

[1] Buell, pp. 201–2.
[2] *Concise Statistical Year-book of Poland,* 1938.
[3] Morgan, p. 280.

and so forth. In 1929, for example, a 200 per cent *ad valorem* export duty was fixed for butter, and exporters who complied with the regulations regarding packing and quality were exempted from the duty.

Polish import duties were the highest in Europe.[1] The protection of the sugar industry, which was closely linked up with the landed estates, created one of Poland's many anomalies. The duty on sugar was the highest in the world[2], and the sugar industry was therefore able to obtain high prices at home and sell cheaply abroad. Thus Poland became one of the most important sugar exporters in the world, while its home consumption was one of the lowest.

The proceeds of foreign trade were not sufficient to pay for imports, a considerable proportion of which were capital goods and this necessitated an influx of foreign capital. The important influence of the latter on Polish economic life can be judged by the fact that according to the last available figures (1930–37) about half of the capital of all Polish joint stock companies was foreign-owned; of this two-thirds were in the mining, oil, chemical, electricity and insurance joint stock companies, and nearly all the larger private banks were foreign-owned.[3] (A considerable proportion of foreign capital had been invested before 1914.)

In order to overcome the reluctance of foreign entrepreneurs to invest in a small market with its uncertainties of return on capital, the ordinary risks had to be removed from commercial undertakings which became more monopolistic with each influx of capital. For instance, one of the more important loans contracted by Poland was that with the Kreuger-Toll Match Trust in 1925, on condition that a match monopoly be established in Poland and leased to the trust for twenty years. Although that monopoly had never existed in the former Russian, Prussian or Austrian parts of Poland, the Polish Government had to comply with the conditions of the loan. At times the estimated risks involved in credit transactions with Poland was so great that in 1926 no London banker was prepared to float a Polish loan without concomitant control over customs, railways and the national budget.[4]

To encourage foreign capital private enterprise was sometimes combined with Polish State enterprise. Mr. Buell quotes the case of the Italian Fiat company whose motor cars were exempted from all customs duties, until the State Engineering Works were able to begin production of the "Polish Fiat." This meant in practice that the State Engineering Works imported Italian cars without duty and sold them in Poland. At the same time (1932) new and heavy duties were imposed on all other automobiles, which in some instances proved prohibitive, and the State Engineering Works, therefore, acquired a monopoly of the Polish market.[5]

Before 1914 Russian Poland had an alcohol monopoly and Austrian Poland a tobacco monopoly, both owned by the State; these monopolies were extended

[1] Bell-Morrison, p. 30.
[2] *Royal Institute of International Affairs, World Agriculture*, p. 183.
[3] Wellisz, pp. 145–6. [4] Fischer, Vol. II, p. 716. [5] Buell, pp. 180–1.

after 1918 to the whole of Poland, and new State monopolies, such as salt, were introduced. The growth of private monopolies, particularly strong after the seizure of power by Pilsudski in 1926, is shown in the following table:

TABLE 6.
Number of Domestic and International Cartels in Poland.[1]

	Domestic Cartels	International Cartels in which Polish enterprise participated
1919	9	3
1920	11	4
1926	53	8
1931	168	69
1936	274	106

The service of Poland's foreign debt formed a not inconsiderable item in the Polish balance of payments. These debts were largely contracted before 1920 in the form of subsidies granted by the Allied Powers during the World War to Polish organisations for political propaganda and for the equipment of Polish military detachments and formations, as well as for the repatriation of these troops to Poland, and to cover the cost of delimiting and fixing the Polish frontiers. They were rather a political than an economic debt, and according to M. Wellisz were granted " not only in the interests of Poland herself but also in the well-conceived interests of international solidarity. . . . Without entering into any detailed justification of this point of view, it is necessary only to stress the fact that the consolidation of the Polish Republic and its victory over the Bolsheviks during the Polish-Bolshevik War in 1920 effectively checked the advance of destructive social revolutionary waves threatening the economic structure of Western Europe."[2]

Direct participation of the State in Polish economic life was very extensive. The Government owned or controlled railroads, forests, post and telegraph services, mines, factories and banks. In many large enterprises the State was the largest shareholder. It owned 93 per cent of all the railroads, 100 per cent of commercial aviation, and 95 per cent of the Merchant Marine, post, radio, telegraph and telephone services. It owned 70 per cent of the iron production, 30 per cent of the coal output, 99 per cent of the salt mines, 80 per cent of the chemical industry, 20 per cent of the oil refineries, 50 per cent of the metal industry, and three-eighths of the forests of the country. It owned also the armaments industry and manufactured automobiles and aeroplanes. In addition, State banks dominated the credit situation; altogether the Polish Government had on its pay roll 1,000,000 workers. It has been pointed out by Mr. Buell that the monopolies were distributed by patronage, and that people who knew little about business received licences, while others who

[1] *Concise Statistical Year-book of Poland*, 1937.
[2] Wellisz, pp. 52, 78–9.

had been in trade for generations were driven out. Often the persons who received licences rented them to those with experience. Thus the monopolies created a class who really did nothing but lived on the country by offering their business connections for sale.

The price policy of the monopolies was in general unfavourable to the mass of the people.

In terms of corn, for instance, a peasant in 1914 could get 10 kg. of salt for 6 kg. of corn, 1 litre of alcohol for 11 kg. of corn, and 1 kg. of tobacco for 115 kg. of corn. In 1938 in order to get the same quantities of the monopolised articles, he had to sell 16, 21 and 379 kg. of corn respectively.[1]

Polish financial policy was mainly directed towards the mirage of a balanced budget and the stabilisation of foreign exchange. The pegging of the currency to gold, of which Poland had very little, made any expansion of credits very difficult; the inability of the banks to build up a superstructure of credit on the basis of cash held by them (as is the case in Great Britain and the United States) contributed to its stringency. As a result the bank-rate was one of the highest in Europe:

TABLE 7.

Bank-rate in certain countries, 1928 and 1937.[2]

	1928 Per cent	1937 Per cent
Poland	8.0	5.0
Rumania	6.0	4.5
Italy	6.0	4.5
Germany	7.0	4.0
France	3.5	3.8
Czechoslovakia	5.0	3.0
United Kingdom	4.5	2.0
Belgium	4.3	2.0
Holland	4.5	2.0
U.S.A.	4.5	1.3

Although the maximum legal rate was 12 per cent, rates of interest on the private market varied in 1925 from 24 to 60 per cent, in 1926 from 12 to 24 per cent, and in 1927 from 18 to 36 per cent.[3] According to an estimate of the Institute of Social Economy in Warsaw, the peasants paid up to 36 per cent interest on credits obtained from private sources.[4] The high rate of interest considerably increased the cost of production and acted as a deterrent to investment. Another factor impeding industrial activity was the high cost of transport. Transport costs of coal from the mines in Western Poland constituted about 59 per cent of the price of coal on sale in the eastern provinces. In spite of the facilities for cheap water transport, the rates were 70 per cent of those on the railways, while in western Europe

[1] Buell, pp. 158, 165–6.
[2] *Concise Statistical Year-book of Poland*, 1938.
[3] Rychlinski, p. 63.
[4] *Credit Conditions among Smallholders*, p. 31.

they were only 25 per cent. Because of high railway rates cattle were often driven over 100 kilometers to market and to the slaughterhouses.[1]

The main features of this very inadequate economic policy were the lack of agrarian reform, the low purchasing power of the people, the growth of monopolies and their policy of high prices and high profit margins, producing a further deterioration in Poland's already backward society and rendering her more vulnerable to the vicissitudes of the trade cycle.

In 1929 the national income was 600 zloty per head of population; the respective figures for France, Germany, the United Kingdom and the United States were 2,100, 2,500, 4,200 and 5,800 zlotys.[2] The relative position, according to a different estimate, was about the same in 1938 (the income per head, for instance, in the Baltic States being twice as much as in Poland).[3]

Other indications of the lack of economic development are given by the consumption of iron in Poland which was, per inhabitant, 80 per cent of the corresponding figure for Czechoslovakia, 20 per cent of the German and British figures, 17 per cent of the Belgian figure and 10 per cent of that for the United States.[4] The annual consumption of cotton per head of population, in 1932–34, was 1.7 kg. in Poland, 4.7 kg. in Germany 7.0 kg. in France, 11.6 kg. in the United Kingdom and 11.9 kg. in the United States.

According to a report of the Polish Inquiry Commission on Trade and Industry the annual consumption of timber per head of population was 0.26 cubic metres in Poland, 0.44 cubic metres in Germany and 0.25 cubic metres in France. While timber consumption in Poland was low, she was, after the U.S.S.R., Finland and Sweden, the largest exporter of timber in the world. The consumption of bricks in Poland was in the Western Provinces 170 bricks per inhabitant per annum, in the Eastern Provinces 10; in Germany 400. The annual consumption of cement was in Poland 21 kg. per inhabitant, while in Rumania 36 kg., in Germany 100 kg., and in the United States more than 200 kg. The consumption of hides and skins in Poland was 0.75 kg. (in 1913 1.3 kg.), in Germany 2.03 kg. per inhabitant. The consumption of fertilisers was 35.7 per cent lower in 1926 than in 1913.

In 1924 Poland consumed per head of population 10.8 kg. of oil, the corresponding figures for Germany, France, Belgium, Rumania, United Kingdom and the United States being 13.7, 39.4, 43.7, 51.2, 127.0 and 890.0 kg. The output of crude oil in Poland in 1937 was about 44 per cent of that in 1913, in spite of the great increase of the various uses of oil since 1913.[5] Poland had in 1937 eight motor cars per 10,000 inhabitants; the figures for Rumania, Czechoslovakia, Germany, the United Kingdom and the United States were 12, 71, 214, 476 and 2,197.[6] According to Leslie Buell the number of taxicabs in Warsaw decreased from 2,447 in 1929 to 1,629 in 1935, while the horse-cabs increased from 1,282 to 1,682 in the same period.

The output of blast furnaces in Poland in the peak year 1929 reached 68

[1] Rychlinski, pp. 103–5.
[2] *Statistical Year-book of Poland*, 1938.
[3] Landau, p. 129.
[4] Klarner, p. 35.
[5] Rychlinski, pp. 25–7, 103–5.
[6] *Concise Statistical Year-book of Poland*, 1938.

per cent of the pre-1914 figure, that of steel works 83 per cent, of zinc works 90 per cent and of rolling mills 80 per cent.[1]

Another result of the backward development of the country was the growth of structural unemployment. According to Mr. Woytinsky the index of wage earners in employment, which he considers more reliable evidence than the numbers of officially registered unemployed, varied as follows:

	1927	1928	1929	1930	1931	1932	1933	1934
Poland ...	89.5	99.7	100.0	86.8	73.9	63.3	62.9	68.0[2]

In 1937 the index, with 1928 as base year, was still below 1928, although the population of Poland increased between 1928 and 1937 by more than three million; on the other hand, almost every other country showed in 1937 an increase in the number of employed as compared with 1928.

The fall in the numbers of employed was accompanied in coal mines by an increase in the intensity of labour and by a rise in output per head:

TABLE 8

Output per man shift in certain countries (Belgium = 100).

	1935	Percentage of increase between 1929 and 1936
Belgium	100	38.1
France	112	23.6
Great Britain	153	8.4
Czechoslovakia (bituminous) ...	172	40.0
Germany (Ruhr)	220	34.5
Netherlands	231	42.8
Poland (Upper Silesia) ...	261	52.9

In spite of the highest output per man and the longest working hours per week, the miners' wages were some of the lowest in relation to the sale value of coal.

TABLE 9

Relative labour costs per ton of coal, 1935 (*British costs* = 100).[3]

France	148
U.S.A. (Anthracite)	121
Germany (Ruhr)	97
Czechoslovakia	87
Poland	52
Japan	23
Union of South Africa (native workers) ...	13

Sweated labour and high profits were not limited to the coal mining industry. Employment conditions in the prosperous years of 1926–28 were investigated by an official Inquiry Committee which emphasised

[1] Klarner, p. 35. [2] Woytinsky, pp. 149–50.
[3] *I.L.O., Coal Mining Industry*, pp. 109, 167, 175.

" the disregard of the laws relating to the protection of labour. The breaking of the regulations follows from a too weak control of factory inspection which has too small a personnel and is only supplied with small funds. In 1926 the factory inspectors called at 19.8 per cent of the industrial enterprises, in 1927 at 23 per cent.

". . . Not only small-scale industry violates the regulations but also large (mining, textiles). Those infringed are not only the regulations dealing with the length of the day's work, the Saturday half-holiday, work on holidays, and the non-payment of overtime, but also with night-work in the textile industry, so dangerous for women and children, or in bakehouses, which ruins the health of the worker and has harmful consequences even for the consumer.

". . . In small-scale industry, in flour mills and the bakery and meat trades, holidays are not usual. The mill owners contend that the workers do not ask for holidays, and that they sometimes receive special grants instead of holidays.

". . . On the whole there is no concern for human life and health, not only in the small industry and handicrafts, which are situated in slums, but also in larger factories which may be old buildings, dark and stuffy, where there is sometimes a lack of elementary hygienic measures. In the textile industry, even in large firms, the ventilation leaves much to be desired.

". . . The poverty of the worker prevents his having a special set of clothes for working. Even in larger firms one seldom finds clothes lockers, wash-basins, baths, dining-rooms or even lavatories. If they do exist, they are in a frightful condition.

". . . Disease decimates the workers. The most common is tuberculosis, which develops in a dusty atmosphere, in sudden changes of temperature, humidity, etc. (textiles, flour mills, bakery). In Lodz 53 per cent of deaths between the ages of 10 and 40 result from tuberculosis; 24 per cent of the patients in hospitals are treated for tuberculosis. Dust also causes inflammation of the eyes and cataract. Primitive methods of labour in the bakeries such as hand-kneading of the dough, cause persistent eczema.

" Safety devices on machinery are also inadequate. In the woollen trade the Inquiry Committee confirmed the existence of factory equipment which threatens the lives of the workers. This applies not only to small but also to large factories. In 1924 accidents caused by machines formed 17 per cent of the total accidents in the textile industry, in 1925, 43 per cent.

" In coal-mining every sixth worker has an accident annually. After the war the percentage increased (from 12.9 per cent in 1913 to 15.6 per cent in 1927).

" Safety equipment will not abolish the possibility of accident, if the worker is not taught to be careful during his work. It is worth mentioning that low wages cause nervous exhaustion on the part of the worker because of insufficient feeding, and the piece and premium systems which speed up the pace of the work.

". . . The Inquiry Committee has serious doubts about the system of wages in our industry. The report on coal-mining especially condemns the exploitation of the worker. According to such authorities as Gantt and Taylor the premium should not fall below 30 per cent or even 20 per cent of the basic wages, because otherwise the worker will not make the effort to obtain it. Meanwhile in the coal mines the premiums do not on the whole reach 20 per cent . . . the worker works for premiums in spite of the fact that theoretically he should not be interested in them. Why? Because the rates of pay are fixed so low that he must work with all his strength to reach the minimum subsistence level. Therefore he exerts himself to the very utmost to get the low percentage of the premium.

" According to the Inquiry Commission there is in several important industries a regulation of conditions of work and wages without agreement. On the whole, in factories where collective agreements exist, the conditions of work are considerably better; in one of the enterprises the cost of living index number was even applied.

". . . The Inquiry Committee also draws attention to the omissions in the existing agreements. The agreements in the bakery trade break the legislative regulations of the working day by fixing the minimum amount of work at such a level that the worker must work 10 or 11 hours a day.[1]

". . . Social insurances are fully applied only in larger industrial concerns. In small-scale industry the workers are either not insured, or contrary to the law are made to pay the whole of the insurance rates."[2]

Madame Krahelska, factory inspector and pre-1914 associate of Pilsudski, gave the following account of conditions prevailing in the Lodz textile industry:

" Lodz gives generally the impression of a large factory settlement rather than a town. The factories dominate the town, they overwhelm it not only by their quantity, but the whole pulse of its life and temperament is subordinated to the interests of industry. At night, when the life of the town dies down and the streets become quiet and empty, the louder is the noise of the motors, the clearer the language of work expressed by lighted windows and whole floors of factory buildings. The work of the night drums through the air. Windows shine, motors hum. But there is not the other phenomenon of night work: the shifts. The stream of workers going on to the night shift and releasing the stream of those who are just ceasing. Why is there not this other phenomenon? Because there is no eight-hour day in the factories.

" Lodz cancelled the 8-hour day. Therefore the 24 hours consists not of three normal shifts, as laid down by law, but is divided into two shifts of 12 hours each, from 5.0, 6.0 or 7.0 p.m. to 5.0, 6.0 or 7.0 a.m., usually without any break during the twelve hours.

". . . The 12-hour shifts are not ' record ' figures to-day; there can sometimes be found a 16-hour working day, without a break. In a considerable number of factories of the Lodz district the staff work a 16-hour day; and in the town itself this occurs even in the largest firms.

". . . In the weaving mill of L. Geyer about 100 women weavers worked in September 1926 for 16 hours a day. At G. Steigert's some of the dyers

[1] The Act of 23rd November 1918 introduced the 8-hours' working day and the 46-hours' working week.

[2] Rychlinski, pp. 35–50.

worked a 16-hour day during the same month. The finishing department of Geyer's worked from 7.0 a.m. to 7.0 p.m., as also did the finishing department of Kindermann's.

"The trade unions have very exact information concerning 50 factories: in 27 work lasts for 12 hours, in seven 16 hours, in the rest 10 hours. (Among these are the largest factories: Scheibler, with 7,364 workers; Poznanski with 5,722 workers; Geyer with 4,036 workers; Widzewska Manufaktura with 3,983 workers).

"... There are factories where the workers are told when they are taken on that the shift lasts 12 hours and that they are only employed on this condition; there are factories where the management publishes the lengthening of the working day in writing; the tone of such notices is peremptory, the workers are not consulted.

"In the factory of I. K. Poznanski in July (1926) the 10-hour day had been introduced in the weaving departments, on the understanding that it was only to be temporary; at the beginning of August the working day was lengthened to 12 hours a day. . . . The Police investigation revealed that . . . the Widzewska Manufaktura, like other factories, employed women at night.[1]

"... In I. K. Poznanski's factory women started the day shift at 3.30 a.m.; the day shift at the Kroening factory began at 3.0 a.m."[2]

Professor Krzywicki, the director of the Institute of Social Economy in Warsaw, commenting on the state of affairs in Lodz declared that the same disregard for social legislation could be observed in other parts of Poland.

"A tragic situation is created: the world of profiteers exposes in the plainest manner to the working masses the weakness of the Polish State, and arouses suspicion that this State does not take its obligations seriously. At the same time it kills their belief, so vital for the interests of the State, in Independent Poland, in the principles of law. Herein lies the gravity of the situation."[3]

The Act of 1918 which laid down the 8-hours' day and the 46-hours' week was amended in December 1919, and provision was made that they could be exceeded in exceptional circumstances; permission had, however, to be obtained from the Ministry of Labour. The number of these permissions increased almost twenty-fold between 1920 and 1928 (from 32 in 1920 to 597 in 1928).[4]

Industry also lengthened the working day without permission. Factory inspectors brought before the courts the following number of cases where the Act of 1919 had been violated:

1923, 931; 1924, 749; 1925, 1,233; 1926, 2358[5]

The enforcing of the law, however, was not effective. According to an inquiry of the Trade Unions in 1928, "the courts apply very mild penalties.

[1] The Act of 2nd July 1924 forbade night work for women.

[2] Krahelska, pp. 15–19.

[3] Krahelska, preface.

[4] Rychlinski, p. 3.

[5] Rychlinski, p. 18.

. . . In Ciechanow the court took the attitude that the meaning of the law of 18th December 1919 about the time of work was the protection of workers from overwork, but in mills the worker does not use much energy. . . . The courts (in Poznania) put off dealing fully with the statements of the factory inspectors; half a year or more elapses before judgment is passed, and the amount of the fine is low and does not carry any weight with the defendants. . . . Even if one passes over the extremely numerous cases of complete acquittal of the employers who break the law relating to the hours of work, it must be stated that the fines fixed by the courts are so low that the employer naturally disregards them completely. The tolerance of the breaking of the law of the working day lowers in the eyes of the employer as well as the employee, the authority of the factory inspector who is responsible for supervising the carrying out of this law."[1]

The Institute of Social Economy made an inquiry into the household budgets of industrial workers in 1928. It came to the conclusion that the budget most similar to the Polish workers was that of the Indian worker in Bombay.[2]

Unemployment insurance was compulsory only in enterprises employing more than five workers. Out of 234,697 industrial enterprises in 1936, 207,969 (i.e. 89 per cent) employed less than five persons and were thus not subject to insurance. Insured workers, when unemployed, received insurance benefit for sixteen weeks (after 1933 only for thirteen weeks); after that period they became, together with the uninsured unemployed, dependent on public assistance, mostly in kind. The Institute of Social Economy in Warsaw made an experiment in 1931 and asked the unemployed to write down their memoirs, offering some prizes. In 1933 the Institute published fifty of these memoirs which gave some insight into the conditions of living and the mentality of the unemployed.

According to the information contained in them, the principal source of income of the family of an unemployed worker seemed to be casual work. Women tried to find washing or charing. Most of the period of unemployment was spent in the search for work of this kind. Secondly, there was the assistance granted by various institutions, which was almost as difficult to obtain, and demanded much perseverence on the part of the worker. Thirdly, help was also given by relations and by individuals. Another important, although limited and merely temporary, source of income was the sale or pawning of furniture and personal possessions.

According to the particulars contained in the memoirs the Institute found that the help provided by unemployment insurance benefit and relief from special organisations came last.[3]

[1] Rychlinski, pp. 19–21.

[2] *Conditions of Living of the Working Classes*, p. 109; also *Ministry of Labour Gazette*, London, May 1923.

[3] *International Labour Review*, Geneva, March 1933.

One of the youngest competitors described his state of mind during the early period of his unemployment as follows:

"To-morrow will be another day, a day on which I shall find work. Every day I cling to this thought as to a lifebuoy. Sometimes, indeed, I think that it is my last link with life, this mysterious faith in a to-morrow which will bring me the glad news of work. Work! I want to work. The will to work is all I have left, so utterly all that when I think about it it seems quite strange. I am walking over an abyss covered with thin planks. These planks are my faith in to-morrow. To-morrow creates the illusion that things will be better. To-day I am a pauper, but to-morrow? To-morrow I may find work. Not may, but must, to-morrow I must find work. I must be able to eat my fill, and so must my father, my mother, and my brothers. Do you know how a man acts when he is hungry? Have you ever heard of creatures driven by hunger? Needless to say, they are like animals. They are hungry. Hunger reigns supreme. Everything they do is dictated by hunger. There is a law of hunger beside which all human laws are mere phantasms."

Another unemployed worker living in Upper Silesia related in his essay that his neighbours had christened him 'Hungermeister' because he had reached the point of eating only once in two days. The unemployed walking through the towns

"have ample opportunities of seeing the shops full of meat, cooked food, bread, sugar, butter—all the good things that they have no money to buy. Thus they are often led to ponder on the social injustice which condemns them to hunger while around them the world is at a loss to dispose of its wheat, coffee or sugar. They repeat things they have read in the papers: that in South America wheat is being burnt or thrown into the sea, that coffee is used to make briquettes for locomotives, that in England pigs are fattened on the Polish sugar which the unemployed Polish worker cannot afford to buy for his children. And in contrast to this they think of their own menu, nearly always composed of the same things: potatoes, pickled cabbage, rye flour, barley meal, suet, and oil. No meat, no sugar, no butter; even bread is often looked on as a luxury.

"On such a diet the worker rapidly loses his strength. His clothes become ragged, obliging him to pass more and more of his time at home. In winter, when it is cold both inside and outside the house, the unemployed and their families try to sleep as long as possible and spend most of their time in bed.

"These conditions inevitably have an evil effect on family life. The crowding of several people into a single room where soon there is not enough furniture for them to sit down, eat or sleep, and where there is less and less food to be divided and the atmosphere becomes more and more hopeless and depressing—all this cannot but lead to constant quarrelling. 'Where there is poverty, there is discord'—so runs a proverb which an unemployed woman has invented and quotes in her memoirs. The break-up of family life is accelerated and the road lies open to a life of vagrancy or prostitution.

"... First there is the larger group of those who have not yet lost all hope of regaining employment in their former occupation and winning back their former social status. All of them have fallen to a very much lower standard of living and support themselves by means of casual employment and what rare outside help they can obtain in the form of the assistance in cash or in kind provided by institutions for the relief of the unemployed. Some are resigned to their fate, especially among the older workers. But the younger members of this group nearly always voice a more or less open spirit of revolt against the existing social and economic order. Generally speaking, they are men imbued with a social sense; they bring to bear on the problems of life a reflective and critical spirit. But in practice they do not overstep the limits traced by their former life.

"The second group is that of the 'outcasts.' After struggling to retain their status for as long as possible, they have resigned themselves to dropping out of their own class, the men becoming tramps, beggars, thieves or gangsters, and the women prostitutes.

"Critical ideas are found most frequently among the first group. These out-of-work workers suffer as much from the constant humiliations to which they are subjected as from their privations. The weaker ones see enemies in all those on whom their fate directly depends: the head of the factory, the landlord, the official of the employment exchange or assistance institution. But many of those who have a modicum of culture and some comprehension of the complexity of social life formulate criticism of a much more general order on the basis of their own experience; they discuss national policy, international economic and political problems, the distribution of wealth, the state of mind of the working classes, etc. In spite of this atmosphere of depression and all these tragic tales, the volume leaves the reader with the impression that a powerful moral force is holding back these men on the very brink of the abyss. The further one reads, the clearer becomes the realisation that this force is a deep-seated love of work, a love which resolves itself here into an apotheosis of the work they have lost—one is almost tempted to write the paradise they have lost, so deep is the love of work which runs like a *leitmotiv* through all the 'Memoirs.'"[1]

A report upon unemployment published by the Royal Institute of International Affairs in London threw further light upon the life of the unemployed in Poland:

"There has been an increase since 1931 in the spread of typhus in countries where that disease is endemic. The figures began to rise in 1931 and have been augmented each year since ... the figures for Poland were 3,490 for the first half of 1934, compared with 1,820 and 2,132 in the corresponding period of the two previous years.

"... Part of the increase in suicide in certain European countries has been attributed to unemployment—in Warsaw, for instance, 5.2 per cent of deaths by suicide were ascribed to unemployment in 1928, and 18.3 per cent in 1931.

[1] *International Labour Review*, ibidem.

"... Inquiries by the Institute of Social Problems in Poland showed that rent formed an insignificant part of the budget of unemployed families, the reason being that in 83 per cent of the cases the accommodation consisted of a single room for each family, the average number of persons to a room being 4.5. As the beds had often been sold with the other furniture, there was on an average only one bed for each 2.7 persons. Most families were in arrears of rent for ten years, but eviction is not permitted. The greater part of the coal used by unemployed persons was obtained by theft. The inquiries showed that marked increases in cases of suicide and in prostitution were among the direct effects of unemployment."[1]

Neither the unemployed nor the employed were adequately fed; the general standard of food consumption in Poland was one of the lowest in Europe.

TABLE 10.

Consumption of dairy products, meat and sugar in certain countries per head of population (average 1932–4).[2]

Country	All dairy products (liquid milk equivalent, in gallons)	Meat (lbs.)	Sugar (lbs.)
Belgium	80	90	62
Czechoslovakia	—	73	56
Denmark	92	125	120
France	69	72	57
Germany	79	110	52
Italy	23	35	18
Netherlands	80	91	68
Norway	98	73	70
Poland	50	41	23
Switzerland	112	105	98
United Kingdom	89	140	110

Meat consumption in Poland decreased by 34 per cent[3] between 1899 and 1932–34, while it increased in most European countries in the same period. It may be mentioned that Poland had on the average in 1926–35 the largest number of head of cattle and pigs after Germany and France, but while the two latter countries did not export meat, Poland ranged as third meat exporter in Europe.

The consumption of almost all other foodstuffs with the exception of rye and potatoes, of which Poland consumed more than any other country, shows a similar state of affairs.

[1] Royal Institute of International Affairs, *Unemployment*, pp. 20–25.

[2] League of Nations: *The Problem of Nutrition*, Geneva, 1936.

[3] U.S. Department of Agriculture. Report No. 109, Washington, 1916.

TABLE 11.

Annual Consumption of certain Foodstuffs in various countries per head of population (1932–4)[1]

Country	Wheat (kg.)	Rye (kg.)	Potatoes (kg.)	Coffee (kg.)	Tea (kg.)
Belgium	193	87	463	5.5	0.03
Denmark	190	134	365	7.1	0.16
France	247	21	383	4.5	0.04
Germany	81	128	705	2.1	0.07
Italy	186	4	—	0.9	—
Netherlands	135	73	349	4.9	1.61
Poland	48	159	768	0.2	0.05
Sweden	136	75	325	6.9	0.06
United Kingdom ...	158	—	125	0.4	4.39

Country	Wine (litre)	Beer (litre)	Alcohol 100% (litre)	Tobacco (kg.)
Belgium	3.4	182.1	1.12	3.1
Denmark	1.1	53.5	2.10	2.0
France	176.4	33.2	2.54	1.3
Germany	—	42.1	0.69	1.7
Italy	84.3	—	0.36	0.6
Netherlands	1.0	19.4	1.07	3.5
Poland	0.0	3.6	0.77	0.5
Sweden	—	41.7	—	1.4
United Kingdom ...	1.3	71.9	0.57	1.5

Hessel Tiltman described the situation of the peasants in the East European agrarian countries, including Poland, during the crisis of 1930–1:

" Those peasant territories remain to-day almost virgin soil for the world's manufactures, populated by millions of potential customers clad in home-made clothing and living on the produce of the soil. In this immense region governmental neglect, oppressive taxation, the fall in world agricultural prices, and political persecution in some of the most populous of the areas concerned first called a halt to development and then set the pendulum swinging back to conditions reminiscent of the serf-states of a century ago. That neglect and repression, unreported but nevertheless real, existed before the oncoming agricultural crises left the peasant millions too poor to buy matches, salt and oil—the three essentials of a village life—and will, unless the course of history changes, continue to exercise their baneful influence long after the world crisis has passed.

"... Taxation remains at an oppressive level, making the poor peasant poorer and preventing progressive spirits among the large landowners from doing anything to improve the lot of their workers. I asked an official of the Polish Ministry of Finance if he could give me a list of all the taxes demanded of the peasant and estate owners. 'It is impossible,' he answered. 'I do not know the answer to that question myself, and it would

[1] *Concise Statistical Year-book of Poland*, 1938.

take days to get the facts.' He volunteered the information, however, that less than 5 per cent of the farm holdings in the Eastern, Southern and Central regions were paying their way at the present time, and added that every quintal of grain sold on the markets is being produced at a net loss of from six to eight zlotys. Even so, the actual facts prove that official to be an optimist! "[1]

The low level of peasant existence was indicated by the diet, the chief articles of which were rye and potatoes. The great increase in potato production during the depression of 1930–32 was an illustration of advancing poverty. A peasant on a small holding could grow enough potatoes to keep himself alive, but not enough wheat or rye. With such meagre rations, the Polish peasants were more or less self-sufficient in food, but had very low purchasing power. Their poverty was proverbial. It was said that during the depression the peasant would split a match four or five times, and would boil potatoes over and over again in the same water to save the salt. Even at this low level, it was estimated that there was a surplus peasant population of between six and nine millions. According to Mr. Buell net receipts on farms ranging from two to 50 hectares (five to 125 acres) over the period from 1931–2 to 1934–5 averaged less than one per cent of the capital invested. On farms of five hectares or less, net receipts were less than one half of one per cent. According to the Polish Minister of Finance the average cash income of the peasant in 1934–5 was eleven groszy (about one penny) a day; and the farm population, although nearly 70 per cent of the total, contributed only 15 per cent to the national budget.[2]

The position of agricultural labourers was from many points of view less favourable than that of the peasants or industrial workers. In 1933 they were exempted from the general scheme of health insurance, which was under State control, and were put under a private insurance scheme of the individual landowner. They were also exempted in 1933 from the general scheme of unemployment insurance and no special provisions regulated this important question; insurance was left to private agreements of the landowners with the labourers or their unions. Agreements which were concluded on that basis usually contained a provision that dismissed workers were to receive a fixed bonus and not cash benefit for a certain period of unemployment. Agricultural labourers were also deprived of a delegate to the International Labour Organisation; the only Polish delegate to the Permanent Agricultural Committee of the I.L.O., who represented the Association of Landowners in Poland, was against any international regulation of hours of work or of minimum wages for agricultural labourers.[3]

One of the greatest evils left over from the past was inadequate housing. It may be said that while there was hardly any other European country where the need for building was greater, there was no country in which the results were so negligible as in Poland:

[1] Tiltman, foreword and pp. 183–5. [2] Buell, p. 30, 197–8.
[3] *I.L.O., Social Problems in Agriculture*, pp. 127, 130, 138.

TABLE 12.

Dwellings and Density of Habitation in three principal towns of Poland in 1921 and 1931.[1]

	Number of dwellings (percentages)					
	Warsaw		Lodz		Lwow	
	1921	1931	1921	1931	1921	1931
1-room dwellings ...	39.1	42.7	59.7	63.0	27.0	31.9
2- „ „ ...	25.1	24.4	19.8	19.2	32.3	33.7
3- „ „ ...	17.5	16.3	9.8	9.0	19.5	16.9
4- „ „ and over	18.3	16.6	10.7	8.8	21.2	17.5

	Number of persons per room (averages)					
	Warsaw		Lodz		Lwow	
	1921	1931	1921	1931	1921	1931
In dwellings of 1 room ...	3.7	4.0	3.6	3.8	3.2	3.4
„ „ 2 rooms ...	2.4	2.4	2.3	2.2	2.1	2.1
„ „ 3 „ ...	1.8	1.7	1.6	1.6	1.6	1.5
„ „ 4 „ and over	1.2	1.1	1.2	1.1	1.1	1.1

The proportion of 1- and 2-room dwellings in the main three cities of Poland was on the increase between 1921 and 1931 and the proportion of dwellings of 4 rooms and over on the decrease. The number of 1- and 2-room dwellings formed in 1921 from 59.3 per cent (Lwow) to 79.5 per cent (Lodz) of the total

TABLE 13.

Number of dwellings built in each year between 1920 and 1929 *(per* 1,000 *dwellings existing in* 1921*).*[2]

Country	1920	1921	1922	1923	1924	1925	1926	1927	1928	1929
England (whole country)	5.3	14.4	10.2	10.8	17.2	21.7	27.3	29.9	21.2	25.3
Netherlands (6 towns)	—	32.8	50.8	42.3	50.9	51.0	57.3	55.6	44.9	44.9
Sweden (3 towns)	—	13.6	7.1	17.7	28.9,	37.6	45.7	51.7	52.7	—
Denmark (Copenhagen)	16.7	30.9	17.1	26.2	19.5	25.9	24.6	30.8	28.5	29.5
Norway (Oslo and Bergen)	6.1	13.2	13.6	12.1	13.7	15.4	9.6	6.5	8.2	19.2
Czechoslovakia (5 towns)	—	15.2	11.8	17.9	28.3	20.5	21.8	39.9	64.5	52.1
Finland (Helsinki)	—	18.1	14.3	24.0	15.4	37.4	54.2	86.1	116.3	128.5
Poland (5 towns) rooms	—	—	—	—	3.0	3.7	4.7	10.8	6.0	—
Germany (46 towns)	3.7	4.3	5.7	5.8	4.4	9.0	14.1	20.2	24.3	28.0

[1] *Concise Statistical Year-book of Poland*, 1937. [2] *I.L.O. Housing Policy*, p. 19.

number of dwellings; these percentages were in 1931, 65.6 and 82.2 per cent. Thus, the tenants of the 1- and 2-room dwellings lived in overcrowded conditions in 1921 as well as in 1931.

Table 13 shows that building activity in Poland was on a much smaller scale than in other countries. It should be added that newly-built houses were erected in Poland mainly by private enterprise and consequently for the richer sections of the population.[1]

The following table shows the comparison between the housing figures of the 1921 Census of the whole population and that obtained from an enquiry into the conditions of living of working-class families carried out in 1927 and 1933 by the Institute of Social Economy in Warsaw:

TABLE 14.

Number of dwellings in 1921, 1927 *and* 1933.[2]

		Percentage of dwellings with		
		1 room	2 rooms	3 & more rooms
Warsaw ...	1921 (whole population)	39.1	25.1	35.8
	1927 (working-class	70.7	29.3	5.4
	1933 families only)	78.4	18.0	3.6
Lodz	1921 (whole population)	59.7	19.8	20.3
	1927 (working-class	76.8	22.2	1.0
	1933 families only)	100.0	—	—
Dombrowa Basin	1921 (whole population)	41.2	40.3	18.5
	1927 (working-class	36.8	60.1	3.1
	1933 families only)	79.8	20.2	—

The above figures show a substantial deterioration between 1927 and 1933. According to the enquiry of 1933, 49.7 per cent of the workers' dwellings examined were sunny, 44.2 per cent dark, 6.1 per cent partly sunny and partly dark; 41.3 per cent of the dwellings were dry, 52.6 per cent damp, and 6.1 per cent partly dry and partly damp. Bathrooms in the dwellings did not exist. In 85.3 per cent of the dwellings the lavatories were in the courtyard; 91.0 per cent of the dwellings had neither running water nor waste pipe. With regard to the lighting 16.9 per cent of the dwellings had electric light, 3.2 per cent gas, 78.1 per cent oil lamps, 1.8 per cent, method of lighting unknown.

Infant mortality in Poland was one of the highest in Europe; 136 babies died in 1938 per 1,000 living births, while the corresponding numbers for Sweden, Switzerland and the United Kingdom were 41, 43 and 61. Similarly, the number of persons surviving the age of 50 was one of the lowest in Europe (Table 15).

In order to grasp the discrepancy between the actual state of affairs and the possibilities of industrial development it should be remembered that Poland was one of the largest States in Europe, one of the most densely popu-

[1] *I.L.O. Housing Policy*, ibidem.

[2] Zdanowski, p. 19.

TABLE 15.

Number of persons surviving the age of 50 years out of 100,000 born.[1]

	Males	Females
Sweden (1931–35)	78,956	81,106
Germany (1932–4)	76,322	79,620
England and Wales (1930–32) ...	74,794	78,958
Poland (1931–32)	59,950	62,970

lated and, above all, one of the richest in industrial raw materials. Poland had large deposits of coal, zinc, lead, iron ores, crude oil, salt, potash salts and other minerals. She had the natural foundation for an important chemical industry (coal, oil, salt), metal industry (coal, iron ores); she had abundant resources of energy (coal, oil, natural gas, wood, water) and millions of unemployed, many of whom were highly skilled workers. The methods which were devised to utilise these tremendous resources were, to say the least, most inadequate.

REFERENCES

Bell-Morrison, R., *Tariff Walls*. London, 1930.
Buell, R. L., *Poland—Key to Europe*. London, 1939.
Dmowski, R., *Odbudowanie*, etc. (Polish Policy and the Restoration of the State). Warsaw, 1926.
Fischer, Louis, *The Soviets in World Affairs*. London, 1930.
Graham, Malbone W., *New Governments of Eastern Europe*. New York, 1928.
Gruber, Dr. H., *Uwagi*, etc. (Observations about the Capitalisation Process). Warsaw, 1928.
Guest, Dr. L. Haden, *The Struggle for Power in Europe*. London, 1921.
Institute of Social Economy, *Przyczynki*, etc. (Credit Conditions among Smallholders). Warsaw, 1931.
Institute of Social Economy, *Warunki*, etc. (Conditions of Living of the Working Classes). Warsaw, 1929.
International Labour Office, *The World Coalmining Industry*. Geneva, 1936.
" " *Social Problems in Agriculture*. Geneva, 1938.
" " *Housing Policy*. Geneva, 1930.
Klarner, C., *Silesia and Pomerania*. Torun, 1934.
Krahelska, H., *Lodzki*, etc. (The Lodz Industry and Labour Legislation). Warsaw, 1927.
Landau, L., *Gospodarka Swiatowa* (World Economy). Warsaw, 1939.
League of Nations, *The Problem of Nutrition*. Geneva, 1936.
Machray, Robert, *The Poland of Pilsudski*. London, 1936.
Morgan, O. S., *Agricultural Systems of Middle Europe*. New York, 1933.
Rose, W. J., *Poland*. London, 1939.
Royal Institute of International Affairs, *World Agriculture*. London, 1932.
" " " *Unemployment*. London, 1935.
Rychlinski, S., *Marnotrawstwo*, etc. (Waste in Industry). Warsaw, 1930.
Skrzynski, A., *Poland and Peace*. London, 1923.
Szturm de Sztrem T., *Zywiolowosc*, etc. (The Inflation Tax). Warsaw, 1924.
Tiltman, H. Hessel, *Peasant Europe*. London, 1934.
Wellisz L., *Foreign Capital in Poland*. London, 1938.
Woytinsky, W., *Three Sources of Unemployment*. International Labour Office. Geneva, 1935.
Zdanowski, A., *Warunki*, etc. (Conditions of Housing amongst Workers), Institute of Social Economy. Warsaw, 1936.
Zdziechowski, G., *The Finances of Poland*. London, 1925.

[1] *Statistical Year-book of the League of Nations*. Geneva, 1939.

Chapter VIII

DOMESTIC POLITICS

THE basis of Poland's political life was laid down in 1921, when a freely elected Assembly passed the Constitution of the Republic of Poland. According to the Constitution freedom of speech, Press and association was granted to everyone; all Polish citizens were declared equal and the use of hereditary titles made illegal. Legislative, executive and juridical powers were separated. Parliament was to consist of two chambers (Seym and Senate) elected by a universal, equal, direct, secret and proportionate vote. The Government was made responsible to Parliament which was also to elect the President of Poland. Courts were to be independent and judges could not be dismissed except for criminal offences.

The Constitution of 1921, however, was seldom fully observed. Polish democratic parties had a majority in the Constituent Assembly of 1921 as well as in Parliament up to 1926, and they had all the power necessary to uphold the Constitution and to plan and to execute the necessary reforms in the economic, political and social spheres. Nevertheless the democracy of Poland, although perhaps more virile than that of the Weimar Republic, proved to be divided, and too weak to impose its will and to defend the people's rights and liberties against the onslaught of autocratic forces. This timidity is to be attributed largely to the successful use of the Bolshevik bogy which the chauvinistic elements were continuously discovering in even mild liberal reforms. It was also due to the prevaricating attitude of the peasant parties which, as yet unconscious of their strength, often supported the oligarchic reaction. The failure of the Governments, which were controlled by a democratically elected Parliament, to solve the many outstanding problems in Polish life and to enforce the existing legislation, contributed greatly to the discrediting of parliamentary democracy in Poland. Internal peace was unknown; in 1922–23 and in 1926, as well as later in 1929–30, 1934 and 1937, domestic strife threatened to engulf Poland in civil war.

The first open challenge to the Constitution of 1921 came a year later, when the National Assembly, composed of the Seym and Senate, elected in December 1922 Gabriel Narutowicz as first President of the Republic of Poland. He was a democrat, a former professor of the University of Zurich and the candidate of the liberal groups, supported in the final ballot by the peasants, Socialists and the parties of the National Minorities. His defeated opponent was Count Maurycy Zamoyski, the Nationalist candidate. Narutowicz was called a " non-Polish " President and riots were organised with the undisguised aim of upsetting the decisions of the deputies and senators chosen by popular election. According to Robert Machray great excitement reigned in Warsaw; there were violent incidents in the streets; the Right absented itself *en bloc* from the ceremony of oath-taking by the President; one of the ministers resigned; the chief of police was dismissed. Next day the working-class of Warsaw organised a twelve-hour strike in protest against the excesses of the partisans of the Right.[1] The police had to take measures to protect the members of the diet and foreign diplomats who appeared for the ceremony of oath-taking. The President had to be smuggled in. When his inauguration was over, the Nationalists formed barricades and the police had to charge. " The automobile of M. Narutowicz made slow progress back to the Palace, and all along the way the first President of Poland was pelted with snowballs and mud. Five days after he took the oath of office he was assassinated. The crime was explained as the act of an insane man without accomplices, but there can be no doubt that it was prompted by the feeling aroused over the defeat of the Nationalist candidate."[2]

In succession to President Narutowicz, the National Assembly elected Stanislas Woyciechowski, the representative of the Peasant Party. Although he was a former leader of the Polish Socialist Party, he did not show any initiative in curbing the anti-social tendencies of the Nationalists during his period of office (1923–26).

A year after Woyciechowski's election grave events occurred in Cracow. Embittered by low wages and the excesses of inflation, the workers, led by the trade unions and the Polish Socialist Party, went on strike in November 1923. The Government decided to suppress the strike by force and the military were called in; twenty-five persons were killed and forty-nine seriously wounded. (*Manchester Guardian*, 8th November 1923.) The workers defeated the army detachments (mainly cavalry units composed of Ukrainian peasants and commanded by landowning officers) and a general strike was proclaimed in Poland. Industry, transport and communications stood still until the Government decided to accede to the demands of the workers. However, bitterness and unrest, in particular amongst the workers, continued unabated, since the succeeding Governments were mainly under the control of the Nationalists, who together with the peasant parties had a majority in Parliament; they shirked the task of solving the economic deadlock and enforcing social legislation, and they even hesitated to send to the courts those of their members who were publicly accused of corruption and of embezzlement of public funds. Democratic government became very much discredited with the people in consequence, and an atmosphere was created propitious to the overthrow of the Government by force.

Pilsudski acted as head of the State from 1918 until the election of President Narutowicz and retired from public life after the latter's assassination. In

[1] Machray, p. 165.
[2] Gibbons, p. 254.

the three years between 1923–26, therefore, he became dissociated from the Government and his popularity increased considerably. Hence, when he decided to " cleanse " Poland's public life of corruption and " party rule " with the help of former officers of the Austro-Polish legions, he found enthusiastic supporters among the working classes. Pilsudski struck in May 1926, marching on Warsaw at the head of a few regiments. The trade unions, and the Socialist and Communist parties, organised a general strike and the railway workers diverted the Government troops from the battle zone. Pilsudski, at the cost of a thousand soldiers killed, became master of the situation and the Government and President capitulated.

* * *

It soon became evident that the *coup d'état* meant not the " moral cleansing " of public life, but the abolition of parliamentary democracy and the establishment of an oligarchy, which aimed at a fusion of Fascist elements of the Right and of the Left and relied on their support.

From the moment of his return to office, Pilsudski " set himself to bring into public service people who had never been there, chiefly because they hated party politics. Two approaches gave hints of his plans. One was to the heads of the great families, when he visited the Radziwills at Nieswiez, the other—not made by the Marshal himself—to the big industrialists in Lodz."[1] The visit of the small nobleman Pilsudski to the magnates of the Eastern Borderlands, the Radziwills, was described by Pilsudski's biographer as follows:

> " At times in Socialist days, he had remembered with satisfaction that he was a noble, as well born as the greatest Polish families. Prince Albert Radziwill, the bearer of one of the most ancient and powerful titles in the country, invited him to Nieswiez, his castle on the Russian border, to visit the grave of Prince Stanislas Radziwill, Pilsudski's favourite adjutant, who had fallen in the Bolshevik war. He accepted and went to Nieswiez. The house-party which had been asked to meet him was composed of guests who bore the most historic Polish names, Radziwills, Sapiehas, Tarnowskis, Tyszkiewiczs, Lubomirskis, and Potockis. When, after dinner, by candle-light, in the wide and ancient hall, a prince stood up to drink his health, the Prime Minister was made to feel that a secret alliance had been cemented between him and the Polish aristocracy. He was fêted by the assembled nobles as the chief citizen of Poland, a great patriot and soldier; Prince Eustachy Sapieha, who in 1920 had conspired to overthrow his government, said, before he emptied his glass: ' To-day we have among us a man whose courage is consolidating the State. Marshal, we are all behind you—ready with all our help to make your task a success.' But Prince Radziwill's toast pleased the Marshal best of all. He drank to ' Josef Pilsudski, a dear cousin of our family.' "[2]

[1] Rose, p. 91. [2] Landau, p. 253.

In order to set these events in the right perspective it may be mentioned that the vast estates of Nieswiez and Olyka had been confiscated by the Tsarist Government a hundred years before. They belonged to the oldest branch of the Radziwill family, whose last legal heir, Dominik Radziwill, fought in the Polish legions of Dombrowski and was killed in the battle of Hanau in 1813. Tsar Alexander threatened to expropriate him unless he returned to Russia. Dominik refused and was expropriated in his own lifetime. His son, Alexander Dominik, took part in the insurrection of 1830–31, while his cousin, Leon Radziwill, fought against the Poles in the ranks of the Russian army. Ultimately the Tsar accorded the confiscated estates to Leon Radziwill (also related to the Hohenzollerns) whose descendants owned the Nieswiez castle in 1926.[1]

The host at Nieswiez was Janusz Radziwill, who played an important part later as Chairman of the Foreign Affairs Committee of the Polish Senate. Count Burian, the last Foreign Minister of the Austrian Monarchy, described Prince Janusz Radziwill's political role on the eve of Germany's collapse in 1918 as follows: "Towards evening (14th August 1918) Count Hertling appeared and said to me with an expression of satisfaction that the Polish question was now settled. He informed me that the day before, Prince J. Radziwill, the Head of the Foreign Department (of the Council of Regency) at Warsaw, and the councillor, Count Ronikier,[2] had been at Spa and offered the Emperor William the crown of Poland for a Hohenzollern. The Emperor had declined the offer and had recommended the Archduke Charles Stephen (Hapsburg) as a candidate for the throne. The Polish delegates had accepted this suggestion with great enthusiasm."[3]

The tentative "self-conscious" period of the autocracy lasted three years, a period of trial in which the democratic parties, opposed in principle to a violent overthrow of the government, failed, and in which the Fascist elements, convinced of the weakness of the people, gained the ascendancy in the Pilsudski-ist camp. Various democratic institutions, including local self-government, were abolished one by one, and it became obvious that the turn of Parliament must come sooner or later.

In the election of 1928, held in relatively free conditions, the government party, which bore the title "non-party bloc" (B.B.W.R.), failed to obtain a majority. The opposition parties chose as Speaker of the Seym the leader of the Socialist Party, Daszynski. One of the functions of the Speaker was to act as Deputy President of the Republic. The Government was therefore confronted with the alternative of reaching a compromise with Parliament or rendering it impotent. The oligarchy chose the latter course.

The first attack came in October 1929, when a group of officers, with Pilsudski at their head, appeared in the lobbies of the Seym. The Speaker

[1] Almanach de Gotha, 1939, pp. 592–9; Radziwill, p. 69.

[2] Count Ronikier afterwards went with a false passport as a political agent to Soviet Russia. He described his arrest and his release in his book *Dzierzynski*, *The Red Executioner*. (London, 1935.)

[3] Burian, p. 352.

considered this a hostile demonstration and an attempt to influence parliamentary proceedings, and refused to open the session. The military left and later in the day Pilsudski issued the following order:

> "On 31st ult. a painful incident happened when officers, coming into the Seym building for various motives, were insulted.
>
> "The officers considered it an insult that the representative of the Seym authorities should ask them to leave the lobby, which is normally open to the public and which at the time in question was occupied by civilians who were not compelled to leave the place as were the officers without being given any reason.
>
> "The request was the more painful to the officers in that it was repeated at the moment when I personally was in the Seym building, that is, when they had the right to expect that such or any other orders should come from me and from no one else. The officers saw—not without justification—the slight and disrespect for their uniforms in this tactless behaviour of the representative of the deputies.
>
> "I affirm therefore that since a Member of Parliament cannot be held responsible, the officers must consider the incident closed, leaving no stain upon their honour. J. PILSUDSKI."[1]

This order shows that the influence of the Prussian, Austrian and Russian military castes, against whom Pilsudski strove in his youth, proved to be stronger in him than that of the Polish insurgent tradition. In the subsequent months and years the former editor of the revolutionary *Robotnik* developed still further in an anti-democratic and even terroristic direction.

According to Hessel Tiltman, "There were dark hints concerning the mysterious fate of General Zagorski, who was called from Vilna to Warsaw, where he disappeared without leaving any trace—until next day, when his corpse—headless—was found and quickly buried. Senator Trompczynski, a leader of the Right, raised the subject of this murder in Parliament, and newspapers began to make pointed comments upon it. Whereupon several journalists were attacked at night and severely handled, one of them having an eye knocked out. The culprits who carried out these attacks arrived and drove away in a motor car belonging to Police Headquarters!

"Hand in hand with methods of repression, attempts were made to discredit the Seym and its members who stood in the path of Pilsudski and his wishes. Foreign visitors to Poland were informed that 'the Members of the Seym in general lack experience and authority, they do not constitute the *élite*; they are inferior to their mission.'"[2]

The methods which the Pilsudski camp began to use reacted as a unifying factor on the democratic parties. The policy of the peasant parties was finally directed towards full co-operation with the Socialists, and a congress of six democratic opposition parties was held "in the defence of the people's rights" in Cracow on the 30th June 1930. The parties which organised the congress had 160 deputies in the Seym and represented about five million voters; they

[1] Pilsudski, *Speeches*, pp. 247–48.

[2] Tiltman, pp. 341–2.

now formed an alliance, the "Centre-Left" Bloc (Centrolew). The resolution passed by the Congress said that the nation's confidence in law had been shaken and Parliament silenced; the whole country should therefore mobilise in defence of freedom against dictatorship; it also asked for the resignation of the President of the Republic who backed the régime. (*New York Times*, 30th June 1930.)

The Government considered the activities of the Congress as an incipient revolutionary movement and decided to suppress it by force. The Members of Parliament who attended the Congress were charged for bringing the head of the State into contempt under the Austrian Penal Code, which was still in force in Cracow in 1930. In August a new Government was formed with Pilsudski as Prime Minister and Colonel Beck[1] as Foreign Minister. Parliament was dissolved and a writ for a general election issued. Pilsudski declared that the Polish Constitution of 1921 "is like a piece of rotting meat mixed with foul bacon and putrid cabbage, and as much unwashed as the spirit of the deputies who in Poland are an infamous band. The entire work of Parliament stinks so that the air is poisoned." (*The Times*, 28th August 1930.)

The Government decided to take an active part in the elections and were prepared to use any methods, however drastic, which would gain a majority in Parliament. Life in Poland in that decisive year was described by the *Manchester Guardian Weekly* (4th July 1930) as follows:

> "In Soviet Russia the old 'Ochrana' has been replaced by the Tcheka. In Poland it has been replaced by the 'Defensive.' The 'Defensive' is more than an intelligence service, more than a political police. Members of the Government either belong to it or are approved by it. No one is safe from its interference. It spies everywhere and shadows everyone who is at all suspect or at all important. It pries into the most intimate personal affairs, and will bring pressure to bear on any person by threatening to reveal secrets of his private life. It is a national system of spying, blackmail, and terrorisation.
>
> "Polish elections are not a fair and equal fight between the different parties. The Radical Opposition are so handicapped by the 'Defensive,' the police, and the bureaucracy that it is a wonder they can do as well as they do. Their candidates are arrested, their meetings broken up, their newspapers are censored or confiscated, their 'lists' (Poland has an advanced system of proportional representation) are declared invalid on all kinds of false pretences. Sometimes even the totals of actual returns are falsified."

On 1st September 1930, *The Times* reported that the leader of the peasant party, Dombski, was assaulted outside his home in a Warsaw suburb by four persons alleged to have been wearing the uniforms of a major, a captain, a lieutenant and a corporal in the Polish army; his housekeeper and nine-year-old daughter who came to his rescue, were also said to have been bruised.

[1] See p. 162.

Shortly afterwards a number of opposition leaders were arrested, among them the former Prime Minister and great peasant leader Witos, and imprisoned in the military fortress of Brest Litovsk. After having verified the reports about the treatment meted out to arrested leaders, forty-seven professors of Cracow University[1] signed the following protest:

"We are deeply convinced that many events of recent years shake the moral foundations of the social and political life of Poland and thereby threaten the development and, as a further consequence, the very existence of the Polish realm. Among these events the affair at Brest Litovsk cannot be sanctioned by the silence of the thinking social classes.

"We fear that their interest with regard to Brest Litovsk is not adequate. In addition it can easily be incorrect and falsified when it comes from people who have an interest in concealing the truth. We therefore submit a short extract of our information on the events of Brest Litovsk:

"The arrested, former Ministers of the Polish Republic, Members of the Seym (including men who are decorated with the highest civil and military orders), were without exception compelled to undertake the meanest tasks.

"In particular, they were compelled by the most brutal methods of moral and physical force to clean the floors in the cells, in offices and in the corridors of the prison, to carry and empty the refuse pails from their own cells, and also to clean the latrines set apart for the administrative staff of the prison, being compelled to remove the refuse from the pails with their bare hands.

"The prisoners were starved for two months. They were served with a quarter of a loaf of bread daily and cattle food consisting of rotten cabbage, cattle turnips, uncleaned carrots and potatoes.

"The most severe internal regulations of the military prison were aggravated still further against the political prisoners, who were after all imprisoned pending trial, by means of a whole system of chicanery and provocation.

"If an order was not obeyed quickly or correctly enough, or if a military salute (standing to attention and saluting) was not given exactly in accordance with the regulations, the prisoners were humiliatingly cursed, and various punishments, such as hard beds, darkness and fasts, were imposed upon them. Their stay in the dark chamber (a dark, unheated cell without a straw mattress) lasted as long as nine days.

"The prisoners were often awakened during the night and conducted to a dark and cold cell under the pretext of a body inspection. There they were completely undressed and placed with their faces to the wall, while wails and shots were heard nearby.

"All these events which have no parallel in the world must be described as a scandal of the twentieth century. We must condemn them from the standpoint of humanity. We must brand them as a serious injury to

[1] In November 1939, the German authorities interned almost all the professors of Cracow University in the concentration camp of Dachau (for protesting against an abusive speech by a German professor) where many of them died.

Poland. Brest Litovsk disgraces the name of Poland in Europe. Brest is an element of decay and corruption in the life of Poland."[1]

On the 14th November 1930, soon after the election campaign to the first totalitarian Parliament of Poland, the *Manchester Guardian* devoted an article to the terroristic methods used:

"There is no doubt whatever that if the Polish elections were being held by fair means they would sweep Pilsudski and his Government out of existence by an overwhelming majority. But they are, to use a continental expression, being 'made,' and it is the Government that is 'making' them. . . . It must not be supposed that it is the Germans alone who are being oppressed in Poland . . . the fate of the purely Polish opposition is no more enviable. The fate of the extremer opposition (particularly the Communists) is far worse, and most dreadful of all are the atrocities committed by the Polish punitive expeditions in the Ukraine. These, indeed, are the most tragic thing in these tragic elections, which are farcical only on the surface—to look a little way beneath the surface and to realise the implications of all that is being done is to be filled with a sense of disgust with a dictatorship and of tragic pity for the highly-gifted peoples, whether Polish, German or Ukrainian, who are doomed to live beneath it. . . . Warsaw looks like a city under martial law. Khaki-clad infantry, cavalry and machine-gun detachments clatter through the streets all the day. . . . Even more conspicuous than the soldiers are the blue-uniformed police. They have special detachments of these that wear steel helmets . . . and carry rifles and steel shields that make them look like medieval warriors. Besides the soldiers and the police there are the gangsters. They co-operate (though not openly) with the police and resemble the 'Squadristi' of Italian Fascism. It is chiefly they who commit the innumerable acts of brutal violence that are part of the system. It is they who go about in armed bands tearing down the posters of the opposition parties and 'beating up' the messenger boys of opposition newspapers. It is they who deal with politicians or journalists who are inconvenient to the dictatorship, beating them till they faint, or kidnapping them (often in motor-cars borrowed from the police) and beating them almost to death in some remote spot where screams for help cannot be heard."

Pilsudski had more in common with Mussolini than his methods of suppressing opponents for they had both been some-time members of the Socialist International and advocates of terroristic methods in the struggle against capitalism. The following two documents show Pilsudski's relations with the Socialist International at two stages of his life. In October 1912 he addressed a Socialist Congress in Vienna, saying: "Comrades, in the name of the Polish Socialist Party of Russian Poland I have the honour and the great pleasure to greet your party congress. . . . If the war breaks out, we will, of course, work for the fulfilment of our ideals, which the revolution (of 1905) has refused us, and then, within the walls of free Warsaw we will be able to prepare the reception for the dear guests of the International Con-

[1] Tiltman, pp. 349–51.

gress."[1] In September 1930, the Socialist International issued the following proclamation:

"To the workers of all countries!

"Pilsudski's plan for the creation of a docile Parliament by means of a general election was built up from the beginning on terror and corruption. The Government has now made a stroke, the like of which has never been known in Parliamentary history. Members of the Seym which has just been dissolved have been arrested with the undisguised intention of depriving the opposition parties, both labour and peasant, of their leaders during the election campaign.

"This wholesale arrest of men, whose parties undoubtedly represent the majority of the people in Poland, shows through what shameless outrages Pilsudski's minority Government wishes to retain power.

"Democracy in Poland is in the most serious danger! The Polish Republic, which has already been groaning for a long period under the domination of a military clique, threatens to be overcome by open Fascism!

"But the Fascist outrages of the clique of colonels around Pilsudski are by no means simply an internal affair of Poland; they are at the same time a real danger to European peace. The unlimited power of Polish militarism means the violation of the vital rights of the national minorities in Poland and a dangerous aggravation of the relations between Poland and the neighbouring States. These frightful dangers can only be checked by Polish democracy, headed by Polish Socialism.

"Workers of all countries!

"Demonstrate everywhere against the infamous actions of the Pilsudski Government!

"Demonstrate everywhere against the menacing absolute rule of militarism in Poland!

"Condemn everywhere the violation of the liberties of the Polish electorate!

"The cause of democracy in Poland is the cause of the international working class, of world democracy, and of all who desire to preserve the peace of the world!

"The Bureau of the Labour and Socialist International."[2]

The elections and the terror of autumn 1930 meant the end of Parliamentary opposition in Poland; far from bringing order to the country, they embittered the political struggle of the following years. The scene of that struggle was not Parliament, but city and village streets. Strikes of workers and peasants, not only economic, but also distinctly political in character became frequent; many men and women were killed in encounters between strikers and police or military detachments. The mass struggle of the Polish people against the régime was usually attributed by the Government to Communist inspiration, an argument which served in turn to justify a further intensification of terror. Oppression bred further resistance, and the internal life of Poland followed a vicious circle of repression and demonstrations, demonstrations and repression.

[1] Pilsudski, *Works*, Vol. III, pp. 279–80.

[2] *The Fourth Congress of the Labour and Socialist International*, pp. 323–34.

The Pilsudski camp received a majority in the elections of 1930 and began to prepare a new Constitution in order to make the system as permanent as possible. The Constitution was ready in 1934; in spite, however, of having been approved by Parliament, which was dominated by the régime, the Constitution was scrapped as it did not receive Pilsudski's consent. The framework of the Polish State was thus made dependent and changed at a moment's notice at the will of one person. In 1935 the new Constitution was at last ready and became law. Its aim, according to the official explanation, was to give exclusive control over the State to the *élite* of the nation. Although the Constitution granted freedom of speech, personal liberty and freedom of assembly to every citizen regardless of origin, sex and religion, all rights were limited by the proviso of the " common good," the interpretation of which lay in the hands of the régime. A new electoral law, also passed in 1935, was intended to give the *élite* control over Parliament. According to the new law candidates to the Seym could be nominated only by special electoral committees consisting of representatives of local authorities, professional and trade organisations under the chairmanship of a Government commissioner. These committees were in fact controlled by the Government. Members of the Senate were to be nominated, as to one-third, by the President, and as to two-thirds to be elected only by those Polish citizens who received certain decorations or held certain educational degrees. All the opposition parties replied to the new laws by announcing that they would not put forward a single candidate for a seat in Parliament and would boycott the elections. That declaration was implemented and the Polish Parliament from 1935 onwards became a one-party parliament, which worked on lines very similar to the German Reichstag.

The revolt of the people took various forms. The workers adopted new strike methods; they developed sit-down strikes into so-called occupation strikes. The miners of the Dombrowa Basin were the first to apply this form of strike, when they refused for weeks to come up from the mine until their demands were granted. The peasant strikes, with their strong demands for the democratisation of home and foreign policy, stand out as probably unique in their form and intensity.

In June 1933, ten people, including one policeman, were killed in a peasants' riot in a village in Western Galicia. The peasants, who had chased a tax-collector out of the village, and begun to lay waste a forest belonging to a large landowner, attacked a body of police who arrived to restore order, and the police used firearms. In another riot arising from the firing of shots at a religious procession in the district of Lancut, in Galicia, also in June 1933, two policemen and six peasants were killed. (*The Times*, 21st and 27th June 1933.) Grave riots occurred in Cracow in March 1936. The riots followed a general strike proclaimed at a meeting of about ten thousand workers to protest against harsh police methods used in ejecting strikers from one of the local factories. When the meeting broke up several thousand workers formed a procession in the streets, in spite of strict police orders prohibiting street demonstrations. The police attempted to disperse the crowds, and a battle ensued. The demonstrators put up barricades in the main street and stoned the police from behind the barricades; the police charged several times with sabres. Fifteen policemen were wounded, some seriously. Three demonstrators were shot on the spot, and three died from wounds; a number of women were among the wounded. For several hours Cracow was almost cut off, and it was difficult to establish telephone communication. (*The Manchester Guardian*, 24th March 1936.)

A few weeks later street battles took place in Lwow. The disorders began with the funeral of an unemployed man who had been shot a few days before in a demonstration. The arrangements for the funeral procession, including the route that it would take, had been agreed between the police and a committee representing the Lwow trade unions. The Committee had given an undertaking that the funeral would pass quietly, and had made themselves responsible for keeping order. At the last minute, the procession suddenly changed its route, and, instead of making for the cemetery which had been agreed, turned into the centre of the city, which it should have avoided, and marched towards a different cemetery. The police intervened, battles ensued and a few persons were killed. (*The Times*, 17th, 18th and 22nd April 1936.)

These events, however, instead of calling a halt to the terror and eliminating Fascist elements from the Government, brought about the removal of the more liberal leaders who were still supporting the dictatorial *régime*. The old Government party (B.B.W.R.), which had been established in 1928, was dissolved in 1935 when the new Constitution came into force. The Constitution failed to win recognition from the people and to abolish political parties, replacing them by corporative associations, as was intended. The Government decided, therefore, to create a new party, under the title of " Camp of National Unity " (O.Z.O.N.). Its programme called not only for the proclamation of a leader equivalent to the Fuehrer or Duce, but also for the appointment of a Grand Council equivalent to the Fascist Grand Council. In addition it provided for the creation of one totalitarian, authoritarian and apparently self-perpetuating political organisation that was ultimately to supplant the political parties of the moribund Polish democracy. In it were to be merged all the classes and interests in the country under the banner of nationalism, military preparedness, and social and economic reform. The Poles, numbering about 22 millions out of 34 million inhabitants of Poland, were to be " the ruling nation." The 1935 Constitution limiting Parliament's powers was to be fully upheld. The army and its leaders were held to be the nation's great uniting forces. Land distribution was promised to the peasants in a vague form and the problem of over-population of the Polish countryside was to be settled by emigration of peasants to towns to seek employment in trade and industry. The programme was received in German political circles with " satisfaction bordering on enthusiasm." (*New York Times*, 12th, 22nd and 23rd February 1937.)

Colonel Koc, the creator of O.Z.O.N.'s programme, also established the

Union of Young Poland, headed by a leader of the Polish Fascists, M. Piasecki. The programme called for a national revolution, a totalitarian régime on the Nazi model, a national State, the assimilation of the Slavic national minorities. The Jews were to be expelled from Poland. Until their expulsion they were to be refused all civil rights, and their fortunes were to be confiscated. Key industries were to be nationalised, but peasant ownership and small independent businesses were to be encouraged.[1]

All available evidence points to the fact that the great majority of the people did not accept the O.Z.O.N. programme. On the contrary, the internal struggle against the dictatorship seemed to have reached a new peak.

In April 1937, two peasants were killed and several wounded in a clash between peasants and police on the battleground of Raclawice where Tadeusz Kosciuszko defeated a Russian army in 1794. A commemorative celebration of Kosciuszko's victory had been planned by the Peasants' Party, but was banned by the authorities. Arrangements were cancelled too late, however, and groups of peasants assembled on the battleground, only to come into conflict with the police. (*New York Times*, 19th April 1937.) Seventeen peasants were killed in August in various parts of Poland in clashes with police and soldiers which arose from a nation-wide farmers' strike. Six were killed and twenty wounded when troops fired on a mob attempting to raid military ammunition stores at Jaroslaw. Five thousand members of the group camped in a forest after the fight, in which they used clubs, hoes and spades. It was estimated that over one million people took part in the peasants' strikes. The movement extended to industrial workers and there was a twenty-four hour general strike in Cracow, Tarnow, and other towns. (*The Times*, 22nd, 24th and 25th August 1937.)

The strike was announced by the central body of the Peasant Party in a resolution, which also protested against dictatorship, demanded a change in the Constitution and electoral laws, honest elections, a government that enjoyed popular confidence, a reversion to the French from the German alliance in foreign policy, agricultural reform and the return from Czechoslovakia of their exiled leader, Wincenty Witos. (*The Manchester Guardian*, 27th August 1937.)

In October 1937 school children throughout Poland were ordered home when their teachers struck. The strike was a demonstration against the authorities for suspending the left-wing executive committee of the teachers' union and appointing in its place a Government commissioner, who was a member of the newly formed "Union of Young Poland." The general council of the Polish Trade Unions decided to call a one-day general strike in support of the teachers and in defence of labour's freedom of coalition. The reprisals against the teachers' union were also strongly opposed by the left group in the Pilsudski camp.

The creation of the "Camp of National Unity" brought about a split in Government circles. The more progressive Pilsudski-ists and legionaries

[1] Buell, p. 111.

decided finally to break away and formed a new party, the "Union of the Patriotic Left" in order to counter-balance the "Camp of National Unity" with its Fascist leanings. The Union promised to continue in the true spirit of Pilsudski, to follow his ideologies and his work in building a strong modern progressive Poland. (*New York Times*, 5th and 8th October 1937.)

Even intellectuals who tended to remain passive in political life, expressed their protest by founding the Democratic Club under the leadership of Professor Michalowicz of Warsaw University. While the club had no large mass basis, it united in one group intellectuals who played an important role in the social and intellectual life of the country.

The Times (5th March 1938) summed up the situation which had developed in Poland: "With some 20 million peasants and 10 million of the minorities (out of a total population of 35 millions) definitely opposed to the Koc programme and demanding a return to the democratic forms of government, the promoters of the national unity camp find themselves in a dilemma." Thus, the result of the policy of the dictatorial régime was the re-creation of a social structure similar to that which largely contributed to the fall of Poland in the eighteenth century. Behind an almost imperial facade, maintained by the leaders of the Government and of the "Camp of National Unity," stood only a small minority of the Polish population. The active supporters of the dictatorial régime were comparable in mentality and behaviour with the Fascists in other European countries.

References

Buell, R. L., *Poland—Key to Europe*. London, 1939.
Burian, Stephan Count, *Austria in Dissolution*. London, 1925.
Gibbons, H. A., *Europe since 1918*. New York, 1923.
Labour Party Publications Department, *The Fourth Congress of the Labour and Socialist International*. London, 1932.
Landau, Rom, *Pilsudski, Hero of Poland*. London, 1930.
Machray, Robert, *The Poland of Pilsudski*. London, 1936.
Pilsudski, J., *Mowy*, 1926–30 (*Speeches*, etc.). Warsaw, 1931.
,, *Pisma* (*Works*). Warsaw, 1930.
Radziwill, Prince, *Losy*, etc. (The History of the Eldest Line of the Princes Radziwill). Vilna, 1926.
Rose, W. J., *Poland*. London, 1939.
Tiltman, H. Hessel, *The Terror in Europe*. London, 1931.

Chapter IX

NATIONAL MINORITIES

THE frontiers of Poland, as established in 1921, included within the Polish State millions of citizens of different race, tongue and religion from the bulk of the ethnographic Polish people. According to the census of 1921 and 1931 about one-third of the population was made up of national minorities, of which the largest groups were the Ukrainians, Jews, White-Russians (Byelorussians) and Germans.

The Allied Powers when recognising the Polish Government of Paderewski (January–February 1919) and the right of Poland to an independent existence, considered it necessary to impose certain restrictions on Polish sovereignty. Fair treatment for national minorities was to be guaranteed by an international treaty, which was signed at Versailles on 28th June 1919, between the United States, the British Empire, France, Italy and Japan on the one hand and Poland on the other.

In the preamble of the Treaty the following letter from Clemenceau to Paderewski is quoted:

> ". . . I must also recall to your consideration the fact that it is to the endeavours and sacrifices of the Powers in whose name I am addressing you that the Polish nation owes the recovery of its independence. It is by their decision that Polish sovereignty is being re-established over the territories in question and that the inhabitants of these territories are being incorporated in the Polish nation. . . . There rests, therefore, upon these Powers an obligation, which they cannot evade, to secure in the most permanent and solemn form guarantees for certain essential rights which will afford to the inhabitants the necessary protection whatever changes may take place in the internal constitution of the Polish State."

The principal provisions were as follows:

(1) Poland undertook to assure full and complete protection of life and liberty to all inhabitants of Poland without distinction of birth, nationality, language, race or religion. (Art. 2.)

(2) All Polish nationals were to be equal before the law and enjoy the same civil and political rights without distinction as to race, language or religion. Differences of religion, creed or confession were not to prejudice any Polish national in matters relating to the enjoyment of civil or political

rights, as, for instance, admission to public employments, functions and honours, or the exercise of professions and industries. (Art. 7.)

(3) Poland was to provide, in the public educational system in towns and districts in which a considerable proportion of Polish nationals of other than Polish speech were resident, adequate facilities for ensuring that in the primary schools the instruction was to be given to the children of such Polish nationals through the medium of their own language. (Art. 8.)

(4) Poland undertook that the above stipulations were to be recognised as fundamental laws, and that no law, regulation or official action was to conflict or interfere with these stipulations. (Art. 1.)[1]

The evidence of 1919–39 shows that Poland failed to observe the provisions of this Treaty, which was signed on the same day as that with Germany, although it was undoubtedly in the interest of the Polish Republic both to uphold the *status quo* created at Versailles and to give the right of full citizenship to the millions of Ukrainians, Jews and White-Russians.

The psychological heritage of the past and other considerations, how-

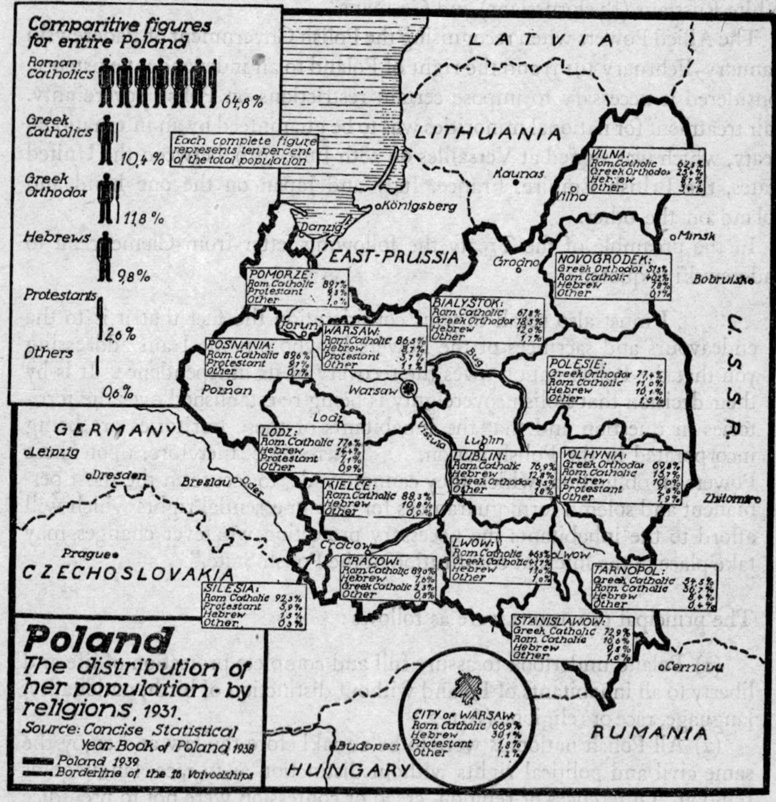

Poland The distribution of her population - by religions, 1931. Source: Concise Statistical Year-Book of Poland, 1938

[1] *The Treaty of Peace.* H.M. Stationery Office, 1920.

ever, predisposed the Poles to another course of action. Ukrainians and White-Russians had generally been serfs in Poland before the partitions; the Jews were a religious minority and also to some extent racially different. Although the democratic struggle of Poles, Ukrainians, Jews and other inhabitants of Poland in the nineteenth century created a genuine spirit of equality amongst them, the prejudices of old Poland against the serfs and the Jews were still alive amongst the landed barons and the lower middle-class gentry; and these strata of the population had a great influence upon Government, Press and public opinion, particularly after 1926.

The attempt to assimilate the Ukrainians, did not only evoke hatred, but brought results similar to those of the Prussian action against Poles in the nineteenth century; its extent can be gauged from data of primary schools. In 1922–23 there were 2,996 primary schools with Ukrainian as the language of instruction; in 1936–37 the number of these schools decreased to 496, i.e. by 83 per cent.[1]

The policy towards the Ukrainians was particularly hostile, because their national struggle was bound up with their demands for land reform. It rose to a peak in 1930, when simultaneously with the attack upon Polish democracy, ruthless " pacifying " expeditions were organised against the Ukrainian peasants of the Eastern Borderlands, who set ablaze many haystacks and outhouses of Polish landowners. *The Manchester Guardian Weekly* (14th July 1930) described the Ukrainian problem in general terms as follows:

> " Like Tsarist Russia, Poland is an Imperialist Power whose conquests are not made overseas but by the expansion of her own frontiers. She has her colonies at home. The Western Ukraine is a Polish colony under Polish military and police occupation and administered by Polish officials. It is a kind of Polish Ireland within the Polish frontiers before the days of Home Rule. . . . The Ukrainians have appealed to the League several times, but in vain. They are fighting their own battle and believe in their own strength. They are fighting by constitutional means, like the Germans and the Jews. Only, if the need and the occasion arise their ultimate appeal will surely be to arms."

Miss Mary Sheepshanks, former head of Morley College, London, who went to Poland to investigate the alleged terroristic action against the Ukrainians in 1930, reported that the so-called " pacification " was carried out with a ferocity which could only be compared with the atrocities committed in the early nineteenth century by the Bash-Bazouks in the old Turkish territories; there was no question of the punishment of crime, but of wholesale atrocities inflicted without trial on an entire population; they were executed by command of the Government strictly according to plan and were not merely the excesses of subordinates; the victims were denied all medical assistance and every effort was made to prevent the appearance of any reports or statistics showing the extent of the repression. According to

[1] *Concise Statistical Year-book of Poland*, 1938.

an estimate the " pacification " was carried out in about 500 to 800 villages and hundreds or perhaps thousands of peasants and workmen were flogged. Imprisonments were also carried out on a great scale, and when the prisons were full the barracks and other buildings were requisitioned. (*The Manchester Guardian*, 29th December 1930.)

The pacification had repercussions abroad. About seventy British Members of Parliament signed a petition in which they asked Sir Eric Drummond, the Secretary-General of the League of Nations, to lay the facts before the League on behalf of the Ukrainian minority in Poland, alleging infractions of the Minority Treaty signed between Poland and the Allied Powers in 1919 and placed under the guarantee of the League of Nations. In the United States the Ukrainian National Association addressed an appeal to Secretary of State Henry L. Stimson asking for an international investigation of the events in Poland. Thousands of American Ukrainians demonstrated by wearing black bands on their sleeves and mourning for the death of Polish Ukrainians killed during the pacification. (*New York Times*, 16th November 1930.) *The Times* (12th December 1930) reported that Ukrainians in Canada also, who were the largest foreign-born racial group in the Dominion, were much agitated over reports of the ill-treatment of their compatriots in Eastern Galicia. " In each Ukrainian community committees have been formed for the purpose of helping their brethren, and these committees have been disseminating pamphlets in which they accuse the Polish authorities of outrages upon defenceless people. They have also appealed to the Dominion Government to make representation and demand that an international commission investigate the situation in Eastern Galicia, and have been bringing pressure to bear on members of Parliament to force the Government's hand."

Terroristic methods were not used against the Jews, the second largest national minority in Poland, mainly because the mass of Polish Jews were deeply attached to their faith and politically inactive in spite of the fact that they were living in abject poverty in semi-medieval ghettoes. Nothing, however, was done to alleviate their plight; on the contrary, they could hardly get employment in any Government factory, in gas or electrical works, in the post office and telegraphic services or in the Civil Service. After a long and obstinate struggle a few got employment on the Warsaw Tramways. The main weight of anti-semitism fell upon poor Jews or professional men; Jewish industrialists and people of independent means were little affected and Jews in important positions in the Government, the Army or the Pilsudski-ist party were left untouched until about 1937.

During the period of collaboration with Germany the policy of the Polish Government towards the Polish Jews moved along much the same lines as that of the Nazi party towards the German Jews before 1938. In 1937–38 anti-Jewish measures reached their climax. The Supreme Council of the Camp of National Unity declared in May 1938 that the Jews were an " element weakening the State; that the best solution was emigration; that the percentage of Jews in certain professions should be lowered; and that it was necessary to defend the centres of Polish cultural and social life, such as the Press, theatre, libraries, music and radio, against their influence." The National Democratic party demanded that Jews be prohibited from voting, holding any public office, or owning land. The programme of the Fascist wing of the National Democrats demanded expulsion of the Jews from Poland and confiscation of their fortunes. According to this programme the Jews were to be deprived of their political rights, eliminated from all social associations, and denied the right to serve in the Polish army. They would be forbidden to participate in Polish enterprises, to employ Poles, or to work for Poles. Polish schools would be purged of Jews, and Polish cultural life would be closed to them. A systematic and radical elimination of the Jews from Poland was regarded as the ultimate solution of the Jewish problem.

In 1933 a law was passed by the Diet limiting university autonomy and permitting the intervention of the police within the universities. In 1937 that law was extended to allow the introduction of 'ghetto benches.' Under such a provision, Jewish students could be compelled to sit in seats specially reserved for them. "Scores of Polish intellectuals and professors all over the country protested against the ghetto benches, and some refused to introduce them in their classrooms. Senator Michalowicz, Professor at the University of Warsaw and President of the Democratic Club, who saved the late Marshal Pilsudski from a Tsarist prison in 1901, refused to abide by the Rector's instructions. . . . M. Kulczycki, Rector of the University of Lwow, resigned, refusing to introduce ghetto benches. In an open letter of 11th January 1938, explaining his resignation, he said: 'For the blackmail going on in the universities, not only do those venerable institutions pay with their prestige, but their autonomous régime is being destroyed, and their ability to work is vanishing. It is easy to see that, under the lofty slogans of national solidarity and defence of the Polish character of our culture the dignity of the autonomous authorities is being brutally challenged and the freedom of science, without which science cannot exist, is being undermined. Science cannot develop under conditions of constraint—not because of the professors' fancy but because science signifies free thinking. Thought that is not free is not scientific. Without science it will be difficult to live, not only for the professors but also for those who are to-day destroying the Polish scientific institutions'."[1]

The White-Russians living in Poland were of peasant stock to an even greater extent than the Ukrainians. The chief White-Russian party in Poland was the Hromada, whose aim was to reach approximately the same status as the White-Russians were enjoying as a federal republic in the U.S.S.R. Its agrarian policy aimed at making the peasants independent of the landlords, who owned nearly all forests and pastures, and were exacting payment in money or kind for all wood, grass and hay which the peasants needed. The Hromada was singled out in 1928 for exemplary punishment. Its leaders were

[1] Buell, *Poland*, pp. 288–91.

tried on a charge of high treason for having plotted to establish Communism in Poland and taken Russian money for that purpose. The accusation was not proved, yet thirty-seven of its members, among them four deputies to the Polish Parliament, were sentenced to terms of penal servitude varying from three to twelve years. Since these men were known as moderates, it became clear that the trial was intended to discredit not so much the extreme wing as the party itself, and with it the whole national movement. When the sentences were pronounced in court, the prisoners, amid the cheers of the public, sang a national song, whose opening words are: " We slept for centuries, now we are awakened."[1]

White-Russians were " polonised " in a higher degree than the Ukrainians, for, as most of them were Catholics, they were considered more assimilable. The language of instruction in the schools was universally Polish, only three or four hours in the week being given to White-Russian, which was taught by Polish teachers as a foreign language. From 1930 onwards the White-

[1] Stephens, pp. 67–8.

Russians had no representation in the Seym and almost all their political parties and newspapers were suppressed.

The position of Germans in Poland was more favourable than that of other national minorities. Although various official and non-official restrictions, occupational and otherwise, were imposed upon them—very similar in character to those on Jews—the Germans could count on Berlin's support in Geneva. Their position was still further improved when Hitler came to power. While German democrats and socialists in Poland, particularly numerous in Upper Silesia and Lodz, were being suppressed, together with the Polish democratic parties, various Nazi organisations were left intact. According to the *Slavonic Review* three-fourths of the German minority were in 1937 in sympathy with the Third Reich, even though they may not have consistently accepted the Swastika programme. At the most one-quarter frankly rejected it. This division of forces was due to the fact that the Germans in Poland from a long time back had been seriously dependent on various kinds of help from the Reich, and from 1933 this had naturally been given only to such as accepted the Nazi creed. The Polish Government, moreover, had done nothing to encourage those who opposed the Hitler movement, much less to support them. No more Germans got into Parliament by election, and only two by nomination of the President. Both of these were disciples of Hitler. It was true that Polish public opinion expressed general sympathy with the smaller German groups, who wanted no truck with Berlin; but the material worth of this attitude was small indeed. Many individual Germans had the feeling that they might have to leave Poland owing to the ultra-nationalist policy of the administration, and they saw no other asylum open to them than the Reich.[1]

In November 1934, the Polish Foreign Minister Beck denounced the Versailles Peace Treaty, concluded between the Allies and Poland in 1919, which protected the national minorities. This step was undertaken in agreement with Germany and formed one of the first Polish contributions to the German-Polish action against the *status quo* in Central and Eastern Europe. The German minority continued to be under the protection of the Reich, and on 5th November 1937, a declaration was published in Berlin which said that in a friendly exchange of views, the German and Polish Governments had discussed the position of the German Minority in Poland and the Polish Minority in Germany. They were in complete agreement that the treatment of these minorities was a matter of great importance for the further development of friendly relations between Germany and Poland, and that in both countries the well-being of the minority was better protected when it was certain that the same principles would be observed in the other country. On the same day Hitler declared :

"The identical German-Polish Declaration regarding the protection of foreign racial groups in each country, which has been made public

[1] *Slavonic Review*. London, 1937, Vol. XVI, pp. 95–6.

to-day by both states, should improve and strengthen the friendly relations between the two peoples. The practical execution of the principles contained in this declaration can materially contribute to the attainment of this aim. . . . The principal aim of the Pact which I concluded with the Great Polish Chief of State, Marshal Josef Pilsudski, will, by this reciprocal German-Polish Declaration regarding the minorities question, be brought nearer to its complete fulfilment."[1]

The *volte-face* in Polish policy towards the German minority was particularly noticeable in the Free City of Danzig. In execution of Article 104 of the Versailles Treaty Poland concluded in 1920 a separate treaty with Danzig which accorded to Poland the right to represent Danzig abroad and to guard the rights of her racial, religious and linguistic minorities. It also included Danzig in the customs area of Poland. Up to 1927 innumerable disputes arose between the Polish and the Danzig authorities and the decisions made by the High Commissioners of the League of Nations in these disputes filled six volumes.[2] After 1926 relations greatly improved and, after 1933, the persecution of German anti-Nazis in Danzig and the violation of the Danzig constitution and international Treaties met with no interference from Poland. On the contrary, while the relations between the League of Nations and the Government of Danzig were full of friction, Beck usually defended Danzig's case in Geneva. For instance, in the report submitted by Colonel Beck in January 1937, at Geneva he advised that High Commissioners " should take care to see that the internal administration of the Free City of Danzig is not hampered."[3] The result was the appointment of a High Commissioner, M. Karl Burckhardt, who was " *persona grata* in National Socialist eyes."[4] In September 1939, M.Burckhardt left Danzig and Forster and Greiser, leaders of the Danzig Nazi party and of the Senate respectively, both favoured by Beck, proclaimed the incorporation of the Free City into the German Reich.

References

Buell, R. L., *Poland—Key to Europe*. London, 1939.
Morrow, I. D. W., *The Peace Settlement in the German-Polish Borderlands*. London, 1936.
Royal Institute of International Affairs, *Documents of* 1936. London, 1938.
Stephens, John S., *Danger Zones of Europe*. London, 1929.

1 *Documents of* 1936, pp. 199–201.
2 Morrow, pp. 75–6.
3 *Documents of* 1936, p. 447.
4 *Documents of* 1936, p. 420.

Chapter X

FOREIGN AFFAIRS

POLISH foreign policy seems to have been the outcome of two tendencies. On the one hand, the landed barons, accustomed to hold high posts in the great empires of Austria, Russia and, in a smaller degree, Germany, cherished the idea of recreating the Polish Empire of the eighteenth century. Loss of property as a result of the Russian revolution made them all the more outspoken about their wishes. On the other hand, a large part of the lower middle-class *Szlachta* regarded itself as the traditional defender of the West against the " barbarism " of the East; possessed by the spirit of servility to the mighty, similar in essence to the *Landsknecht* cult in the Nazi movement, it was fanatically anti-Russian. At the outset, therefore, Polish foreign policy was directed towards expansion and towards an anti-Bolshevik crusade.

Just as at home, so in foreign affairs, Polish democracy proved to be too weak to impose on the Government a peaceful policy, in spite of the fact that peace was vital for Poland's existence; as Dr. Haden Guest put it after his visit to Poland in 1921: " The only national policy for Poland between Germany on the one side and Russia on the other is a policy of peace. And democratic Poles know it and wish to follow it, because they wish to develop the social programme of reconstruction to which they have set their hands. It may be that anti-democratic Poles engineer disturbance and war for the same reason from the opposite side. . . . And despite an intense nationalism and the intrigue of its feudal and business classes in international politics, it is probable that the economic necessities will prevail over the political preferences. But Poland is still hesitating between progress and reaction."[1]

According to Sir Robert Donald, the Polish leaders " were smitten with the microbe of megalomania " before the Allies resurrected their country into a State. When the tide of battle turned in favour of the Allies they had visions of a great Poland stretching from the Baltic to the Black Sea.

> " Poland likes to pose as the buffer State between Sovietism and Teutonism, as the protector of Western Civilisation from the Russian peril and as the force which will hold German chauvinism in check.
>
> " Militarily, Poland is not strong enough to guard against either of these so-called dangers: the Russian steam-roller, if or when it is ready,

[1] Haden Guest, pp. 113, 135.

will roll over Poland as it pleases, as there will not be another ' miracle of the Vistula '; Germany re-armed could conquer Poland with as little difficulty as in 1917. Should these two military forces ever get together through the blundering diplomacy of the former Allies of the West, Poland will be in a vice; its life blood will be squeezed out of it. . . . Whatever may happen about frontier changes, or if nothing happens, Poland's safety lies in a non-aggressive policy. Poland can only prosper by cultivating friendly relations with its neighbours. Towards this end it should encourage an interchange of goods. On the contrary, it is chauvinistic, both economically and militarily."[1]

The leaders of the N.D. party (which was the Government party until 1926) although on the whole democratic in word and deed, were nevertheless advocates of Poland's territorial expansion. These, for instance, were the views of S. Grabski, Chairman of the Seym Commission for Foreign Affairs, as outlined in 1923:

" As regards Poland's *Machtpolitik* the same fundamental dilemma which has overshadowed the whole of our history still continues to exist—namely the question of what direction the expansion of the Polish people shall follow? Shall it expand northwards to the Baltic or to the south-east, in the direction of the Ukraine and the Black Sea? . . . One of two things: either we turn the Polish policy of ascendancy eastwards, against Russia by taking advantage of the successive periods of weakness which the next half century will bring, and thereby leave the decision of the merely provisional settlement of the East-Prussian problem to Germany, or we stake all the power at our disposal on the solution of the East-Prussian problem by Poland in a sense favourable to Poland."[2]

S. Bukowiecki, Attorney-General of Poland, expressed a similar opinion on foreign policy:

" As matters stand now, we must reckon with the fact that Germany's endeavour to secure union with East Prussia to a certain extent represents a historical necessity which Poland must oppose with all her might, as such a union would undermine our whole political position; and our opposition must take the form of a trend toward the east. When I am speaking of such a trend I am by no means thinking of an aggressive policy; that would be in contradiction to our general tendencies, which are definitely pacific. But a State of moderate size in the position of Poland has certain natural tendencies towards development, which, even if they do not find expression in concrete political action, yet represent a fundamental aim which can wait through generations for an opportunity of realisation, but which is constantly kept in mind in the nation's various political and economic activities. Poland might, for instance, direct her aspirations mainly towards the east, towards the Ukraine or White-Russia; or she might even endeavour to extend her influence northwards to East Prussia, in order to turn at a given opportunity, in one direction or the

[1] Donald, pp. 243, 260. [2] Grabski, p. 142.

other. But the tendencies to extend northwards could only become a real and active effort if whole generations were to lend themselves to the work, for the forces opposing it are enormous."[1]

Politicians of the Dmowski orientation rather favoured an expansion to the West; on the other hand the large landowners of the Eastern Borderlands and the former Austro-Polish statesmen sponsored an expansionist policy towards the East. The latter's counsel prevailed after Pilsudski's *coup d'état* and Government practice seems to suggest that it was accepted as one of the guiding principles of Poland's foreign policy.

The maximum plan of the dictatorial régime in the matter of territorial expansion was presented by W. Studnicki, a former Austro-Polish politician and leading Pilsudski-ist[2] as follows:

"The geographical conditions of restored Poland are infinitely worse than the geographical conditions of pre-partition Poland. The present area of the State comprises only 57 per cent of the Polish Empire of 1772. We ceded to Russia much land which, in view of its ethnographic and economic structure and of its scanty population, should have been incorporated in Poland with advantages both for Poland and for the inhabitants of those areas . . . I consider a Polish-German war would be a calamity for Poland and dangerous for Germany, and the participation of Poland in an anti-German coalition as a blow directed against European civilisation. . . . The anti-Russian front of the Polish State, established by history, is unshaken, although it does not always enter the political consciousness of the nation.

"Poland ought to take advantage of the present anti-Bolshevik movement in Germany, to make an agreement with her. Poland cannot be in alliance with her eastern neighbour.

". . . Where do the frontiers of Poland end? They end where Aryan blood flows unmingled with Mongolian-Finnish, where Catholicism has been a factor of civilisation, where Roman law shaped the economic conditions. I do not speak of the present frontier defined by the Riga Treaty, but of frontiers which history has created. Russia, Slavonic by language, is Asiatic by blood and history.

". . . The security of Europe requires on the one hand its political consolidation, on the other a further amputation from Russia in the west, south and east. Particularly important would be the cutting off of the Caucasus with its abundant sources of oil and manganese. The separation of Turkestan, with its cotton, would be important. . . . For humanitarian reasons the frontier of Finland should be pushed further eastwards. The Polish-Russian frontier should be corrected for strategic as well as economic reasons. . . . The Far East up to the Baykal Lake should belong to Japan.

". . . The taking away from Poland of the Corridor would be a violation of the right of national self-determination, which the Germans cannot deny, since they are a nation of strong national feeling and therefore

[1] Bukowiecki, p. 73.

[2] Studnicki carried his policy to a logical conclusion. After the German occupation of Poland in 1939 he was reported to be one of the first to co-operate with the invaders.

have the right to annex Austria and Northern Bohemia with its German majority. . . . The question of the Corridor, which is unimportant to Germany, has been presented to the civilised world as a most vital question. Why should a great nation be hypnotised by a small idea, when its great numbers, its economic and civilising forces, allow it not only to preach great ideas, but also to practise them?

". . . A great idea is the *Anschluss*, because the union of Germany with Austria means the foundation of a Central-European bloc. The Central-European bloc depends on a *rapprochement* between the two largest countries of Central Europe, Poland and Germany. Such a bloc will give to Germany world hegemony and to Poland conditions of safety and development.

". . . The creation of the Central European bloc will probably be as follows: After the incorporation of Austria with Germany, Hungary and Rumania will enter into an economic bloc with these countries, not on the lines of a customs union, but on one of preferential duties. . . . Poland would also enter on the basis of preferential duties. . . . Yugoslavia, not wanting to be alone, will seek agreement with the bloc. . . . Czechoslovakia, encompassed by countries of the Central European bloc, will not be able to stay aloof. . . . Subsequently other Balkan and Baltic States will begin to enter the bloc.

"Poland in the first years of her existence had the hope of gaining influence over the Baltic States. We wanted to create a Baltic Union, of which we would have been a member as a Baltic country. Poland wanted to gain the support of Latvia and Estonia for this union, recognising already in 1919 their independence and helping Latvia in her struggle with Bolshevik Russia and giving her Courland, to which not Latvia but Poland has historic rights. The Baltic Union was to be a part of the chain of the union of countries, which rose from the ruins of Russia. The liberated Ukraine, the republics of the Caucasus, Georgia, Asserbeidshan, Armenia, were to be members of the new union, which under Poland's hegemony was to be the power which would be able to exist between Russia and Germany. This plan, however, did not reckon with the fact that for its realisation Poland had no allies among the European powers.

". . . Latvia and Estonia had no history, i.e. they were not subjects of history, but objects.

". . . Czechoslovakia . . . is a great monstrosity, a kind of European appendix."[1]

Although the conceptions outlined above may seem to have been fantastic, nevertheless they undoubtedly represented the views of that group of politicians who reigned over Poland after Pilsudski's death in 1935. It may be mentioned here that the Foreign Minister Beck was at one time military attaché in Paris and was reported to have been recalled to Warsaw at the request of the French Government, which was disturbed by his close relations with the German Intelligence Department. (*Nineteenth Century*, October 1936.) The rule by brute force over an economically backward and poverty-stricken country and an adventurous foreign policy, fitted well together. It

[1] Studnicki, pp. 6–10, 319–20.

cannot be said that the pro-Nazi policy was due to a misapprehension; it was the logical application to foreign affairs of Fascist principles blended with feudal conceptions and prejudices and it tried to ignore the all-too-numerous anti-Polish tendencies in Germany.

The German attitude towards the Polish State was made abundantly clear by many German statesmen, politicians and soldiers. Prince von Buelow declared in 1916:

> "It is very well known that Prince Bismarck considered an independent Polish State incompatible with the interests of our existence. . . . The work of German colonisation in the Eastern Marches, begun a thousand years ago, suspended for four centuries, and taken up anew less than 30 years ago, cannot be completed in a short time. This is not like an ordinary political action, which is soon followed by success or failure; we are in the midst of a great historical evolution in which generation after generation will have to co-operate."[1]

In 1919, Field Marshal von Hindenburg declared, "There could be no graver danger for us than the existence of a Polish State, if that State were destined to a continued independent existence."[2] In March 1928, the Congress of the German People's Party (*Deutsche Volkspartei*) passed a resolution opposing the conclusion of a commercial treaty with Poland and declaring that the Eastern frontier should never be accepted. In May of the same year Herr Hergt, German Vice-Chancellor, declared that no government would ever guarantee the permanence of the frontier with Poland.[3]

Alfred Rosenberg, the Nazi leader and theoretician, declared bluntly in his book, *Der Zukunftsweg einer deutschen Aussenpolitik*:

> "It is understood that the disappearance of the Polish State is the chief necessity for Germany, then the conclusion of an alliance between Kiev and Berlin and the delimitation of a common frontier becomes from a racial and national standpoint an indispensable object to be pursued by German foreign policy in the future."[4]

In 1933 Hitler declared in an interview that the Corridor was "a hideous injustice" and "must be restored to us." (*Sunday Express*, 12th February 1933.) Nevertheless, three months after Hitler's declaration the pro-German orientation of Poland's foreign policy began. According to Professor Toynbee the actual improvement in Polish-German relations was unmistakable and prompt. On 4th May 1933, the Polish Minister in Berlin was received by Herr Hitler, and the German Minister in Warsaw, simultaneously by the Polish Minister for Foreign Affairs; and it was publicly announced that, at both these meetings, the representatives of the two countries had declared the

[1] Buelow, pp. 252, 265.
[2] *New Poland*, London, May 17th, 1919.
[3] Toynbee, *Survey of International Affairs*, 1932, p. 62.
[4] Quoted by Morrow, p. 463.

intention of their respective Governments to keep their attitude and their actions strictly within the limits of existing treaties and dispassionately to examine their common interest. On the 15th November there was an equally friendly conversation in Berlin between Hitler and the newly accredited Polish Minister, Lipski, who was entrusted with the execution of the new Polish policy. These mutual acts of deliberate goodwill in 1933 prepared the way for the conclusion of the German-Polish pact of 26th January 1934.[1]

On 15th November 1933, Hitler said to Lipski that he was anxious first and foremost to define his attitude in principle towards Poland. He took Poland into account as a reality which nothing would be able to change or cause to disappear. It was, perhaps, the error of preceding German Governments that they did not sufficiently understand this reality. Poland was a reality for Germany, just as Germany was for Poland, and the two nations were obliged to live side by side. The life of nations was not measured by ten or fifteen years, but by hundreds and thousands of years. German-Polish relations had not been established on an ideal basis, especially as the result of the Treaty of Versailles, which was calculated to render them difficult. The Chancellor affirmed none the less, very emphatically, that he had no intention whatever of effecting any change by resort to war. He was anxious for good relations with Poland, and a favourable atmosphere, so that the common life of the two nations would take a normal course.[2]

On 26th January 1934, the following declaration was made officially:

> " The Governments of Poland and Germany consider that the time has arrived to begin a new era in the political relations of Poland and Germany by means of reaching direct understanding between the two States. They have, therefore, decided by the present declaration to lay the foundation for the future shaping of these relations. Both Governments proceed from the assumption that the maintenance and stabilisation of a permanent peace between their respective countries constitutes an essential condition of a general peace in Europe. . . . Both governments declare that it is their intention to reach direct understanding on problems concerning their mutual relations. In the event of disputes arising between them on questions which could not be settled by direct negotiations, both Governments will seek such a solution in each particular case by way of other peaceful means mutually agreed upon, without, however, excluding the possibility of applying, if necessary, such modes of procedure as are provided for such cases by other agreements by which they are mutually bound. In no case, however, shall they have recourse to force in order to settle such question under dispute.
>
> " The guarantee of peace established upon the above principles will facilitate for both Governments the important task of finding, for political, economic and cultural problems, solutions based upon just and equitable consideration of the interests of both parties. Both Governments are convinced that the relations between their respective countries will thus develop fruitfully and will lead to the firm establishment of good neigh-

[1] Toynbee, *International Affairs*, 1933, p. 186.
[2] *The Polish White Book*, Paris-London, 1940.

bourly relations, which should have salutary consequences not only for their own countries but also for the other nations of Europe."[1]

Conferences between officials of the Polish Foreign Office and the German Foreign Office and Ministry for National Enlightenment and Propaganda took place frequently to implement the declaration. They were designed to maintain permanent contact between Berlin and Warsaw for the purpose of "enlightening public opinion" in the two countries. As a result the Polish censorship permitted newspapers to make the bitterest attacks on France while no unfavourable criticism of Germany was allowed to be published. (*The Times*, 8th October 1934.)

From 1934 up to the seizure of Czechoslovakia in March 1939, the foreign policies of Germany and Poland seem to have followed a similar course with regard to the *status quo* in Europe. The White Book, published by the Sikorski Government in 1940 in France, contains many diplomatic documents referring to that period and mainly dealing with Russia.

In January 1935, Lipski reported to Warsaw a conversation he had had with Hitler, who expressed the opinion that the theory of Polish-German hereditary enmity was very unsound. In the history of the two countries, he said, there had been periods of co-operation against the mutual danger threatening from the East, and they had also formed dynastic alliances. Hitler declared that after eight or nine years quite different relations would surely exist between the two States, when both nations had come to know each other better and the old prejudices had disappeared. He mentioned, however, that naturally there were certain elements in Germany hostile to Poland. There were, undoubtedly, people who did not wish his Government to be successful in its foreign policy. No doubt there were similar elements in Poland.

Subsequently, Hitler discussed at length the Russian question and the danger threatening from the East. He pointed out that, according to the information of his military authorities and intelligence services, Russia had made great progress with her military preparations. The moment might come when both Germany and Poland would be compelled to defend themselves against aggression from the East.

According to Lipski, then Polish Ambassador in Berlin, Goering was very outspoken in his conversations during a hunting visit which he paid to Poland in February 1935, especially while talking to generals. He outlined far-reaching plans, almost suggesting an Anti-Russian Alliance and a joint attack on Russia, and he gave it to be understood that the Ukraine would become a Polish sphere of influence and North-Western Russia would be Germany's. In view of these confidences the Ambassador was afraid that Goering might, when visiting Marshal Pilsudski, make over-definite proposals in regard to the Russian question. For this reason also, before he should call at the Belvedere Palace, M. Lipski advised the German Ambas-

[1] *Documents*, 1934, pp. 424–5.

sador that Goering should maintain some reserve in his conversation with Pilsudski. Nevertheless, Goering did touch on the Russian military question with the Marshal, hinting at a joint Polish-German attack on Russia and pointing out the advantages to Poland of the Ukraine in such an event. Pilsudski in reply stiffened, as Goering later put it, and gave it to be understood that, even so, it was impossible to stand continually at the ready on such a long line as the Polish-Soviet frontier.

In August 1935, Foreign Minister Beck visited Finland, and, according to Mr. Machray, was well received there. Finland was then watching with close attention the Comintern Congress in Moscow—as were Poland and other countries. On 27th August the *Gazeta Polska*, the semi-official Polish Government paper, contained a sharp criticism of the discrepancy between the official policy of the Soviet Union to friendly States and the policy of the Comintern, which was aimed at stirring up the peoples of other countries with a view to overthrowing their existing governments by revolution from within. The strained attitude of the United States to Russia at this time did not go unremarked either in Poland or the Baltic States, and Warsaw's continued opposition to the Eastern Pact and her dislike of the Franco-Soviet and Czechoslovak-Soviet Pacts, especially the latter, were resented by Moscow.[1]

In February 1936, Count Szembek, Polish Under-Secretary for Foreign Affairs, described a conversation he had with Herr Frank, German Minister of Justice, also a frequent guest in Warsaw. Frank opened the conversation by declaring that Poland, Germany and France must march together; he stressed that in this regard Poland had great opportunities. Polish-French-German collaboration was the only means to an effective struggle against the barbarism which would come from the East. The Russian nation was to be pitied for being lost in the confusion of Bolshevism, but they had to defend themselves against it with all their strength, since it aimed at destroying everything which had been most sacred to Poland, France and Germany for a thousand years. Speaking of the Polish-German *rapprochement*, Frank stated that Poland and Germany together were a force which it would be difficult to resist in Europe, for it was a bloc comprising a solid mass of a hundred million people.[2]

During another visit to Poland (February 1937) Goering declared in a conversation with Marshal Smigly-Rydz, Ambassador von Moltke and Count Szembek, that he had been instructed by Chancellor Hitler to emphasise that Germany was more than ever determined to continue the policy of *rapprochement* with Poland. It was obvious that this policy, which was desired by both Governments, could not yet completely win over public opinion in both countries, since there were still traces of former prejudices in both peoples. Years of enmity between the two States had left their mark in certain memories and resentments in both countries. In this sphere some uncertainties still existed. The task of both Governments was to influence

[1] Machray, p. 411–12.

[2] *The Polish White Book*, p. 31.

public opinion so as to dispel them. On the German side there was no desire whatever to deprive Poland of any part of her territory. Germany was completely reconciled to her present territorial status. Germany would not attack Poland and had no intention of seizing the Polish " Corridor."

The new Germany had come into existence in the same way as the new Poland, and Germany would never return to a pro-Russian policy. For it should always be remembered that there was one great danger coming through Russia from the East, and menacing both Germany and Poland alike. This danger existed not only in the form of a Bolshevik and Communist Russia, but of Russia generally, in any form, be it monarchist or liberal. In this respect the interests of Poland and Germany were identical.

On the eve of the seizure of Austria, in February 1938, the Polish Commander-in-Chief, Marshal Smigly-Rydz, had a conversation with Field-Marshal Goering in the presence of Count Szembek. Goering stated that Chancellor Hitler had instructed him to say how gratified the Chancellor felt that in his last Reichstag speech he had been able to refer to relations with Poland. Those relations found expression in a clear and reasonable policy. The Chancellor was also glad that Polish-Danzig relations were on the road to improvement, and he was anxious to emphasise that Polish rights in the Free City would not be violated. He had already given expression to these views on previous occasions. Only in his last speech he had again defined his attitude. He was firmly and irrevocably resolved to carry on this policy in the future. Goering devoted the next part of the conversation to the Soviet Army. After reviewing its present condition, he expressed the opinion that from the point of view of equipment, and also of human material, it stood at a very low level. He gave the Marshal to understand that in his opinion, in the event of war, it would not be difficult to inflict a military defeat on the Soviets. He stressed that politically the Soviets were, however, a permanent and very serious danger, and in this respect Polish and German interests completely harmonised. For these two States formed a bulwark against Bolshevism. In Germany they perfectly realised that if Poland were defeated in a conflict with the Soviets, then the logical result of this would be the swift Bolshevisation of Germany.

At the height of the Czechoslovak crisis, on 10th September 1938, Herr von Ribbentrop emphasised the necessity for good Polish-German relations; it was his personal conviction that good relations were in the common interest of both States. His view was confirmed by the line adopted by the Chancellor. As long as the Chancellor desired to maintain him in his present post, therefore, he would work positively for the development of Polish-German relations. Granted this general assumption, minor issues disturbing Polish-German relations should be settled in a friendly spirit.

On 14th September 1938, Hitler declared in his speech at Nuremberg:

> " In Poland a great patriot and a great statesman was ready to make an accord with Germany; we immediately proceeded to action and completed

an agreement which was of greater importance to the peace of Europe than all the chattering in the temple of the League of Nations at Geneva."[1]

German-Polish relations, however, underwent a rapid change after the Munich agreement. On 25th October 1938, von Ribbentrop put to M. Lipski a proposal for a general settlement of issues between Poland and Germany. This included the reunion of Danzig with the Reich, while Poland would be assured the retention of railway and economic facilities there. Poland would agree to the building of an extra-territorial motor road and railway line across Pomorze. In exchange von Ribbentrop mentioned the possibility of an extension of the Polish-German Agreement by twenty-five years and a guarantee of Polish-German frontiers. As a possible sphere for future co-operation between the two countries, the German Foreign Minister specified joint action in colonial matters and the emigration of Jews from Poland, and a joint policy towards Russia on the basis of the Anti-Comintern Pact.

On 5th January 1939, Beck paid a visit to Berchtesgaden and afterwards asked " M. von Ribbentrop to inform the Chancellor that whereas previously, after all his conversations and contacts with German statesmen, he had been feeling optimistic, to-day for the first time he was in a pessimistic mood."[2]

After the absorption of Czechoslovakia by Germany, on 26th March 1939, Ambassador Lipski wrote to Warsaw that he was received by von Ribbentrop, who gave him a distinctly cold reception.[3]

Six months later Poland was overrun by German armies.

No evidence is available on the question whether Polish foreign policy towards Czechoslovakia and Lithuania was concerted with that of Germany during the period 1934–39. There is no doubt, however, that Poland pursued an aggressive policy towards these small neighbouring States. A few weeks after the conclusion of the German-Polish pact, on 18th March 1934, a mob of members of the Pilsudski-ist Legion of Youth stoned and smashed the windows of the Czechoslovak Legation in Warsaw as a demonstration against the " persecution of the Polish Minority " by the Czechs. The official telegraph agency published dispatches describing the arrest of Polish leaders in Teschen, the closing down of Polish schools and the prohibition of Polish papers. The semi-official *Gazeta Polska* warned the Czechoslovak Government that the entire Polish nation would react against the " policy of exterminating the Polish Minority " and declared that " Poland could not remain indifferent." The Czechoslovak Press was equally bitter, criticised the Polish-German Ten Years' Pact as enabling Germany to concentrate against Austria, and even hinted that the pact had something in it or behind it that allowed Poland to take a sharp, bullying attitude towards Czechoslovakia. Why, it was asked, should this Polish outburst occur so soon after the signature of the Ten Years' Pact?[4]

Professor Toynbee, in the " Survey of International Affairs of 1935," wondered whether the increase of tension between Poland and Czechoslovakia

[1] *The Polish White Book*, p. 46.
[2] *The Polish White Book*, p. 54.
[3] *The Polish White Book*, p. 66.
[4] Machray, p. 352.

which first became noticeable in the spring of 1934, and which showed no sign of diminishing, was not one of the more sensational of the many changes in the European political situation which followed directly or indirectly from the resurgence of Germany. Its interest lay rather in its close connection with more important problems, such as the possibility of the eastward or south-eastward expansion of Germany, or of changes in the policy of the successor States and especially of Poland.

> "The aristocrats, who still enjoyed considerable power in Poland, together with those Poles of all classes who were under the influence of the 'legionary' spirit of the Pilsudski régime, felt much more in sympathy with the Hungarians than with the Czechs. They were, indeed, inclined to despise the latter as a grasping and bourgeois race, inhabiting a country far inferior in status to their own beloved Poland, whom they believed to be at last about to fulfil her divinely appointed mission as a Great Power. (The Czechs for their part were apt to give way to a corresponding prejudice against the clerical and aristocratic traditions of Poland.) Whether Marshal Pilsudski and his government of Colonels were actually harbouring any sinister designs against Czechoslovakia or whether they merely wished to accustom public opinion to their newly established reconciliation with Germany by promoting Czechoslovakia to the position of public enemy, formerly held by that country, the signing of the German-Polish non-aggression pact certainly coincided with the opening of a campaign of propaganda in defence of the Polish minority in Teschen."[1]

According to Mr. Stephen Heald, throughout 1937, as in 1936, the Little Entente was under fire from Berlin and Rome and also from Warsaw, the eventual objective of this campaign being the isolation of Czechoslovakia by the disruption of the Little Entente—an objective which it was hoped to secure by detaching Rumania and Yugoslavia.[2] At the height of the Czechoslovak crisis *The Times* reported that

> "Polish attention was being increasingly focussed on 'the persecution of our kinsfolk beyond the Olza' in a manner which suggested that the 20-year-old conflict over Teschen was on the verge of being 'liquidated', if necessary by drastic measures. An ultimatum to the Prague Government was being spoken of as the next step. Appropriate resolutions demanding the 'revindication of these ethnographical Polish lands' were being submitted at organised demonstrations in all Polish towns of any importance.
>
> Troop movements took place, a 'volunteer' corps was organised and popular demonstrations were held in favour of redeeming the 'lands beyond the Olza'. The Polish-Czech frontier was closed by the Prague government; Poles and Czechs were killed in clashes. Meanwhile, the Polish and Hungarian authorities asked Hitler and Mussolini for help in advancing their claims. When the Soviet government warned that it might

[1] Toynbee, *International Affairs*, 1935, pp. 279–81, 289.
[2] *Documents of* 1937, pp. 337–39.

denounce the non-aggression pact of 1932 if Polish troops crossed the frontier, Poland replied that this affair did not concern Russia, while Colonel Beck proceeded to confer with the Japanese Ambassador."[1]

After Munich, Poland received the Teschen area, and a few months later, when Czechoslovakia was annexed, Poland was surrounded by Germany from the North, West and South.

After the seizure of Vilna by General Zeligowski, Lithuania refused to enter into diplomatic relations with Poland. In March 1938, simultaneously with the stroke of Germany against Austria, incidents occurred on the Polish-Lithuanian frontier, and the Polish Government, in an ultimatum, asked the Lithuanian Government to resume diplomatic relations with Poland. According to *The Times* the counter-proposal of the Lithuanian Government that the incident, which resulted in the shooting of a Polish soldier, should be the subject of inquiry by a mixed commission was stated to be unacceptable to the Polish Government. The time limit to the Polish ultimatum delivered to the Lithuanian Government, " outlining the conditions necessary for avoiding in the future incidents dangerous to peace," was 48 hours. The consequences of a negative reply were indicated by the arrival at Vilna of Marshal Smigly-Rydz, accompanied by officers of the General Staff, " and preparations have presumably been made to occupy at least a small part of Lithuanian territory adjacent to the Polish Lithuanian border—in case the Lithuanian Government refuse to begin diplomatic conversations. . . . There has been much loose talk about a Polish-German-Hungarian ' deal ' involving the absorption of Lithuania by Poland and the partitioning of Czechoslovakia, but it is altogether too fantastic to be believed." (*The Times,* 16th and 19th March 1938.)

The Spectator (25th March 1938) commented on the incident as follows:

> " Poland is a member of the League of Nations. She is a Member of the Council of the League, accorded by a two-thirds majority of the Assembly the honour of a ' semi-permanent ' seat. It is the fundamental rule of the Covenant of the League, the very foundation on which the rest is built, that no Member shall take or threaten warlike action without first submitting disputes to third-party judgment by the impartial organs which the Covenant provides. Poland has set that rule aside; she has exploited a frontier incident, the shooting of a frontier sentry, to demand immediate satisfaction of her claims within a period of hours, she has mobilised 50,000 troops to back that ultimatum . . . she has made warlike demonstration in Vilna and elsewhere . . . to-day Poland has gravely compromised her good reputation throughout the world. From now on her weaker neighbours must inevitably regard her with suspicion. Whatever else she has obtained she has not advanced towards her real objective of confident and friendly co-operation with a neighbour State. . . . A precedent has been created which some day may be used against the Poles themselves by either of the mighty nations between whom they live."

[1] *The Times,* 22nd September, 1938; Buell, p. 328.

The attitude of the Polish Government towards other questions, such as the pacts of mutual assistance proposed in 1934 by Mr. Eden and M. Barthou, the minority treaties, colonies, the Spanish Republic, German rearmament, the occupation of the Rhineland and the reintroduction of compulsory military service in Germany, all fell in line with Poland's expansionist policy.

With regard to the colonial problem, for instance, Beck declared in Geneva (December 1936):

> "I cannot maintain silence on the fact that during the current year I put forward in the Assembly of the League of Nations, in the name of Poland, the problem of our Colonial interests. This problem might be divided into two parts. First the securing for our population of territories for emigration. . . . The second part of the colonial question for Poland is access to raw materials in a better way than by ordinary commercial exchange."[1]

The Polish Colonial League, founded in 1930, carried on propaganda in favour of colonies. Although the organisation at first did not receive government support, later on every member of the O.Z.O.N. (Camp of National Unity) was asked to join. The Old German Maritime League seems to have been the model for the Polish organisation. Membership had grown from 40,000 in 1930 to 753,000 in 1937. The Polish Government showed considerable interest in the Cameroons, and it was even demanded that Poland be given a mandate over Tanganyika in compensation for the service rendered Europe in the war against the Soviets in 1920.[2]

The attitude of the Polish Government to the Republican Spanish Government, which was with Poland a member of the League of Nations, was openly hostile. When the Secretary-General of the League consulted the Government which were represented on the Council (December 1936) in regard to the action to be taken on the Spanish Government's appeal, the majority of them found themselves obliged to agree that it was not possible to refuse the request that a meeting of the Council should be summoned at an early date. There was a minority to which Poland and Chile belonged which would have preferred to refuse the Spanish Government's appeal. M. Komarnicki, for Poland, expressed with unexpected bluntness the view that the Council ought never to have been summoned to discuss the situation in Spain; while Mr. Jordan, the representative of New Zealand, put the opposite view with no less bluntness.[3]

The Times gave the following analysis of Poland's foreign policy on 12th August 1938:

> "While the Polish Government have always professed loyalty to the principles and ideals of the League, they have never, since the Pilsudski *coup d'état* in May 1926, been resolute supporters of collective security. The story is even told that the first instruction given by Marshal Pilsudski

[1] *Documents of* 1936, pp. 412–13. [2] Buell, pp. 224–26.
[3] *Documents of* 1937, Vol. II, pp. 262–277.

to Colonel Beck. . . . in 1932 was to 'open all the windows at the Foreign Office and let out the smell of the League of Nations.' . . . The so-called 'Vilna School'[1] which includes publicists who were at one time very close to Pilsudski, now has one eye on Lithuania and the other on Czechoslovakia . . . both significantly regarded as 'Bolshevik breeding grounds'—and its leading spokesmen write openly of a greater Poland marching side by side with Germany to dismember Russia; their assumption being that all the present-day activities of the Third Reich are merely preparatory to a war of aggression against Russia. . . . With the Peasant and Socialist masses wholeheartedly in sympathy with the democratic Powers . . . it would seem that the foreign policy of Poland ought not to be so much a matter of doubt. . . . Although they constitute a good three-quarters of Poland's 35 millions, the Peasants and Socialists, who could be expected to bear the brunt of the fighting in case of war, have no effective voice in national affairs, and no influence on foreign policy."

The attitude of the majority of the Polish people towards the foreign policy of Poland can be judged to a certain extent from a resolution passed in October 1935 by the Central Executive Committee of the Peasant Party. The resolution stated that recent events of international life indicated that peace rested on delicate foundations and that no one could guarantee that Poland would not be facing danger in the not distant future. In these conditions each citizen should be anxiously aware that the principles and aims of Polish foreign policy were kept hidden from the public. Apprehension had been aroused by such facts as came to the knowledge of the public and which could be therefore observed, such as the loosening of the alliances with France and Rumania, the great tension in relation with Czechoslovakia, and the cooling of the friendship with the Baltic States. In the name of the Peasant Party the Central Executive Committee declared:

"(1) If one can admit without difficulty that the proceedings of Polish diplomacy should in each particular case remain secret from the State, nevertheless public opinion must know and approve of the general lines of foreign policy, for the State is not the property of the Government and it is the whole nation which has to bear the brunt of a bad foreign policy.

"(2) Poland, inspired by considerations of her own security, ought to demand respect for treaties and collaborate with the States which are supporting them; the rural masses, to whom the preservation of peace is of importance, since it is above all on them that will fall the weight of war, therefore demand that Poland's foreign policy shall be based on a sincere alliance with France and Rumania as well as on friendly relations with Czechoslovakia and with the Baltic States. To base this policy on 'friendship' with Germany, in which direction the Polish magnates are pressing, would be a contradiction both of the interests of the State and

[1] The *Slowo* of Vilna wrote on 19th December 1934: "We have already forgotten that we have a Polish Minsk, Mohylew, Vitebsk, a half-Polish Kiev." Closely connected with that "School" was the "Promethean" movement, which demanded the liberation of Siberia. The leader of the "Vilna School" was Prince Janusz Radziwill, the Chairman of the Senate Commission for Foreign Affairs.

the views of the rural masses who have an extreme and justified mistrust of ' friendship ' with Germany.

"(3) In the present situation, in view of the great tension of international relations at a time when Poland may find herself faced with internal difficulties, a government should be called which has the support of the most numerous class of the population, which has the moral right to speak and to decide in the name of the whole nation and which knows how, in the moment of danger, to draw from the people the maximum of effort in the defence of the country."[1]

The foregoing analysis of Polish foreign policy supports two conclusions. Firstly, it is a fallacy to assume, especially in the case of Poland, that a small country is *ipso facto* a peaceful neighbour or is content to follow a bigger country's lead in foreign affairs (e.g. France or Germany if Poland is concerned). Secondly, it is the *régime*, and not the size or power of a country, which seems to determine its foreign policy.

References

Buell, R. L., *Poland—Key to Europe*. London, 1939.

Buelow, Prince von, *Imperial Germany*. London, 1916.

Bukowiecki, S., *Polityka*, etc., Warsaw, 1922, as quoted by E. R. B. Hansen, *Poland's Westward Trend*. London, 1928.

Donald, Sir Robert, *The Polish Corridor and the Consequences*. London, 1929.

Fiala, V., *La Pologne d'aujourd'hui*. Paris, 1936.

Grabski, S., *Uwagi*, etc., Warsaw, 1923, quoted by E. R. B. Hansen, *Poland's Westward Trend*. London, 1928.

Guest, Dr. L. Haden, *The Struggle for Power in Europe*. London, 1921.

Machray, Robert, *The Poland of Pilsudski*. London, 1936.

Morrow, I. D. W., *The Peace Settlement in the German-Polish Borderlands*. London, 1936.

Polish White Book, The. Paris-London, 1940.

Royal Institute of International Affairs, *Documents on International Affairs*. London, 1934, 1936 and 1937.

Studnicki, W., *System polityczny*, etc. (The Political System of Europe and Poland). Warsaw, 1935.

Toynbee, A. J., *Survey of International Affairs*. London, 1932, 1933 and 1935.

[1] Fiala, p. 251.

Postscript

1939 AND ITS AFTERMATH

THE military position of Poland in 1939 was the logical outcome of her home and foreign policy. Before the occupation of Czechoslovakia Poland faced Germany, excluding Danzig and the coast, on 34.5 per cent of her frontier. That percentage increased to 52.3 after March 1939, the common frontiers with Russia, Lithuania and Rumania remaining respectively 25.5 per cent, 9.2 per cent and 6.3 per cent of Poland's boundaries. While the frontier with the Soviet Union and other neighbours followed more or less a straight line, the frontiers of Germany stretched round the ethnographic part of Poland and endangered the most vital centres of population and industry.

The weakness of Poland's war potential was admitted by the Polish Government in a memorandum presented to the League of Nations in 1931. This memorandum stressed the power of the neighbouring States, the lack of industrial development in Poland, her unfavourable geographical position, the length of her frontiers, the absence of natural barriers and the unfavourable distribution of existing industrial centres, which were situated near the German frontier.[1] There is no doubt that in the course of 1931–39 Poland's military position became much weaker relatively both to Germany and Russia.

In technical weapons Poland was and continued to be lamentably ill-supplied and ill-equipped for their production. In 1939 cavalry still formed about 40 per cent of the army, the other 60 per cent consisting almost exclusively of infantry. Formations did not possess a full establishment of heavy artillery and were short even of other artillery. The equipment of first-line troops with anti-tank guns and the anti-aircraft defences of the whole country, including the army, were inadequate. The Polish Air Force possessed a total of 377 planes, only a small proportion of which were fighter planes. Infantry weapons were not only of inferior quality but insufficient in number.[2]

The majority of the army leaders were politicians rather than military specialists and their field experience was limited to infantry and cavalry. The latter played a great role in Polish military science as it had been the principal weapon of all East European wars throughout the ages, and was by preference the choice of arm of the landed gentry. As an offensive rather than defensive weapon, and much more adapted to a war in the East than in

[1] *Documents on International Affairs*, 1931, p. 67.
[2] Norwid Neugebauer, pp, 34–40.

the West, it was trained for a possible war with Russia rather than with Germany. According to Liddell Hart the picture of a cavalry charge and even of a strategic decision attained by audacious cavalry manœuvres stood out prominently in Polish military minds. The spirit of the offensive was much stronger than its material backing.[1]

In spite of the possibility of a war with Germany no defences were in existence on the German frontiers, whereas the Russian frontier was strongly fortified, and was even constantly guarded by a specially organised Frontier Protection Corps (K.O.P.).

When Germany turned the spearhead of her aggressive policy towards Poland it was obvious that only a water-tight Polish-Soviet military alliance could save Poland's independence or discourage Germany from attacking Poland altogether; the Polish Government refused, however, to entertain the idea that it was necessary to admit Soviet troops to Polish soil. With regard to the British guarantee to Poland, Lloyd George denounced it as sheer madness to give such a pledge in the absence of military support from Russia. " Russian troops could alone hope to reach the battlefield in time to save the Polish Army from being crushed by an overwhelming German superiority in men and especially in equipment. The Chief of our General Staff was abroad in France when this hare-brained pledge was given. I have good reason to believe that on his return he and his advisers pointed out that we did not possess the means to redeem it." (*Sunday Express*, 23rd July 1939.) Previously, in May 1939, Winston Churchill stated that " there is no means of maintaining an Eastern Front against Nazi aggression without the active aid of Russia." (*Daily Telegraph*, 4th May 1939.)

The events of 1939, leading up to and including the conduct of military operations when Germany struck in September, showed the gross lack of ability and responsibility of the Polish political and army leaders. No large-scale preparations were made until the German attack actually started; millions of reservists were not called up and the people, who were resolute and determined to fight the Germans with all available means, had to take the initiative into their own hands and find weapons wherever they could. From the first day of the war, the Polish army, faced with German aggression simultaneously from Eastern Prussia, Pomerania, Silesia and Slovakia, lost touch with headquarters. According to General Neugebauer the Polish command in the field first received the news that the Polish Government had crossed the Rumanian frontier on 17th September from a German communiqué. " The Polish army found itself in a strange situation. It had no High Command. The information about the general situation, which so far had been scarce, was no longer available at all. The armies acted on previous orders and in accordance with the instructions of 15th September which had reached them by an indirect route. Their actions were not co-ordinated." General Neugebauer also stated that the High Command issued its last communiqué on 16th September.[2] There were many reports of voluntary evacua-

[1] Liddell Hart, pp. 95–6.

[2] Norwid Neugebauer, pp. 186–87.

tions of officers of high rank and their families. " Travellers who have crossed the country (Rumania) during last week, report that again and again they have passed motor cars and taxi-cabs carrying officers evacuating their families and transporting their luggage—trunks, suitcases, perambulators and umbrellas. That is indication enough of the deplorable length to which the demoralisation of the army has gone." (*The Times*, 18th September 1939.)

All the available evidence points to the fact that the defence of Warsaw, Hel, Modlin and other places was organised against the orders of the General Staff either by officers appointed on the spot, commanding a medley of field units which the war had thrown together or even, as in the case of Warsaw, by civilians headed by the Mayor. There is no evidence, however, that the leaders of the dictatorial régime, convinced of the helplessness of Polish resistance, deliberately refrained from mobilising all the energies of the Polish people, and it would be invidious to make such a charge. It would also be unfair to define the Soviet action on Polish territory as unfriendly to the Polish people. The Red Army crossed the borders on 18th September, that is, one day after the Polish Government and High Command fled to Rumania, and after the collapse of Polish resistance was obvious.

The Polish President, I. Moscicki, was said, before leaving Polish soil, to have appointed W. Raczkiewicz as his successor. That fact and the retirement from political life of the principal leaders of the régime, of the Prime Minister Skladkowski, the Commander-in-Chief Marshal Smigly-Rydz and all members of the Cabinet, seem to suggest that they probably realised their responsibility for the catastrophe of Poland; one of the former Prime Ministers of the Pilsudski régime, General Prystor, was reported to have committed suicide.

The leaders of the Polish Opposition refused to leave Poland after the defeat. M. Rataj, leader of the Peasant Party and former Speaker of the Senate, M. Niedzialkowski, N. Barlicki and C. Czapinski, leaders of the Polish Socialist Party, W. Buczek, Communist leader, and S. Starzynski, the Mayor of Warsaw, were still organising Polish resistance after the emigration of the Government and were all caught at different times by the German authorities and executed or killed in action.

Polish political life abroad, and to a certain extent at home, falls after 1939 into two different periods marked by the death of General Sikorski. The first Polish Government in exile was formed by him in September 1939 in Paris. None of the national leaders of the Opposition nor the members of the former Government took part in it, and the personality of General Sikorski, who had lived in France since 1926 and had been refused a command in the German-Polish war, was therefore outstanding in that Government.

It seems that the Sikorski Cabinet was determined to dissociate itself from the defunct dictatorship and to work for a revival of democracy in Poland. It was reported that the Government was preparing a new Constitution, different in structure from that of the autocratic régime; it dissolved the Diet and the Senate elected in 1935 and declared that they had " failed to fulfil the requirements of the State." It was stated that Poland's foreign policy between 1934–38 was quite unintelligible " unless related to the purpose of the rulers of that period and particularly of Colonel Beck, to set up in Poland a totalitarian State on the German model." (*Daily Telegraph*, 13th November 1939.) The holders of posts on lower levels, however, were by no means in agreement with the policy of the Sikorski Government. They consisted, in the great majority, of former officials of the Ministries of War, Foreign Affairs and other Government departments of the former régime, who, when the war broke out, were abroad on various missions, staffing embassies and so forth, or who left Poland in and after September 1939, having much greater facilities to get to Paris and later to London, than the Opposition Poles or those who were not civil servants. The bureaucratic influence was to a certain point controlled and kept in check by General Sikorski. After his death, however, the Polish administration in exile became dominated by the same forces which had ruled Poland before September 1939 and which seem to have been even less representative of the Polish population than they had been when in power in Poland. The people, shocked by their conduct of operations in 1939, had lost all confidence in the pre-1939 régime. Also, the representation in the émigré administration of certain elements, previously domiciled in Eastern Poland, and even in Russia or the Ukraine before 1918, was grossly disproportionate to their numerical importance in Poland. It may perhaps be said that that element is as different from the bulk of the Polish people as the Anglo-Indian from that of the British; the Polish writer from Vilna, Mackiewicz, described this difference, saying that " people from the Borderlands not only do not possess a national inferiority complex but rather have a national superiority complex. This is because in the East we never have been a nation of peasants or labourers, but a nation of masters."[1]

The shift towards the Right in the Polish administration abroad was characterised by the gradual whitewashing of the dictatorial régime in matters of foreign policy and the placing of most of the responsibility for Poland's fate on others; in matters of internal policy it brought about the re-emergence of autocratic methods of government, although it may be said that the absence of any channels through which public opinion may exert pressure is probably inherent in the artificial life led by a government in exile, particularly during a war.

The political situation in Poland does not seem to have developed on similar lines. The German-Polish war and life under German occupation reinforced rather than weakened the popular clamour for a democratic régime. As in other countries, resistance against Germany brought forward new leaders in both the so-called Home Army, which was organised and directed from abroad by the émigré Government, and the so-called People's Army and workers' and peasants' battalions which were formed by the Opposition. Whether the one group was mainly Fascist-led, and the other

[1] S. Mackiewicz, p. 106.

mainly Communist-led, is a matter of conjecture; leaders of both groups, however, declared their intention of fighting for the expulsion of the Germans from Poland and for the restoration of democracy in Poland.

The Soviet Union recognised in 1941 the Government headed by General Sikorski, and financed the formation of a Polish Army from Polish citizens domiciled on Soviet soil. In March and August 1942, that army, commanded by General Anders and numbering 80,000 men, was evacuated to Iran on the orders of the Polish military authorities, the Polish Government having declared previously that "troops of the Polish Republic stationed on the territory of the Soviet Union will fight the German brigands shoulder-to-shoulder with Soviet troops." Some officers and men refused to leave Russia and, in order to redeem the name of Poland in Soviet eyes, offered themselves for "suicide" assignments on the front, which at that time was approaching Stalingrad. Later on these men, together with some civilians, formed in Moscow the Union of Polish Patriots, which was headed by the writer W. Wasilewska and General Berling, a former chief of staff of General Anders's army.

Early in 1943 the German Government accused the Soviet authorities of the murder of thousands of Polish officers in a prison camp in the Smolensk area; that charge was officially taken up by the Polish Government in London which asked the International Red Cross to investigate the German allegations. The Soviet Government declared that it considered the Polish step "as entirely abnormal and violating all regulations and standards of relations between two Allied States," and decided to interrupt diplomatic relations with the Polish Government in London. The Union of Polish Patriots received semi-official status and was permitted to form, on a voluntary basis, a Polish army corps; that corps later fought on the Soviet-German front which was receding to the frontiers of Poland.

The dictatorial tendencies in the Polish Government found expression also in some of the Government organisations in Poland, and cases of fratricidal battles were reported. (*Observer*, 6th August 1944.) The Opposition, which seems to have refrained hitherto from setting up a separate central authority, proceeded to do so now and in December 1943 a congress of delegates of local resistance groups elected the Polish National Council. That body, with the support of the Union of Polish Patriots, formed in the summer of 1944 in the newly liberated areas of Poland the Committee of National Liberation, with its seat in Lublin; the Committee was subsequently recognised by the Soviet Government and granted the right to set up a Polish administration in the Polish territories occupied by the Russian armies. The Committee's manifesto to the Polish people declared that they would administer the liberated areas in conformity with the Constitution of March 1921, as the "only really lawful constitution adopted in a lawful manner"; it recognised that the Polish-Soviet frontier must be settled by means of a mutual agreement according to the principle of Polish lands to Poland, Ukrainian, White-Russian and Lithuanian lands to the Ukraine, White-

Russia and Lithuania. The manifesto proclaimed the restoration of all democratic liberties and announced the speedy execution of land reform.

Both the Government in London and the Committee of National Liberation undoubtedly represented certain political orientations among the Polish people and there are no grounds for the assertion that they were mere nominees of the French, British or Soviet Governments respectively. In both administrations there were at one time or another various members of the same parties, such as the Peasant and Socialist Parties. It is not possible, however, to estimate which of these members represented the opinions of their parties, which had been silenced between 1939 and 1944. Similarly, no information is available as to the relative influence in 1944 of the émigré Government or the Committee of National Liberation.

The changes in the administration and the economy of Poland after September 1939 were also considerable. Out of the 1939 territory of 152,000 square miles with a population of about 34 millions, 74,000 square miles with a population of about 23 millions were occupied by Germany, and 78,000 square miles with a population of about 11 millions, about 9 millions of whom were non-Poles, formed between September 1939 and June 1941, part of the Soviet Ukrainian, White-Russian and, later, Lithuanian republics. The German Government incorporated the major part of western Poland into the Gaue Danzig, Wartheland and Breslau of the German Reich, creating out of the Central and Southern provinces of Poland the so-called *Gouvernement-Général*, which included Warsaw and Cracow; a small stretch of territory in the Tatra range, the Jaworzyna, was annexed by the Slovak State.

Active resistance of any character from whatever part of the population was ruthlessly suppressed. Physical extermination of the more passive elements, however, seems to have been applied rather to the professional and middle classes than to the population as a whole; Jews of all classes were systematically wiped out. Those Poles who declared themselves as *Volksdeutsche*, that is, not Germans proper but of German descent, were treated midway between *Reichsdeutsche* and Poles. Shortly after the outbreak of the Soviet-German war, however, all former Polish inhabitants of the Gaue Danzig, Wartheland and Oberschlesien were made *Reichsdeutsche* by Government decree and the men called up for military service in the German armed forces.

Small industrial undertakings were, on the whole, left in the possession of their Polish owners, although to many of them German observers with considerable powers were appointed. Large enterprises were incorporated into German concerns; mines and factories formerly owned by the Polish State were taken over largely by the Hermann Goering Werke, and private undertakings, including those where foreign capital was invested, by German trusts such as the Roechling Werke, the Preussische Bergwerk and Huetten A. G., I. G. Farben and others. In the course of the war many Polish enterprises, which were of value to the German war effort, were extended, new mines sunk, new furnaces installed, new factories built, and it seems that a just solution of the problem of pre-war ownership, and indeed the reorganisation of Polish economy on the whole, presents at least as much difficulty as the solution of the political and social problems, most of which are to be encountered in all European States which experienced German occupation.

References

Liddell Hart, *The Defence of Britain*. London, 1939.
Mackiewicz, Stanislaw, *Historia Polski* (The History of Poland). London, 1942.
Norwid Neugebauer M., *The Defence of Poland*. London, 1942.
Royal Institute of International Affairs, *Documents on International Affairs*. London, 1931.

POLAND—THE STRUGGLE FOR POWER
1772–1944

By

HENRYK FRANKEL

Mickiewicz:
An der Weichsel fernem Strande
Tobt ein Kampf mit Donnerschall,
Weithin ueber deutsche Lande
Rollt er seinen Widerhall.
Schwert und Sense scharfen Klanges,
Dringen her zu unsern Ohren,
Und der Ruf des Schlachtgesanges:
' Noch is Polen nicht verloren '.

Und wir horchen und wir lauschen,
Stille waltet um und um,
Nur die traegen Wellen rauschen
Und das weite Feld ist stumm;
Nur wie Sterbender Gestoehne,
Lufthauch durch gebrochne Hallen
Hoert man dumpfe Trauertoene:
' Polen, Polen ist gefallen '.

Mitten in der stillen Feier
Wird ein Saitengriff gethan.
Ha, wie schwillet diese Leier
Voller stets und maecht' ger an!
Leben, schaffen solche Geister,
Dann wird Totes neu geboren:
Ja, mir buergt des Liedes Meister
' Noch ist Polen nicht verloren '.

(Ludwig v. Uhland, 1833).

APPENDIX[1]

THE MANIFESTO OF THE POLISH DEMOCRATIC SOCIETY, 1836.

(Printed by H. Hetherington, 126 Strand, London, 1837.)

The partition-iniquity perpetrated on Poland interrupted merely the political existence of the State, but destroyed not the natural life of the nation. Her incessant struggles for independence ever since the confederation of Bar, the torrents of blood shed by Poles in so many parts of the world, their present expatriation, the unparalleled fury of Poland's assassins, and the general sympathy of the people of Europe, are indubitable evidence that the Polish nation still lives, that it regards its future existence as a certainty. . . . At the very moment that the nation had need of all her energies to be brought to bear against her invader, those energies were internally fainting beneath the effects of a long system of anarchical misrule. For a long time previous the nobility had enthroned itself on the ruins of the ancient democracy, during a long period that nobility strengthening and developing itself alone had absorbed the general vitality of the nation. The primitive national principle, imprisoned within this narrow framework, necessarily lost its omnipotence. Liberty, equality and fraternity, once common to all, became the exclusive privilege of a caste. Henceforth, the great mass of the people, excluded from political life, bereaved of all rights, stripped of property, they themselves transformed into property inseparable from the soil, had no means of advancing with the dominant order towards a common point. The interest of the nobility was as opposite to that of the people as freedom to slavery, opulence to misery. This destruction of unity, this division of national strength, led by a natural process to general debility. The privileged caste were unwilling to remedy the evil by renouncing their encroachments, by consciously doing justice to the oppressed. Poland, having therefore no longer any support in the masses reduced to slavery and supineness, was unable to repulse her invaders.

All her efforts for reconquering her independence show on the one hand the impotence of a class which had shut itself up within itself and its infatuated stubbornness in the maintenance of usurpation; on the other hand, they prove that the people nourish in their hearts a deep attachment to freedom, that they were always found ready for the struggle in proportion to the promises made, and to the bright hopes held out to them.

At the voice of Kosciuszko, announcing the approach of better days to the oppressed, the masses flew to arms. The fields of Raclawice and so many other memorable battlefields, bear glorious testimony to the energy of spirit

[1] See p. 39. The following extract contains the salient points of the Manifesto.

which animated the Polish people. There, those were the true representatives of the people's devotion for their country's cause, who, with scythe or lance alone, carried the Muscovite cannons; but the unconquerable antipathy of the nobility to social reforms paralysed and blasted the sublimity of patriotic enterprise.

The November revolution, whose tendency was of a still more pronounced nature, encountered the same obstacles, and met with the same fate. The inopportuneness of the period selected for its outbreak, the preponderancy of the enemy's forces, the military blunders and partial treachery of our commanders, the malevolence and bad faith of the neighbouring States, above all, France's and England's abandonment of Poland, are not the true causes of the fall; they were but the secondary or apparent causes. That which really rendered fruitless the mighty sacrifices then made, was the arresting and throwing back of the revolutionary movement, a movement which was a solemn manifestation of the national mind, and of its conception of its great mission upon earth. The heirs of prejudice and the representatives of the old dominant class perceived from the first moment, that their usurpations would be undermined and demolished if the revolution were not diverted from this original tendency. After having, therefore, by craft, seized upon the reins of government, they changed the revolutionary movement into a mere military campaign, and instead of arousing the masses, instead of combating with the whole strength of the nation, they chose rather to throw themselves into the arms of false and hypocritical cabinets, to crouch before, and sue for aid, even the accomplices of the murderer of Poland, to negotiate with the enemy himself. In fact, they would rather witness the destruction of their own country's cause than part from their usurpations. By this infamous and anti-revolutionary conduct they weakened the nation's confidence in its own resources, chilled the enthusiastic, discouraged the brave. Poland, as she once more sank into the grave, beheld, in her own sons, her defender and her executioners; once more she fell, not by the brute force of the invader's hordes, but—too truly—by the selfishness of her own privileged class.

Nevertheless the first emotions of the people, at the sign of the November revolution, promised the more brilliant future. Had the movement been unrepressed, it would have produced its natural and inevitable results; it would have emancipated the whole of society, have lighted up real national war, and most certainly have brought about the triumph of our country's cause. The people would have risen as one man, have braced the gauntlet of war on their vigorous arms, and have crushed the invaders without foreign aid.

. . . The Polish people, with its usual unerring instinct, perceived from the first, the minds of our younger patriots were able to comprehend, in all its extent, this plan and idea of national salvation. The same idea, saved from the national shipwreck, passed into other hands with a handful of the exiles, to be matured in the enlightened West, and gain power hereafter to develop itself entirely in our fatherland. It is this same idea that gave birth to the Polish Democratical Association.

The Association having, at its foundation on the 17th of March 1832, demonstrated the necessity of social reform, determined to labour in the spirit of democratical principles for the recovery of their country's independence, and the consummation of the people's emancipation.

In order to accomplish these purposes they were obliged by the circumstances of the time, first of all to set right public opinion, led astray by traitors to the national cause; to expose the indolence and bad faith of those who, invested fraudently during the last struggle with the majesty of the people, endeavoured, still, in foreign countries, to pass for its representatives.

Lastly came a complete and striking separation of the two antagonistic principles. The aristocracy repulsed, attacked, and declared by the emigration inimical to the national cause, is fled to its last shift—the contrivances of diplomacy: in order, by this pretended patriotic solicitude, to prolong, in credulous eyes, the supposition of its retaining its olden weight in Polish affairs.

For now nearly half a century, the European mind has been developing new principles upon the ruins of the ancient order of things and, seeking out new conditions of social life, this tendency at present manifests itself alike in the intellectual and political world, in all the efforts and movements of nations, even in the concessions of governments, which can no longer effectively resist the urgent demands of the principle of self-emancipation.

. . . We are profoundly convinced that a social system based upon usurpation, in which some enjoy all the advantages of social life, and others are obliged to bear all its burdens, is the sole cause of the calamities of our country and of those of mankind at large. As long as a similar order of things, violating natural justice, exists, there will ever be an internal struggle between the oppressed and their oppressors; between the masses doomed to ignorance, misery, and slavery, and the fortunate few who have appropriated to themselves all the advantages of social life. In the midst of such anarchy, there can never take place a free and harmonious development of national powers.

All men, as being of one and the same nature, possess equal rights, and have equal duties to discharge; they are all brothers, all children of the same Father—God; all members of the same family—man.

All for the people—all by the people; such is the broadcast and most general principle of democracy; it comprehends at once the objects and the means.

. . . It is thus that we understand the principles to the realisation of which mankind is now verging. On them we found the future regeneration of Poland, and in their spirit we labour for the achievement of their independence.

Regenerated and independent Poland will be Democratical. All her inhabitants, without distinction of birth or creed, will receive intellectual, political, and social emancipation. A new order of things, embracing property, labour, industry, education, and every social relation; a new order of things, based upon the principles of equality, will be substituted for that anarchy which the usurping nobles have hitherto dignified with the name of Law. Poland regenerated can never be an aristocratical Republic. Sovereignty will return to the people; the old dominant class will effectually be dissolved, will descend into the bosom of the people, become part of the people; all will be equal, all free, all children of one mother—their country.

. . . Poland possesses in her own bosom gigantic powers for the reconquest of her independence, powers which have never yet been called forth by any earnest and conscientious voice. Powers almost as yet unknown, alike formidable to foes within as to those without. By those powers Poland shall be raised from the dead.

The Polish people, despoiled of all their rights, crushed beneath misery, ignorance, and servitude, cultivate to this very hour, in toil and sweat for the benefit of others, that soil of which they themselves were robbed centuries since. Unto this very hour, in the provinces invaded 60 years ago by Russia, they are considered an integral part of the soil and sold with it. Human nature scandalised and outraged by this iniquity loudly calls for justice; but our domestic tyrants have been hitherto deaf to that appeal. During the last struggle for independence, they, abusing the sacred name of patriotism, wished with sonorous phrases only to satisfy the people tortured by physical suffering.

But Poland, besides her own forces, possesses natural allies. During her sanguinary struggles with the oppressor, every one of her victories was welcomed by Europe with shouts of joy and admiration; and we, the representatives of the misfortunes and hopes of our enslaved country, we have found responsive hearts, and shelter in the bosom of universal sympathy. The people of Europe have allied themselves with the immortal spirit of Poland, and they extended to each other the hand of fraternal amity over the same tomb on which absolutism ratified its infernal alliance. Our enemy is theirs, their foe is ours. Hence, convinced that our ancient national animosities have been entirely extinguished, we rely upon a sincere co-operation of the people of Europe, based on universal fraternity and a common desire for emancipation.

Cabinet Treaties will never restore Poland, and monarchical wars will never render justice to her people. Our country is nevertheless so dear to us, her wounds afflict us so bitterly, that we shall never fail to endeavour to turn to profit every event, every favourable circumstance. We will eagerly grasp at anything which may be beneficial to our country's cause, which can hasten or facilitate the attainment of our principal objects.

. . . We have sworn before our country and mankind never to rest until Poland recovers her independence, and securely establishes her existence upon democratical principles. This solemn obligation, sworn to by us in the enthusiasm of youth, shall be fulfilled to the letter by the perseverance of our manhood.

. . . We will labour by the Democratical Association for Poland, by Poland, for mankind.

Finally we declare emphatically that we are far from having any wish to expose our native land to spoliation and ravage. It is not with the avenging archangel's sword, but with the volume of national annals in our hand, that we go forth; on the one hand to prove to the oppressed that are obliged neither by divine law, nor by centuries of oppression, to remain longer in a state of misery and slavery, revolting to the dignity of man; on the other hand, by awakening the same sentiments of eternal justice, by appealing to the same historical recollections, to urge without cessation the inheritors of usurpation and nobility privileges, in the name of their own interest, in the name of the intellect of the age, more especially by the magic name and spell to us all of love of country, to restore to the people the rights of which they have been robbed. We know not whether the spirit of justice in the one, or rather the impatience and disappointed hopes of the other, will give the signal for Poland's enfranchisement. If, however, the indispensible reform of the social system and its consequent independence cannot be accomplished without violence, if the people should be obliged to become severe judges of the past, avengers of the wrongs they have suffered, and executors of the irrevocable feats of national justice, we will not sacrifice the happiness of 20 million human beings to a handful of the privileged; and if the blood of brethren must be shed, be it on the heads of those who, with criminal obstinacy, shall prefer their own selfish interests to the common weal and the enfranchisement of their motherland.

Signed by 1,135 Members of the Society.

Attested a True Copy by the Central Committee of the Polish Democratical Society.

L. J. Zaczrynski
Victor Heltmann
H. Jakubowski
Th. Malinowski
A. Chrystowski
B. Chmielewski
A. Molsdorf
J. N. Janowski

Poitiers, *4th December* 1836.

INDEX